Marie McLisky

English for
BANKING
in Higher Education Studies

Teacher's Book

Series editor: Terry Phillips

English for Specific Academic Purposes

Garnet
EDUCATION

Published by
Garnet Publishing Ltd.
8 Southern Court
South Street
Reading RG1 4QS, UK

First published 2008
Reprinted 2008

ISBN 978 1 85964 943 5

British Cataloguing-in-Publication Data
A catalogue record for this book is available from
the British Library.

Production
Series editor: Terry Phillips
Project management: Louise Elkins, Martin Moore
Editorial team: Jane Gregory, Rebecca Snelling
Academic review: Sheila Scott
Design: Henry Design Associates and Mike Hinks
Photography: Sally Henry and Trevor Cook; Alamy (Lou
Linwei, Ramer Unkel), Corbis (Jose Fuste Raga, TOPhoto),
Fotosearch, Shutterstock, Clipart.com, Digital Vision,
Stockbyte
container ship on page 105: © Adrian Shafto, Johnson
Stevens Agencies; OECD image on page 141: © OECD.

Audio recorded at Motivation Sound Studios produced by
EFS Television Production Ltd

The author and publisher would like to thank Google for
permission to reproduce the results listings on page 68.
Every effort has been made to trace copyright holders and
we apologize in advance for any unintentional omission. We
will be happy to insert the appropriate acknowledgements
in any subsequent editions.

Printed and bound in Lebanon by International Press

Contents

Book map

Unit	Topics
1 What is banking? Listening · Speaking	• definition of banking • aspects of banking
2 The origins of banking Reading · Writing	• history of banking • development of banking in the US
3 Banking institutions Listening · Speaking	• different types of bank and their ownership, e.g., · commercial · retail · investment · central · cooperative · mutual • banking services
4 Computers in banking Reading · Writing	• e-banking • computers for research
5 Bank performance Listening · Speaking	• financial statements: · statement of financial position · statement of financial performance • capital adequacy ratio
6 Central banks Reading · Writing	• the role of the central bank: · economic stability · regulation ·'lender of last resort'
7 International banking Listening · Speaking	• finance for international trade • payment terms: · cash with order · letter of credit · documentary collection · cash on delivery
8 Offshore banking Reading · Writing	• definition of offshore banking • regulation of offshore banking • offshore banking services
9 Banking in developing countries Listening · Speaking	• definition of developing v. developed countries • World Bank • types of banking institution in developing countries: · multilateral banks · commercial banks
10 Banking and ethics Reading · Writing	• socially responsible investments • 'ethical' banking • Equator Principles
11 Influences on banking standards Listening · Speaking	• factors which affect banking standards: · technological (Internet banking) · globalization · economic · political (regulation) • online fraud and security
12 Banking governance Reading · Writing	• principles of bank governance • compliance • Basel II accord

Vocabulary focus	Skills focus		Unit
• words from general English with a special meaning in banking • prefixes and suffixes	Listening	• preparing for a lecture • predicting lecture content from the introduction • understanding lecture organization • choosing an appropriate form of notes • making lecture notes	**1**
	Speaking	• speaking from notes	
• English–English dictionaries: · headwords · definitions · parts of speech · phonemes · stress markers · countable/uncountable · transitive/intransitive	Reading	• using research questions to focus on relevant information in a text • using topic sentences to get an overview of the text	**2**
	Writing	• writing topic sentences • summarizing a text	
• stress patterns in multi-syllable words • prefixes	Listening	• preparing for a lecture • predicting lecture content • making lecture notes • using different information sources	**3**
	Speaking	• reporting research findings • formulating questions	
• computer jargon • abbreviations and acronyms • discourse and stance markers • verb and noun suffixes	Reading	• identifying topic development within a paragraph • using the Internet effectively • evaluating Internet search results	**4**
	Writing	• reporting research findings	
• word sets: synonyms, antonyms, etc. • the language of trends • common lecture language	Listening	• understanding 'signpost language' in lectures • using symbols and abbreviations in note-taking	**5**
	Speaking	• making effective contributions to a seminar	
• synonyms, replacement subjects, etc. for sentence-level paraphrasing	Reading	• locating key information in complex sentences	**6**
	Writing	• writing complex sentences • reporting findings from other sources: paraphrasing	
• compound nouns • fixed phrases from banking • fixed phrases from academic English • common lecture language	Listening	• understanding speaker emphasis	**7**
	Speaking	• asking for clarification • responding to queries and requests for clarification	
• synonyms • nouns from verbs • definitions • common 'direction' verbs in essay titles (*discuss, analyse, evaluate*, etc.)	Reading	• clauses with passives	**8**
	Writing	• paraphrasing • expanding notes into complex sentences • recognizing different essay types/structures: · descriptive ·analytical · comparison/evaluation · argument • writing essay plans • writing essays	
• fixed phrases from banking • fixed phrases from academic English	Listening	• using the Cornell note-taking system • recognizing digressions in lectures	**9**
	Speaking	• making effective contributions to a seminar • referring to other people's ideas in a seminar	
• 'neutral' and 'marked' words • fixed phrases from banking • fixed phrases from academic English	Reading	• recognizing the writer's stance and level of confidence or tentativeness • inferring implicit ideas	**10**
	Writing	• writing situation–problem–solution–evaluation essays • using direct quotations • compiling a bibliography/reference list	
• words/phrases used to link ideas (*moreover, as a result*, etc.) • stress patterns in noun phrases and compounds • fixed phrases from academic English • words/phrases related to online security	Listening	• recognizing the speaker's stance • writing up notes in full	**11**
	Speaking	• building an argument in a seminar • agreeing/disagreeing	
• verbs used to introduce ideas from other sources (*X contends/accepts/asserts that* …) • linking words/phrases conveying contrast (*whereas*), result (*consequently*), reasons (*due to*), etc. • words for quantities (*a significant minority*)	Reading	• understanding how ideas in a text are linked	**12**
	Writing	• deciding whether to use direct quotation or paraphrase • incorporating quotations • writing research reports • writing effective introductions/conclusions	

Introduction

The ESAP series

The aim of the titles in the ESAP series is to prepare students for academic study in a particular discipline. In this respect, the series is somewhat different from many ESP (English for Specific Purposes) series, which are aimed at people already working in the field, or about to enter the field. This focus on *study* in the discipline rather than *work* in the field has enabled the authors to focus much more specifically on the skills which a student of banking needs.

It is assumed that prior to using titles in this series students will already have completed a general EAP (English for Academic Purposes) course such as *Skills in English* (Garnet Publishing, up to the end of at least Level 3), and will have achieved an IELTS level of at least 5.

English for Banking

English for Banking is designed for students who plan to take a banking course entirely or partly in English. The principal aim of *English for Banking* is to teach students to cope with input texts, i.e., listening and reading, in the discipline. However, students will also be expected to produce output texts in speech and writing throughout the course.

The syllabus concentrates on key vocabulary for the discipline and on words and phrases commonly used in academic and technical English. It covers key facts and concepts from the discipline, thereby giving students a flying start for when they meet the same points again in their faculty work. It also focuses on the skills that will enable students to get the most out of lectures and written texts. Finally, it presents the skills required to take part in seminars and tutorials and to produce essay assignments. For a summary of the course content, see the book map on pages 4–5.

Components of the course

The course comprises:
- the student Course Book
- this Teacher's Book, which provides detailed guidance on each lesson, full answer keys, audio transcripts and extra photocopiable resources
- audio CDs with lecture and seminar excerpts

Organization of the course

English for Banking has 12 units, each of which is based on a different aspect of banking. Odd-numbered units are based on listening (lecture/seminar extracts). Even-numbered units are based on reading.

Each unit is divided into four lessons:

Lesson 1: vocabulary for the discipline; vocabulary skills such as word-building, use of affixes, use of synonyms for paraphrasing

Lesson 2: reading or listening text and skills development

Lesson 3: reading or listening skills extension. In addition, in later reading units, students are introduced to a writing assignment which is further developed in Lesson 4; in later listening units, students are introduced to a spoken language point (e.g., making an oral presentation at a seminar) which is further developed in Lesson 4

Lesson 4: a parallel listening or reading text to that presented in Lesson 2, which students have to use their new skills (Lesson 3) to decode; in addition, written or spoken work is further practised

The last two pages of each unit, *Vocabulary bank* and *Skills bank*, are a useful summary of the unit content.

Each unit provides between four and six hours of classroom activity with the possibility of a further two to four hours on the suggested extra activities. The course will be suitable, therefore, as the core component of a faculty-specific pre-sessional or foundation course of between 50 and 80 hours.

Vocabulary development

English for Banking attaches great importance to vocabulary. This is why one lesson out of four is devoted to vocabulary and why, in addition, the first exercise at least in many of the other three lessons is a vocabulary exercise. The vocabulary presented can be grouped into two main areas:
- key vocabulary for banking
- key vocabulary for academic English

In addition to presenting specific items of vocabulary, the course concentrates on the vocabulary skills and strategies that will help students to make sense of lectures and texts. Examples include:
- understanding prefixes and suffixes and how these affect the meaning of the base word
- guessing words in context
- using an English–English dictionary effectively
- understanding how certain words/phrases link ideas
- understanding how certain words/phrases show the writer/speaker's point of view

Skills development

Listening and reading in the real world involve extracting communicative value in real time – i.e., as the spoken text is being produced or as you are reading written text. Good listeners and readers do not need to go back to listen or read again most of the time. Indeed, with listening to formal speech such as a lecture, there is no possibility of going back. In many ELT materials second, third, even fourth listenings are common. The approach taken in the ESAP series is very different. We set out to teach and practise 'text-attack' skills – i.e., listening and reading strategies that will enable students to extract communicative value at a single listening or reading.

Students also need to become familiar with the way academic 'outputs' such as reports, essays and oral presentations are structured in English. Conventions may be different in their own language – for example, paragraphing conventions, or introduction–main body–conclusion structure. All students, whatever their background, will benefit from an awareness of the skills and strategies that will help them produce written work of a high standard.

Examples of specific skills practised in the course include:

Listening

- predicting lecture content and organization from the introduction
- following signposts to lecture organization
- choosing an appropriate form of lecture notes
- recognizing the lecturer's stance and level of confidence/tentativeness

Reading

- using research questions to focus on relevant information
- using topic sentences to get an overview of the text
- recognizing the writer's stance and level of confidence/tentativeness
- using the Internet effectively

Speaking

- making effective contributions to a seminar
- asking for clarification – formulating questions
- speaking from notes
- summarizing

Writing

- writing notes
- paraphrasing
- reporting findings from other sources – avoiding plagiarism

- recognizing different essay types and structures
- writing essay plans and essays
- compiling a bibliography/reference list

Specific activities

Certain types of activity are repeated on several occasions throughout the course. This is because these activities are particularly valuable in language learning.

Tasks to activate schemata

It has been known for many years, since the research of Bartlett in the 1930s, that we can only understand incoming information, written or spoken, if we can fit it into a schemata. It is essential that we build these schemata in students before exposing them to new information, so all lessons with listening or reading texts begin with one or more relevant activities.

Prediction activities

Before students are allowed to listen to a section of a lecture or read a text, they are encouraged to make predictions about the contents, in general or even specific terms, based on the context, the introduction to the text or, in the case of reading, the topic sentences in the text. This is based on the theory that active listening and reading involve the receiver in being ahead of the producer.

Working with illustrations, diagrams, figures

Many tasks require students to explain or interpret visual material. This is clearly a key task in a field which makes great use of such material to support written text. Students can be taken back to these visuals later on in the course to ensure that they have not forgotten how to describe and interpret them.

Vocabulary tasks

Many tasks ask students to group key business words, to categorize them in some way or to find synonyms or antonyms. These tasks help students to build relationships between words which, research has shown, is a key element in remembering words. In these exercises, the target words are separated into blue boxes so you can quickly return to one of these activities for revision work later.

Gap-fill

Filling in missing words or phrases in a sentence or a text, or labelling a diagram, indicates comprehension both of the missing items and of the context in which they correctly fit. You can vary the activity by, for example, going through the gap-fill text with the whole class first orally, pens down, then setting the same task for individual completion. Gap-fill activities can be photocopied and set as revision at the end of the unit or later, with or without the missing items.

Breaking long sentences into key components

One feature of academic English is the average length of sentences. Traditionally, EFL classes teach students to cope with the complexity of the verb phrase, equating level with more and more arcane verb structures, such as the present perfect modal passive. However, research into academic language, including the corpus research which underlies the *Longman Grammar of Spoken and Written English,* suggests that complexity in academic language does not lie with the verb phrase but rather with the noun phrase and clause joining and embedding. For this reason, students are shown in many exercises later in the course how to break down long sentences into kernel elements, and find the subject, verb and object of each element. This receptive skill is then turned into a productive skill, by encouraging students to think in terms of kernel elements first before building them into complex sentences.

Activities with stance marking

Another key element of academic text is the attitude (or stance) of the writer or speaker to the information which is being imparted. This could be dogmatic, tentative, incredulous, sceptical, and so on. Students must learn the key skill of recognizing words and phrases marked for stance.

Crosswords and other word puzzles

One of the keys to vocabulary learning is repetition. However, the repetition must be active. It is no good if students are simply going through the motions. The course uses crosswords and other kinds of puzzles to bring words back into the students' consciousness through an engaging activity. However, it is understood by the writers that such playful activities are not always seen as serious and academic. The crosswords and other activities are therefore made available as photocopiable resources at the back of the Teacher's Book and can be used at the teacher's discretion, after explaining to the students why they are valuable.

Methodology points

Setting up tasks

The teaching notes for many of the exercises begin with the word *Set ...* . This single word covers a number of vital functions for the teacher, as follows:

- Refer students to the rubric (instructions).
- Check that they understand **what** to do – get one or two students to explain the task in their own words.
- Tell students **how** they are to do the task, if this is not clear in the Course Book instructions – as individual work, pairwork or in groups.
- Go through the example, if there is one. If not, make it clear what the target output is – full sentences, short answers, notes, etc.
- Go through one or two of the items, working with a good student to elicit the required output.

Use of visuals

There is a considerable amount of visual material in the book. This should be exploited in a number of ways:

- before an exercise, to orientate students, to get them thinking about the situation or the task, and to provide an opportunity for a small amount of pre-teaching of vocabulary (be careful not to pre-empt any exercises, though)
- during the exercise, to remind students of important language
- after the activity, to help with related work or to revise the target language

Comparing answers in pairs

This is frequently suggested when students have completed a task individually. It provides all students with a chance to give and explain their answers, which is not possible if the teacher immediately goes through the answers with the whole class.

Self-checking

Learning only takes place after a person has noticed that there is something to learn. This noticing of an individual learning point does not happen at the same time for all students. In many cases, it does not even happen in a useful sense when a teacher has focused on it. So learning occurs to the individual timetable of each student in a group. For this reason, it is important to give students time to notice mistakes in their own work and try to correct them individually. Take every opportunity to get students to self-check to try to force the noticing stage.

Confirmation and correction

Many activities benefit from a learning tension, i.e., a period of time when students are not sure whether something is right or wrong. The advantages of this tension are:

- a chance for all students to become involved in an activity before the correct answers are given

- a higher level of concentration from the students (tension is quite enjoyable!)
- a greater focus on the item as students wait for the correct answer
- a greater involvement in the process – students become committed to their answers and want to know if they are right and, if not, why not

In cases where learning tension of this type is desirable, the teacher's notes say, *Do not confirm or correct (at this point)*.

Feedback

At the end of each task, there should be a feedback stage. During this stage, the correct answers (or a model answer in the case of freer exercises) are given, alternative answers (if any) are accepted, and wrong answers are discussed. Unless students' own answers are required (in the case of very free exercises), answers or model answers are provided in the teacher's notes.

Highlighting grammar

This course is not organized on a grammatical syllabus and does not focus on grammar specifically. It is assumed that students will have covered English grammar to at least upper intermediate level in their general English course. However, at times it will be necessary to focus on the grammar, and indeed occasionally the grammar is a main focus (for example, changing active to passive or vice versa when paraphrasing).

To highlight the grammar:

- focus students' attention on the grammar point, e.g., *Look at the word order in the first sentence.*
- write an example of the grammar point on the board
- ask a student to read out the sentence/phrase
- demonstrate the grammar point in an appropriate way (e.g., numbering to indicate word order; paradigms for verbs; time lines for tenses)
- refer to the board throughout the activity if students are making mistakes

Pronunciation

By itself, the mispronunciation of a single phoneme or a wrong word stress is unlikely to cause a breakdown in communication. However, most L2 users make multiple errors in a single utterance, including errors of word order, tense choice and vocabulary choice. We must therefore try to remove as many sources of error as possible. When you are working with a group of words, make sure that students can pronounce each word with reasonable accuracy in phonemic terms, and with the correct stress for multiple syllable words. Many researchers have found that getting the stress of a word wrong is a bigger cause of miscommunication than getting individual phonemes wrong.

Pair and group activities

Pairwork and group activities are, of course, an opportunity for students to produce spoken language. As mentioned above, this is not the main focus of this course. But the second benefit of these interactional patterns is that they provide an opportunity for the teacher to check three points:

- Are students performing the correct task, in the correct way?
- Do students understand the language of the task they are performing?
- Which elements need to be covered again for the benefit of the class, and which points need to be dealt with on an individual basis with particular students?

Vocabulary and Skills banks

Each unit has clear targets in terms of vocabulary extension and skills development. These are detailed in the checks at the end of the unit (*Vocabulary bank* and *Skills bank*). However, you may wish to refer students to one or both of these pages at the start of work on the unit, so they have a clear idea of the targets. You may also wish to refer to them from time to time during lessons.

1 WHAT IS BANKING?

This introductory unit explores what we understand by the term 'banking'. Students listen to an extract from a lecture which describes different types of bank, such as wholesale, retail and central. They also listen to a series of mini-lectures which introduce different aspects of banking, from bank regulation to the use of technology. The content of the mini-lectures will be explored in more detail in subsequent units.

Skills focus

🎧 Listening

- preparing for a lecture
- predicting lecture content from the introduction
- understanding lecture organization
- choosing an appropriate form of notes
- making lecture notes

Speaking

- speaking from notes

Vocabulary focus

- words from general English with a special meaning in banking
- prefixes and suffixes

Key vocabulary

account	fix (v)	payable
ATM	fixed	rate (n)
bankrupt	floating (adj)	recall (v)
branch	gold standard	regulate
central bank	illegal	regulation
check (AmE)	institution	regulatory
cheque (BrE)	insufficient	retail bank
circulation	interest (n)	return (n)
commercial bank	invalid (adj)	savings
convertible	invest	security
credit	investment	term
creditor	issue (v)	terms
currency	legislation	transaction
debtor	liability	transfer (n and v)
deposit (n and v)	loan (n and v)	variable
depreciation	negotiable	wholesale bank
financial	negotiate (v)	

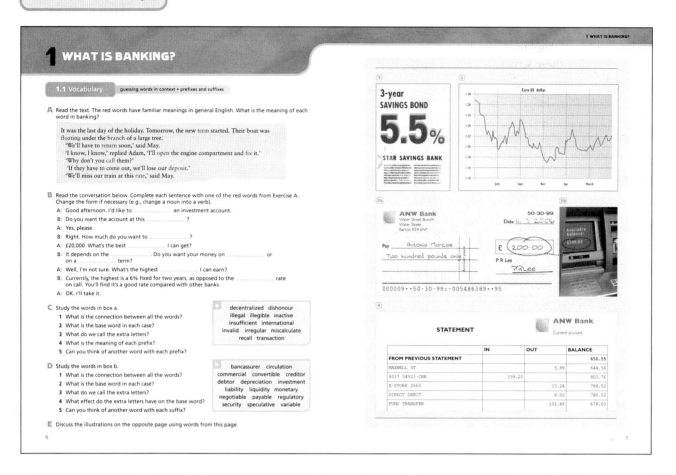

General note

Read the *Vocabulary bank* at the end of the Course Book unit. Decide when, if at all, to refer students to it. The best time is probably at the very end of the lesson or the beginning of the next lesson, as a summary/revision.

Lesson aims

- identify words for the discipline in context, including words which contain affixes
- gain fluency in the target vocabulary

Introduction

Write the word *banking* on the board. Ask students about the origin of the word *bank*. Tell them they will hear the answer in the first listening extract. Elicit *'banker*, and from there get to *'banking*.

Write the word *finance* on the board. Elicit the meaning, related words and the words in context. For example:

finance /'faɪnæns/ noun [U] – (the management of) a supply of money

finance /'faɪnæns/ verb [T] – provide the money needed to pay for something

finances /'faɪnænsɪz/ plural noun – the money which a person or company has

financial /faɪ'nænʃl/ adjective – relating to money or how money is managed

financially /faɪ'nænʃəli/ adverb – *The project is not financially viable* (= will not produce enough money)

financier /faɪ'nænsɪə(r)/ noun [C] – a person who has control of a large amount of money and can give or lend it to people or organizations

Highlight the different pronunciations of the letter *c* – /s/, /ʃ/ – and the alternative pronunciation of *fi* – /fɪ/. Highlight then drill the shifting stress.

Exercise A

Set for individual work and pairwork checking. Point out that this is a text which introduces some important basic vocabulary related to banking – although it may not seem like that, at first glance. Do the first one as an example, e.g., *a term* refers to the periods in the academic year when classes/lectures are held; there are normally three or four terms in a year. In banking, it can mean rules or conditions, and also the period of time when something is legally valid.

Make sure students understand that they should change the form, if necessary, e.g., noun to verb. Ask students if there is a relationship between the meaning in general English and the meaning in banking.

Feed back, getting the banking meanings on the board. Tell students to use these structures where possible:

- *a(n) X is (a(n)) ...* to define a noun
- *to X is to Y* to define a verb

Make sure students can say the words correctly. At the end of the feedback, ask students for any other words they know which have a special meaning in banking.

Answers

Model answers:

term (n)	rules or conditions
floating (adj)	variable, can change
branch (n)	a local bank belonging to a large banking organization
return (n)	profit on money invested
open (v)	start, set up
fix (v)	set for a period of time
call (n)	payable on demand, available when needed
deposit (v)	put money into an account
rate (n)	price or percentage

Other possible words from general English in banking:

basket – a group of prices or currencies

cap – an upper limit

hedge – protect against a possible loss

Exercise B

Set for individual work and pairwork checking. Do the first one as an example. Make sure students understand that they should change the form if necessary, e.g., noun to verb, or past tense to present tense.

Answers

Model answers:

A: Good afternoon. I'd like to <u>open</u> an investment account.

B: Do you want the account at this <u>branch</u>?

A: Yes, please.

B: Right. How much do you want to <u>deposit</u>?

A: £20,000. What's the best <u>return/rate</u> I can get?

B: It depends on the <u>terms</u>. Do you want your money on <u>call</u> or on a <u>fixed</u> term?

A: Well, I'm not sure. What's the highest <u>rate</u> I can earn?

B: Currently, the highest is a 6% fixed for two years, as opposed to the <u>floating</u> rate on call. You'll find it's a good rate compared with other banks.

A: OK. I'll take it.

Exercise C

Set the first question for pairwork. See which pair can work out the answer first. Feed back with the whole class.

Set the remainder for pairwork. Feed back, building up the table in the Answers section on the board.

Answers

Model answers:

1. They all have a base (root) word + extra letters at the beginning/prefixes. Point out that a base word stands on its own as a word, i.e., it has a meaning without the affix.

2. See table; elicit the base word meanings.

3. Prefix.

4. See table; ask students to work out the prefixes which reverse the meaning of a word (*in~*, *il~*, *ir~*, *de~*, *dis~*).

5. See table.

Prefix	Base word	Meaning of prefix	Another word
de	centralized	not	decelerate
dis	honour	not	discount, disallow
il	legal	not	illiquid
il	legible	not	
in	active	not	insolvent
in	sufficient	not	incorrect
inter	national	between	intercontinental
in	valid	not	
ir	regular	not	irrecoverable
mis	calculate	do wrong	misread
re	call	again	refund
trans	action	across	transnational

Language note

English is a lexemic language. In other words, the whole meaning of a word is usually contained within the word itself, rather than coming from a root meaning plus prefixes or suffixes (affixes). In most texts, written or spoken, there will only be a tiny number of words with affixes. However, these often add to a base meaning in a predictable way and it is important that students learn to detach affixes from a new word and see if they can find a recognizable base word.

Some words beginning with letters from prefixes are NOT in fact base + prefix, e.g., *refuse*. In other cases, the base word does not exist anymore in English and therefore will not help students, e.g., *transfer*, *transit*, although even in these cases the root meaning of the prefix may be a guide to the meaning of the whole word.

Exercise D

Repeat the procedure from Exercise C.

Answers

Model answers:

1 They all have a base word + extra letters at the end/suffixes.
2 See table.
3 Suffix.
4 See table.
5 See table.

Base word	Suffix	Effect/meaning of suffix	Another word
bancassur	er	a person who does something	adviser, borrower
circulat	ion	verb → noun	inflation
commerc	ial	noun → adjective	financial
convert	ible	can be	deductible
credit	or	a person who does something	investor
debt	or	a person who does something	depositor
depreciat	ion	verb → noun	stagnation
invest	ment	verb → noun	payment, management
liabil	ity	adjective → noun	accountability
liquid	ity	adjective → noun	
monet	ary	noun → adjective	inflationary
negoti	able	can be	transferable
pay	able	can be	
regulat	ory	verb → adjective	supervisory
secur	ity	adjective → noun	
speculat	ive	verb → adjective	legislative
vari	able	can be	

Language note

Note that with prefixes we rarely change the form of the base word. However, with suffixes, there are often changes to the base word, so students must:
- take off the suffix
- try to reconstruct the base word

Exercise E

Set for pairwork. Try to elicit more than just the words from this lesson. Students should describe the pictures as fully as they can at this stage. Tell students to use adjectives as well as nouns and make complete sentences.

Answers

Possible answers:

1 This is an advertisement for a **fixed-rate**, **fixed-term** savings bond.
   Savings are a form of **investment**.
   The interest **rate** is 5.5%. It is not **variable**.
   The **return** is 5.5% a year/per annum.

2 This shows fluctuations in the exchange **rate** between the euro and the US dollar.
   It shows the **depreciation** of the dollar against the euro.
   The euro and the US dollar are both **convertible** currencies.

3a This shows a personal cheque.

3b This shows an ATM screen.
   The address of the **branch** is printed on the cheque.
   The cheque is **invalid** because the date is **illegible**. There are **insufficient** funds in the account to cover the cheque. In some countries, this is **illegal**.

4 This is a bank statement. It shows the **transactions** on a current account. It shows one **deposit**.

Closure

If you have not done so already, refer students to the *Vocabulary bank* at the end of Unit 1. Tell students to explain how this lesson can help them deal with new words in context. If you wish, make three groups. Group A looks at the first section, *Using related words*. Group B looks at the second section, *Removing prefixes*. Group C looks at the third section, *Removing suffixes*. Then make new groups of three with an ABC in each to explain to each other.

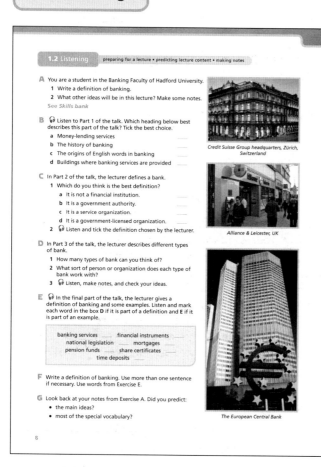

1.2 Listening   preparing for a lecture • predicting lecture content • making notes

A You are a student in the Banking Faculty of Hadford University.
1 Write a definition of banking.
2 What other ideas will be in this lecture? Make some notes.
See Skills bank

B Listen to Part 1 of the talk. Which heading below best describes this part of the talk? Tick the best choice.
a Money-lending services
b The history of banking
c The origins of English words in banking
d Buildings where banking services are provided

Credit Suisse Group headquarters, Zürich, Switzerland

C In Part 2 of the talk, the lecturer defines a bank.
1 Which do you think is the best definition?
a It is not a financial institution.
b It is a government authority.
c It is a service organization.
d It is a government-licensed organization.
2 Listen and tick the definition chosen by the lecturer.

Alliance & Leicester, UK

D In Part 3 of the talk, the lecturer describes different types of bank.
1 How many types of bank can you think of?
2 What sort of person or organization does each type of bank work with?
3 Listen, make notes, and check your ideas.

E In the final part of the talk, the lecturer gives a definition of banking and some examples. Listen and mark each word in the box D if it is part of a definition and E if it is part of an example.

banking services   financial instruments
national legislation   mortgages
pension funds   share certificates
time deposits

F Write a definition of banking. Use more than one sentence if necessary. Use words from Exercise E.

G Look back at your notes from Exercise A. Did you predict:
• the main ideas?
• most of the special vocabulary?

The European Central Bank

General note

The recording should only be played once, since this reflects what happens in a real lecture. Students should be encouraged to listen for the important points, since this is what a native speaker would take from the text. However, students can be referred to the transcript at the end of the lesson to check their detailed understanding and word recognition, or to try to discover reasons for failing to comprehend.

Read the *Skills bank* at the end of the Course Book unit. Decide when, if at all, to refer students to it. The best time is probably at the very end of the lesson or the beginning of the next lesson, as a summary/revision.

Lesson aims

● prepare for a lecture
● make notes
● predict lecture content

Introduction

1 Show students flashcards of some or all of the words from Lesson 1. Tell students to say the words correctly and quickly as you flash them. Give out each word to one of the students. Say the words again. The student with the word must hold it up. Repeat the process saying the words in context.

2 Refer students to the photos and discuss them briefly. (They will look at the different types of banking in more detail in Exercise D.)

Exercise A

1 Set for pair or group work. Feed back, but do not confirm or correct at this time.

2 Set for pairwork. Elicit some ideas but do not confirm or correct.

Methodology note

You may want to refer students to the *Skills bank – Making the most of lectures* at this point.
Set the following for individual work and pairwork checking. Tell students to cover the points and try to remember what was under each of the Ps – Plan, Prepare, Predict, Produce. Then tell students to work through the points to make sure they are prepared for the lecture they are about to hear.

Exercise B

Give students time to read the choices. Check understanding. Point out that they are only going to hear the introduction once, as in an authentic lecture situation. Tell students not to listen for the exact words, but only the main ideas (gist). They should not expect to understand every word of the lecture.

Play Part 1. Feed back. If students' answers differ, discuss which is the best answer and why.

Answer

Model answer:

c The origins of English words in banking

Transcript 🎧 1.1

Part 1

Welcome to 'An introduction to banking'. What do we mean by the term *banking*? We all associate banking with banks, of course, so let's start there. The English word *bank* has 13th-century origins in both German and Italian. When you hear the word *bank* you generally think of money ... right? But actually, the word *bank* is derived from the Italian word *banca*, which evolved from a German word meaning *bench*. What has banking got to do with benches? Well, in the past, Italian moneylenders used a bench or table in a large open area to conduct their business. So the word originally referred to the place where money-lending transactions occurred.

Today the word *bank* refers to the institution which carries out banking services. It also refers to a building where banking services are provided. That is, the offices or buildings in which a bank is located. It can also be a verb: we can say 'Who do you bank with?'

Incidentally, the English term *bankrupt* is used to describe a person who has gone out of business because they could not meet all their liabilities. This term comes from the expression *banca rotta*, meaning a physically broken bench.

The English words *cash*, *debtor*, *creditor*, *ledger*, and the symbols for English currency, pounds and pence, all originate from the 13th century, too.

Methodology note

In many course books with listening activities, students are allowed to listen to material again and again. This does not mirror real-life exposure to spoken text. In this course, students are taught to expect only one hearing during the lesson and encouraged to develop coping strategies to enable them to extract the key points during this one hearing. Listening texts may be repeated for further analysis but not for initial comprehension.

🎧 Exercise C

1 This is a pre-listening exercise. Give students time to read the choices. Check understanding. Tell students to discuss in pairs and try to anticipate the answer.

2 Point out that they are only going to hear the talk once, as in an authentic lecture situation. They are listening for the main ideas. Play Part 2. Feed back. If students' answers differ, discuss which is the best answer and why. Tell students that if the topic is not described at the beginning of a talk, then it is likely to be in the final section.

Answer

Model answer:

d It is a government-licensed organization.

Transcript 🎧 1.2

Part 2

So, we agree that banking is about money. But finance is also about money. Does this mean that banking and finance are the same? Not really. Banks are financial institutions, but so are insurance companies and investment companies. Some financial institutions provide banking services, but they cannot be defined as a bank. Why not? Because they do not fulfil the legal definition of a bank. In Britain, all financial institutions are controlled by the Financial Services Authority, or FSA. There is legislation covering the services provided by each institution. A bank is a government-licensed institution. It is established under a government charter. A banking license gives the right to conduct banking services, particularly services related to the storing, or keeping, of deposits, and the extending, or offering, of credit.

🎧 Exercise D

1/2 Set for pairwork discussion. Ask students to write down their ideas before they listen.

3 Play Part 3. Students take notes. Feed back, building up a diagram on the board. Point out that the lecturer mentions broad categories only. Elicit the examples given for each category and add them to the diagram. Explain that this is a *classification* diagram.

Give feedback on the students' note-taking. Discuss the best examples and why.

Answers

Model answer:

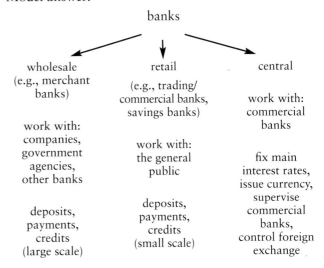

Transcript 🎧 1.3

Part 3

Banks can be categorized into wholesale banks, retail banks, and central banks. It's a bit more complicated than that in reality, but those are the main categories. Both wholesale and retail banks provide the three essential functions of deposits, payments and credits, which are the basis of their services. Wholesale banks, which include merchant banks, provide large-scale services to companies, government agencies and other banks. Retail banks, on the other hand, mainly provide smaller-scale services to the general public. These banks include the trading or commercial banks, and savings banks.

The main government-controlled bank in a country, the central bank, fixes the main interest rates, issues currency, supervises commercial banks and tries to control foreign exchange.

As I mentioned earlier, the term *bank* is generally understood as an institution that holds a banking license. Banking licenses are granted by bank regulatory authorities and provide rights to conduct the most fundamental banking services such as accepting deposits and making loans. Banks generate income through charging interest on loans and charging transaction fees on their financial services.

In the US, banks are under the jurisdiction of the central bank of the United States – the Federal Reserve Bank. In the United Kingdom the central bank is the Bank of England.

🎧 Exercise E

Point out that we often define things before or after classifying them. Give students plenty of time to look at the words in the box. Check understanding and pronunciation. Point out that this time they are listening for very specific information.

Play Part 4. Feed back.

Answers

Model answers:

banking services	D
financial instruments	D
national legislation	D
mortgages	E
pension funds	E
share certificates	E
time deposits	E

Transcript 🎧 1.4

Part 4

The roles and functions of banks have evolved and changed over the years. Today, the variety of services that a bank offers depends on the type of bank, and the country. Many of the larger banks offer services outside those traditionally associated with banking. They may deal in financial instruments such as share certificates, certificates of deposit, and bills of exchange. A financial instrument is a legal document. It shows that money has been lent or borrowed, invested or passed from one account to another.

Some banks also offer banking and insurance to their customers, hence the term *bancassurer*. Notice the spelling, with a *c* not a *k*. However, the essential function of a bank is to provide services relating to the storing and management of money for its customers. These services include most or all of the following: accepting demand and time deposits and paying interest on them, making loans and charging interest on them, investing in securities, issuing bank drafts and cheques, accepting cheques, drafts and notes.

Banks also provide other banking services including deposit facilities, leases, mortgages, credit cards, ATM networks, securities brokerage, investment banking, mutual and pension funds, and so on.

Banking can be defined, therefore, as the management of financial instruments and money, in the form of time deposits, securities, bank drafts, cheques, etc., within the context of specific national legislation.

Exercise F

Set for individual work and pairwork checking. Feed back, building up a model definition on the board. Accept any reasonable answers.

Answer

Possible answer:

Banking is the management of money (e.g., time deposits, pension funds) and financial instruments (e.g., share certificates) which takes place under national legislation.

Exercise G

Refer students back to their notes from Exercise A.

Methodology note

Up to this point, you have not mentioned how students should record information. Have a look around to see what students are doing. If some are using good methods, make a note and mention that. Ask students how they record written information when listening to their own language.

Closure

1 Ask students to give you examples of ways in which modern banking services have changed things for the better in recent times – particularly in students' own countries.

2 Refer students to the *Skills bank* if you have not done so already and work through the section *Making the most of lectures*.

1.3 Extending skills

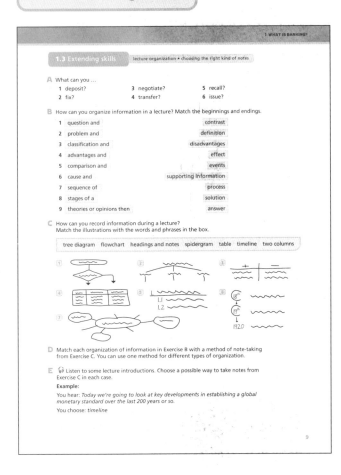

1.3 Extending skills lecture organization • choosing the right kind of notes

A What can you ...
1 deposit? 3 negotiate? 5 recall?
2 fix? 4 transfer? 6 issue?

B How can you organize information in a lecture? Match the beginnings and endings.

1 question and contrast
2 problem and definition
3 classification and disadvantages
4 advantages and effect
5 comparison and events
6 cause and supporting information
7 sequence of process
8 stages of a solution
9 theories or opinions then answer

C How can you record information during a lecture?
Match the illustrations with the words and phrases in the box.

tree diagram flowchart headings and notes spidergram table timeline two columns

D Match each organization of information in Exercise B with a method of note-taking from Exercise C. You can use one method for different types of organization.

E Listen to some lecture introductions. Choose a possible way to take notes from Exercise C in each case.

Example:
You hear: Today we're going to look at key developments in establishing a global monetary standard over the last 200 years or so.
You choose: timeline

Lesson aims

- identify different types of lecture organization
- use the introduction to a lecture to decide the best form of notes to use

Introduction

Tell students to build up the four Ps of preparing for and attending a lecture: Plan, Prepare, Predict, Produce. You could put students into four groups, each group working on one of the stages, then feeding back to the rest of the class.

Exercise A

Set for pairwork. Feed back orally. The more students can say about these words, the better. Accept anything correct but let students explain their choice if they choose a combination not given in the table.

Answers

Possible answers:

1	deposit	money, a cheque
2	fix	interest rates, terms, exchange rates
3	negotiate	terms (e.g., a loan), interest rates, overdraft facilities
4	transfer	money (e.g., from deposit to current account)
5	recall	a cheque, a loan
6	issue	a (share) certificate, a cheque (book), a bond

Exercise B

Point out that you can understand a lecture better if you can predict the order of information. Point out also that there are many pairs and patterns in presenting information, e.g., question and answer, or a sequence of events in chronological order.

Set for pairwork. Feed back orally. Check pronunciation. Point out that lecturers may not actually use these words, but if you recognize that what a lecturer is saying is the first of a pair, or the beginning of a sequence, you are ready for the second or next stage later in the lecture.

Answers

Model answers:

1	question and	answer
2	problem and	solution
3	classification and	definition
4	advantages and	disadvantages
5	comparison and	contrast
6	cause and	effect
7	sequence of	events
8	stages of a	process
9	theories or opinions then	supporting information

Exercise C

Identify the first form of notes – a flowchart. Set the rest for individual work and pairwork checking. Feed back, using an OHT or other visual medium if possible.

Answers

1 flowchart
2 tree diagram
3 two columns
4 table
5 headings and notes
6 timeline
7 spidergram

Methodology note

You might like to make larger versions of the illustrations of different note types and display them in the classroom for future reference.

Exercise D

Work through the first one as an example. Set for pairwork.

Feed back orally and encourage discussion. Demonstrate how each method of note-taking in Exercise C can be matched with an organizational structure. Point out that:

- a tree diagram is useful for hierarchically arranged information, such as when the information moves from general to specific/examples
- a spidergram is more fluid and flexible, and can be used to show connections between things, such as interactions or causes and effects

Answers

Possible answers:

1 question and answer = headings and notes (or spidergram, if one question/several answers)
2 problem and solution = headings and notes or two-column table
3 classification and definition = tree diagram or spidergram
4 advantages and disadvantages = two-column table
5 comparison and contrast = table
6 cause and effect = spidergram
7 sequence of events = timeline or flowchart
8 stages of a process = flowchart (or circle if it is a cycle)
9 theories or opinions then supporting information = headings and notes or two-column table

🎧 Exercise E

Explain that students are going to hear the introductions to several different lectures. They do not have to take notes, only think about the organization of information and decide what type of notes would be appropriate. Work through the example.

Play each introduction. Pause after each one and allow students to discuss. Students may suggest different answers in some cases. Establish that sometimes lecturers move from one information organization to another, e.g., cause and effect then sequence of events.

Answers

Possible answers:

1 two-column table (advantages and disadvantages)
2 table (comparison and contrast)
3 headings and notes (numbered notes or question and answer)
4 timeline (sequence of events)
5 flowchart (stages of a process)

Transcript 🎧 1.5

Introduction 1

Today we'll look at the globalization of private banking. In particular, we'll look at the advantages and disadvantages of foreign banks coming into a country. In recent years, we have seen a worldwide expansion of MNBs, or multinational banks. In many of the less developed nations, branches or subsidiaries of foreign commercial banks dominate the banking system. Incidentally, you may like to note that a subsidiary is independent of the parent bank, whereas a branch is not.

Introduction 2

My topic today is the organizational structure of banks. This is important, because it affects the way a bank operates. I am going to consider the effects of centralization on various aspects of bank management, including authority, accountability, decision-making and leadership. For each element, I'm going to compare the two approaches – centralized or decentralized.

Introduction 3

Today I want to consider the question 'Why are banks regulated?' There are a number of reasons for this. I am going to look at five of these. Firstly, there is the economic role of banks; secondly, the need to protect customers; thirdly, the prevention of a banking collapse, and the central bank's role in this; and fourthly, the competition issue. Finally, there is the issue of the scope of banking activities. What can banks actually do? Let's consider each point in turn.

Introduction 4

OK. Are we all ready? Is everyone here? We seem to have a small class today, so feel free to interrupt me if you have any questions. Right, I'll begin. For centuries, bankers have attempted to establish a global monetary regime or monetary standard. By this I mean the establishing of a fixed exchange rate for a currency. Today we're going to look at key developments in establishing a global monetary standard over the last 200 years or so.

Introduction 5

In this week's lecture, I'm going to discuss some aspects of modern technology and banking. Computers and other electronic machines are widely used in retail banking – for example, in the processing of cheques. A cheque is presented at a bank and an electronic procedure begins. The bank teller enters the details of the cheque onto the system. The computer reads the magnetic code. Money is debited from the payer's account electronically. The cheque is then sent to the clearing house and money is then credited to the payee's account.

Let's look at some more electronic procedures.

Closure

1 Test students on the pairs from Exercise B. Correct pronunciation again if necessary.
2 Refer students to the *Skills bank – Making perfect lecture notes.*

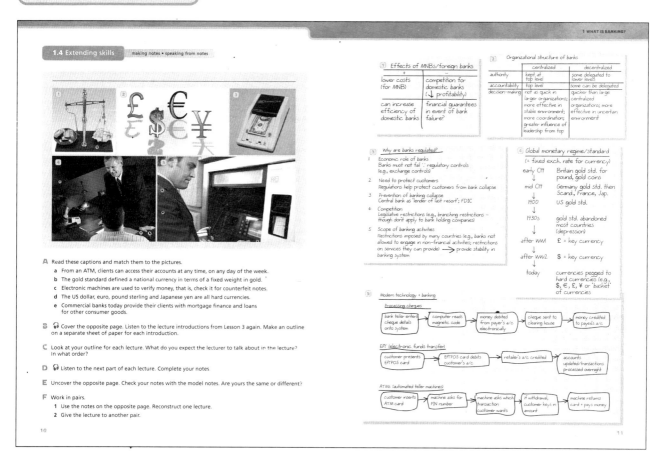

Lesson aims

- make outline notes from lecture introductions
- make notes from a variety of lecture types
- speak from notes

Further practice in:

- predicting lecture content

Introduction

Elicit as much information from the lecture in Lesson 2 as possible. If necessary, prompt students by reading parts of the transcript and pausing for students to complete in their own words.

Exercise A

Set for individual work and pairwork checking. Feed back orally but do not confirm or correct. Point out that they are going to hear about all these things in today's session.

Answers

Model answers:

a From an ATM, clients can access their accounts at any time, on any day of the week. (= picture 5)

b The gold standard defined a national currency in terms of a fixed weight in gold. (= picture 1)

c Electronic machines are used to verify money, that is, check it for counterfeit notes. (= picture 3)

d The US dollar, euro, pound sterling and Japanese yen are all hard currencies. (= picture 2)

e Commercial banks today provide their clients with mortgage finance and loans for other consumer goods. (= picture 4)

Methodology note

It is best that students close the book at this stage, so they are not tempted to look at the model notes. You can give the instructions for the next few stages orally as required.

🎧 Exercise B

Make sure students understand that they are going to hear the introductions from Lesson 3, Exercise E again. Ask them briefly if they can remember any of the content from the introductions. Spend a few moments on this if students are able to contribute. Elicit suggestions for types of notes (Lesson 3, Exercise E).

Explain that this time they must create an outline using an appropriate type of notes. (You can refer them again to the *Skills bank – Making perfect lecture notes*.) Make sure students understand that they don't need to write a lot at this stage – outlines may consist of just a few words, e.g., the start of a flowchart, the first part of a table or diagram. Play each introduction in turn and give students time to choose a note-type, make the outline and check it with other students.

Feed back, getting all the outlines on the board – you may wish to copy them from the first part of the model notes on the right-hand page, or you may prefer to follow your students' suggestions. Clarify the meaning of new words and check pronunciation.

Transcript 🎧 1.5

Introduction 1

Today we'll look at the globalization of private banking. In particular, we'll look at the advantages and disadvantages of foreign banks coming into a country. In recent years, we have seen a worldwide expansion of MNBs, or multinational banks. In many of the less developed nations, branches or subsidiaries of foreign commercial banks dominate the banking system. Incidentally, you may like to note that a subsidiary is independent of the parent bank, whereas a branch is not.

Introduction 2

My topic today is the organizational structure of banks. This is important, because it affects the way a bank operates. I am going to consider the effects of centralization on various aspects of bank management, including authority, accountability, decision-making and leadership. For each element, I'm going to compare the two approaches – centralized or decentralized.

Introduction 3

Today I want to consider the question 'Why are banks regulated?' There are a number of reasons for this. I am going to look at five of these. Firstly, there is the economic role of banks; secondly, the need to protect customers; thirdly, the prevention of a banking collapse, and the central bank's role in this; and fourthly, the competition issue. Finally, there is the issue of the scope of banking activities. What can banks actually do? Let's consider each point in turn.

Introduction 4

OK. Are we all ready? Is everyone here? We seem to have a small class today, so feel free to interrupt me if you have any questions. Right, I'll begin. For centuries, bankers have attempted to establish a global monetary regime or monetary standard. By this I mean the establishing of a fixed exchange rate for a currency. Today we're going to look at key developments in establishing a global monetary standard over the last 200 years or so.

Introduction 5

In this week's lecture, I'm going to discuss some aspects of modern technology and banking. Computers and other electronic machines are widely used in retail banking – for example, in the processing of cheques. A cheque is presented at a bank and an electronic procedure begins. The bank teller enters the details of the cheque onto the system. The computer reads the magnetic code. Money is debited from the payer's account electronically. The cheque is then sent to the clearing house and money is then credited to the payee's account.

Let's look at some more electronic procedures.

Methodology note

Spiral bound or stitched/stapled notebooks are not the best way to keep lecture notes. It is impossible to reorganize or add extra information at a later date, or make a clean copy of notes after a lecture. Encourage students, therefore, to use a loose leaf file, but make sure that they organize it in a sensible way, with file dividers, and keep it tidy. Tell students to use a separate piece of paper for each outline in this lecture.

Exercise C

Set for pair or group work. Feed back, but do not confirm or correct. Students should be able to predict reasonably well the kind of information which will fit into their outline.

Before you play the next part of each lecture, refer students to their outline notes again. Tell them to orally reconstruct the introduction from their notes. They don't have to be able to say the exact words, but they should be able to give the gist.

Remind students that they are only going to hear the next part of each lecture once. Play each extract in turn, pausing if necessary to allow students to make notes but not replaying any section. Tell students to choose an appropriate type of notes for this part of the lecture – it could be a continuation of the type they chose for the introduction, or it could be a different type.

Transcript 🎧 1.6

Lecture 1

There are advantages and disadvantages of foreign bank participation in a national banking market. Of course, one advantage for MNBs is cost: operating costs are often lower in the other country. But there can be advantages for the country in which they are operating, too. One advantage of foreign participation is that it often increases the efficiency of the domestic banks. How can this happen? Well, businesses are often inefficient in a market with little or no competition. When an MNB comes into this kind of market, competition increases and, sometimes, the efficiency of domestic banks increases as a result. However, on the other hand, the arrival of an MNB may be unwelcome competition for other domestic banks. The profitability of domestic banks may go down.

Another problem posed by cross-border banks is that of financial guarantees from the parent bank in the event of a failure in the local branch or subsidiary. The issues that need to be resolved in the event of a crisis in a subsidiary bank include: whose responsibility is it to handle such a crisis? What role should the host nation authorities play? And finally, given that the host nations are often the smaller nations, are they able to handle a crisis of a large cross-border bank?

🎧 1.7

Lecture 2

Let's start with authority. A centralized bank keeps its authority at the top level, whereas a decentralized bank delegates some authority to lower levels. As a result, accountability in a centralized bank should stay at the top level, whereas some accountability may be delegated in a decentralized bank. Of course, ultimately accountability will lie with the highest level of management in either situation.

The decision to be centralized or not can have a significant effect on growth. A small organization can work effectively in a centralized mode, but, as a bank grows, a decentralized organization may be more effective. The main reason for this is that if decisions don't have to go through a long chain of command, decision-making can be quicker. In a rapidly changing or uncertain environment, a decentralized organization is often more effective. It allows the bank to react quickly to changing circumstances. It can also be more flexible.

Centralized decision-making, on the other hand, is more effective in a stable environment. It allows more co-ordination in the organization. It also allows greater influence of leadership from the top.

🎧 1.8

Lecture 3

So, firstly, banks have an important role in the economy of a country. No government can afford to allow the banking system to fail. Therefore, governments maintain regulatory controls over bank operations. For example, they implement exchange controls. These restrict the amount of local currency that can be changed into foreign currencies.

Secondly, the regulations are there to protect the bank's customers. In the event of a bank failure it's important to make sure that small depositors don't lose their savings.

The third point relates to the need to prevent banking collapse. An important objective of bank regulation has been the prevention of a recession, or serious decline in the country's economy. This can occur when thousands of people have become bankrupt or unemployed. A bankrupt is a person whose affairs have been put into receivership, because they have been legally declared incapable of paying their debts.

In the 1930s, a 'bank run' occurred in the United States. Customers rushed to withdraw their deposits from banks which they thought were closing down. A consequence of bank runs is that they can spread to financially healthy banks, and this can have a serious impact on a country's economy.

The banking regulation set up to prevent such an occurrence is the 'lender of last resort' function. This is the ultimate source of credit to which banks can turn. In the United States, the Federal Reserve was created to serve as the 'lender of last resort'. However, it failed in that role during the Great

Depression. Generally, the role of 'lender of last resort' falls to the central bank of a country. For example, in the UK it is the Bank of England, which lends money to commercial banks. And in fact in 2007, the Bank of England did step in to lend money to Northern Rock during the so-called 'credit crunch'.

Because of the failure of the Federal Reserve Bank in its 'lender of last resort' function in the 1930s, the United States set up the Federal Deposit Insurance Corporation. By charging banks a standard premium on their deposits, the FDIC insures deposits in commercial banks and in savings and loan associations.

What's the fourth point? Oh, yes, competition. Legislative restrictions have also been placed on banking industry competition. In the United States until recently, there were 'branching restrictions'. These limited the ability of banks to expand outside their regions or states. However, the branching restrictions didn't apply to bank holding companies. These are firms that own many different banks as subsidiaries.

Finally, many countries place restrictions on the scope of bank activities. For example, banks are not allowed to engage in non-financial activities. Also, different types of banks may be restricted in the type of services they can provide. The purpose of bank regulations is to provide stability in the banking system.

🎧 1.9
Lecture 4

LECTURER: Early in the 19th century, Britain wanted to standardize the value of its currency, so the country adopted the gold standard for the British pound. Until that time, the value of the pound (or pound sterling) was based on an amount of silver in that weight. However, after the gold standard was adopted, the mint produced gold, instead of silver, coins. The mint, of course, is the factory where the government makes money. Almost half a century later, when the German states merged into one country, they also adopted the gold standard. They were followed by the Scandinavian countries, then France and Japan. Although there was an enormous increase in gold supplies, with new discoveries in Alaska, Africa and Australia, the United States didn't officially adopt the gold standard until 1900.

Between 1880 and 1930, the gold standard, which defined a national currency in terms of a fixed weight of gold, became the most common monetary arrangement, allowing a global fixed exchange rate system. Some people believe it

contributed to a period of globalization and economic modernization. However, at the start of the First World War, Britain withdrew gold from internal circulation, and after the depression of the 1930s, the gold standard was abandoned by most countries as a monetary policy.

STUDENT: Excuse me, but wasn't there a recent attempt to back currency with gold, in one of the Asian countries? Why wasn't it successful?

LECTURER: Yes, there was an attempt to produce a gold currency, in 2001. Prime Minister Mahathir of Malaysia proposed a new currency of 425 grams of gold, to be called the gold dinar. Prime Minister Mahathir thought there were good economic reasons for having a gold currency, and he also believed it would be a unifying symbol for Islamic nations, who would use it for their trade. But then Mahathir resigned as prime minister, and his proposal wasn't taken any further.

So, where was I? Oh, yes, for a period of time, between the wars, the pound sterling became the key global currency. Then, following the Second World War, it was replaced by the United States dollar.

STUDENT: Can I ask what has replaced the gold standard? I mean, how are currencies valued today?

LECTURER: Most governments manage money by regulating their economy or the money supply. They also peg their currencies to a currency board. By currency board, I mean a system by which a currency is convertible at a fixed exchange rate with another currency. This can mean that the currency is fully backed by a hard currency. Hard currency, in economic terms, refers to a currency in which investors have confidence. That is, currency from a politically stable country with low inflation and consistent monetary and fiscal policies. In particular, a currency that is tending to appreciate against other currencies on a trade-weighted basis. Examples of hard currencies include the United States dollar, the euro, the pound sterling, the Japanese yen, and the Swiss franc. The Deutschmark was considered the best hard currency until it was replaced by the euro. Today, many countries set their currency against a 'basket' of currencies. This basket of currencies is usually based on those of their trading partners, which are 'weighted' and measured to provide an average. Does that answer your question? Good.

🎧 1.10
Lecture 5

Computers are also used for an electronic funds transfer (EFT). This includes transferring money from and to different bank accounts and for withdrawals. Most of us encounter EFT in our daily lives without thinking about it. For example, using an EFTPOS card as a customer to pay for goods in a shop or supermarket. EFTPOS stands for electronic funds transfer at point of sale.

The procedure works like this. A customer buys some goods at a supermarket. The customer takes the goods to the checkout, where the value is entered onto an electronic point of sale terminal (EPOS). The customer presents his or her EFTPOS card instead of cash. The EFTPOS card debits the customer's account and credits the retailer's account electronically. The customer and retailer accounts are updated after the transactions are uploaded on the computer. They are processed overnight.

Another example of an automated procedure is automated teller machines, or ATMs. ATMs allow bank clients access to their accounts 24 hours a day, seven days a week. This access is also possible in foreign countries. Bank clients are provided with an ATM card.

The bank client inserts the card into the machine. The machine asks for the personal identification number or PIN . The client then keys in their electronic code. The machine checks the code and, if it recognizes it, asks which transaction the client wants to make. The client can now withdraw money, check balances or, in some cases, transfer or deposit money. The most frequent transaction is the withdrawal, in which case the customer keys in the amount and the ATM checks if there are sufficient funds available in the client's account. If so, the machine returns the card and then pays the money, or pays the money and then returns the card. The order is different in some countries.

Exercise E

Allow students to uncover the opposite page or open their books. Give them plenty of time to compare their answers with the model notes. Feed back on the final question.

Exercise F

1 Ask students to work in pairs. Assign one set of notes to each pair. They must try to reconstruct the lecture orally – including the introduction – from the notes.

2 Put the pairs together in groups of four, with different topics. Each pair should give their lecture to another pair.

Closure

Work on any problems you notice during the pairwork (Exercise F).

Extra activities

1 Work through the *Vocabulary bank* and *Skills bank* if you have not already done so, or as a revision of previous study.

2 Use the *Activity bank* (Teacher's Book additional resources section, Resource 1A).

A Set the crossword for individual work (including homework) or pairwork.

Answers

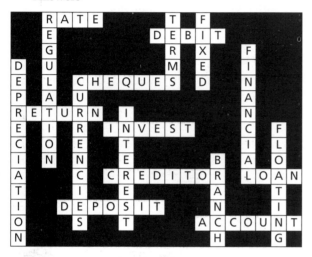

B Play noughts and crosses in pairs. There are two boards. The first contains words with affixes, the second contains other banking terms.

Teach students how to play noughts and crosses if they don't know – they take it in turns to choose a word/phrase/name and try to use it in context or explain what it means. If they succeed, they can put their symbol – a nought 0 or a cross **X** – in that box. If a person gets three of their own symbols in a line, they win.

First board: Tell students to remove the affixes to find the basic word in each case. Make sure they can tell you the meaning of the basic word but don't elicit the meaning of the affixed word, e.g., *legal* not *illegal*. Put students in pairs to play the game. Monitor and adjudicate.

Second board: Put students in different pairs to play the second game. Clearly, this time they have to actually remember the facts from the lectures. Don't let them look back at notes.

3 Each of the mini lectures from Lesson 4 can lead on to a great deal more work. Tell students to research one of the following, according to which group they ended in. Explain that they must come back and report to the rest of the class in the next lesson/next week.

Lecture	Research
1	some examples of MNBs in your own country
2	an example of a bank that you know and an explanation of each of the divisions operating in it
3	some key examples of bank regulations in a country you know of other than the UK and the US
4	a specific example of a currency and the currency board it fixes its exchange rate to
5	new advances in technology that will assist banking in the future

4 Brainstorm note-taking techniques. For example:

- use spacing between points
- use abbreviations
- use symbols
- underline headings
- use capital letters
- use indenting
- make ordered points
- use different colours
- use key words only

2 THE ORIGINS OF BANKING

Unit 2 looks at the history of banking services. The first reading text examines the development of banking from ancient Egypt to 19th-century Britain, identifying services which are still in use today. The second reading text looks at the history of American banks and explores the reasons behind the creation of the Federal Reserve Bank.

Note that students will need dictionaries for some exercises in this unit.

Skills focus

Reading

- using research questions to focus on relevant information in a text
- using topic sentences to get an overview of the text

Writing

- writing topic sentences
- summarizing a text

Vocabulary focus

- English–English dictionaries:
  headwords
  definitions
  parts of speech
  phonemes
  stress markers
  countable/uncountable
  transitive/intransitive

Key vocabulary

advance (n and v)	credit (n and v)	mortgage (n and v)
asset	currency	negotiable
balance (n)	deposit (n and v)	promissory note
(bank)note	depositor	receipt
bankrupt (adj and n)	finance (n and v)	regulate
bankruptcy	financial	regulation
bearer	fraud	reserve(s) (n)
bill of exchange	giro	transaction
bond (n)	invest	vault (n)
borrower	liquid (adj)	withdraw
charter (n and v)	liquidity	withdrawal
circulation	loan (n and v)	
counterfeit	mint (n and v)	

2.1 Vocabulary

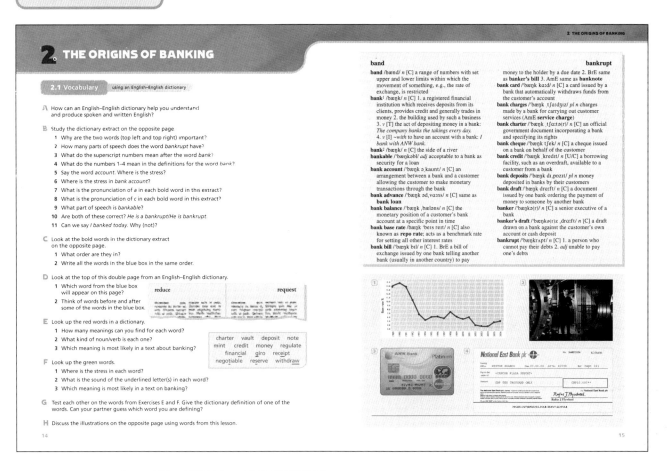

General note

Take in a set of English–English dictionaries. You may also like to take in a specialist dictionary of banking and finance.

Read the *Vocabulary bank* at the end of the Course Book unit. Decide when, if at all, to refer students to it. The best time is probably at the very end of the lesson or the beginning of the next lesson, as a summary/revision.

Lesson aims

- learn how to make full use of an English–English dictionary
- gain fluency in the target vocabulary

Introduction

1 Revise the vocabulary from the last unit. Check:
- meaning
- pronunciation
- spelling

2 Ask students whether they use a translation (bilingual) dictionary or an English–English

(monolingual) dictionary. Elicit the advantages and disadvantages of a translation dictionary.

Answers

Model answers:

+	−
good when you know the word in your own language and need a translation into English	not good when there is more than one possible translation of a word – which is the correct one?
when you look up an English word, the translation into your language is easy to understand	English–English dictionaries often have more examples and precise definitions of each word

Exercise A

Ask the question as a general discussion. Confirm but do not explain anything. Point out that the next exercise will make the value of this kind of dictionary clear.

Answers

Model answers:

The following information is useful for spoken English:
- stress

- pronunciation of individual phonemes – particularly when a phoneme has multiple pronunciations

The following information is useful for written English:

- information about the type of word – C/U; T/I
- the spelling – students might say that if you don't know the spelling, you can't find the word in the first place, but point out that you can often guess the possible spelling – for example, *fractional* could be *frak* but if you don't find it there, you can try *frac* …
- examples of the word in use to memorize
- some synonyms for lexical cohesion – this is a very important point, although you may not want to elaborate on this now

Methodology note

The advantage of monolingual dictionaries is that they introduce the user to the lexical system of L2. Source: Bejoint, H.B. & Moulin, A. (1987). 'The place of a dictionary in an EFL program' in Cowie, A.P. (ed.) *The Dictionary and the Language Learner*. Tübingen: Niemeyer (pp. 381–92). Recent research shows that although students get an instant response from electronic (translation) pocket dictionaries, 'such practices rarely help the student to internalize the word for later recall and use'. Source: Brown, D. (2001). *Teaching by principles: An interactive approach to language pedagogy* (2nd ed.) Harlow: Pearson Longman. (p. 377).

Exercise B

Set for individual work and pairwork checking. Feed back, ideally using an OHT or other visual display of the dictionary extract to highlight points. You might suggest that students annotate the dictionary extract in their books, highlighting symbols, etc., and writing notes on the meaning and value.

Answers

Model answers:

1 These headwords tell you the first and last words on the pages to help you locate the word you want.
2 Two: noun and adjective.
3 That there are two entries giving different meanings of the word *bank*: the first entry gives the meanings related to finance, and the second entry gives the meaning related to geography.
4 That it has four meanings related to finance.
5 On the second syllable.
6 Main stress is on the first word, *bank*; secondary stress in *ac'count*.
7 Four pronunciations: /æ/, /ɑː/, /eɪ/, /ə/. Can students identify the word(s) in each category?

8 Two pronunciations: /k/, /s/. However, if students legitimately come up with /tʃ/, then accept it.
9 Adjective.
10 Yes, because *bankrupt* can be a noun or an adjective.
11 No, because *bank* is either transitive – you must say what you banked – or, when intransitive, must be followed by *with*.

Language note

It is not necessary to go into the precise meanings of all the words in the dictionary extract. However, for reference:

A *banker's draft* is used for local (not international) transactions involving large purchases (e.g., house, car). As it is issued by the bank, from funds in the buyer's account, the payee will almost certainly be guaranteed payment. (Payment of a personal cheque is not guaranteed.)

A *bank bill* has the same meaning as a bill of exchange in the UK. Bank bills form no part of the currency. Also referred to as a *banker's bill*. In the US, a bank bill is used as currency, i.e., a banknote.

A *bank draft* (or international cheque) is drawn on the issuing bank, on currencies that the bank deals with. Signed by the issuing bank's manager, it is not cleared funds and is usually sent back to the originating bank for payment confirmation.

A *bank card* (a debit or credit card, usually plastic) is issued by a bank to persons with a satisfactory credit rating. In general, the bank issuing it guarantees payment for goods bought with it.

Exercise C

Note: If students are from a Roman alphabet background, you may want to omit this exercise.

1 Students should quickly be able to identify alphabetical order.
2 Set for individual work and pairwork checking. Feed back, getting the words on the board in the correct order. Don't worry about stress and individual phonemes at this point – students will check this later with their dictionaries.

Answers

Model answer:

charter, credit, deposit, financial, giro, mint, money, negotiable, note, receipt, regulate, reserve, vault, withdraw

Language note

It may seem self-evident that words in a dictionary are in alphabetical order. But students from certain languages may not automatically recognize this. In the famous Hans Wehr dictionary of written Arabic, for example, you must first convert a given word to its root and look that up, then find the derived form. So *aflaaj* (the plural of *falaj* = irrigation channel) will not be found under A but under F, since the root is *f-l-j*.

Exercise D

1 Set for pairwork. Feed back orally, explaining the principle if necessary.
2 Set for pairwork. Ask students to find words connected with banking if they can. Feed back orally.

Answers

1 *Regulate* will appear on the double page spread.
2 Answers depend on which words students choose.

Exercise E

Give out the dictionaries, if you have not already done so.

Remind students that dictionaries number multiple meanings of the same part of speech and multiple parts of speech. Remind them also of the countable/uncountable and transitive/intransitive markers. (Note that different dictionaries may use different methods for indicating these things. *The Oxford Advanced Learner's Dictionary*, for example uses [V] for intransitive verbs and [Vn] for transitive verbs.)

Write the headings of the table in the Answers section on the board, and work through the first word as an example.

Set for pairwork. Feed back, building up the table in the Answers section on the board. (Students' answers will vary – accept any appropriate meanings and definitions.)

Answers

Model answers:
See table below.

Word	Part of speech	Type	Main meaning(s) in banking	Main meaning(s) in general English
charter	n	C	a written statement of the purposes of an organization	a written statement of the rights and beliefs of a particular group of people
charter	v	T		hire something
vault	n	C	a room with a strong door and thick walls for keeping valuables safe	a room under a church where people are buried
vault	v	T		jump over something
deposit	n	C	money paid into a bank account	a first payment with the rest of the money to be paid later
deposit	v	T	put money into a bank account	put something down somewhere
note	n	C	(banknote) a piece of paper money	1. some words you write down quickly to remember; 2. a short letter; 3. a musical sound
note	v	T		1. write down something to remember it; 2. pay attention to something
mint	n	C/U	(C) a place where money (coins and notes) is made by the government	1. (U) a type of herb; 2. (C) a sweet
mint	v	T	make coins	
credit	n	C/U	1. (U) a sum of money lent by a bank; 2. (U) having money in a bank account	1. (U) buying goods or services and not paying until later; 2. (U) praise, acknowledgement; 3. (C) recognition that a student has completed a course
credit	v	T	add money to a bank account	recognize something that someone has done well
money	n	U	coins and notes used for buying and selling	same meaning
regulate	v	T	control by law	1. same meaning; 2. control a machine, equipment, etc.

Exercise F

Remind students how stress and the pronunciation of individual phonemes are shown in a dictionary. Refer them to the key to symbols in the dictionary if necessary. Check word syllables if necessary. Write the headings of the table in the Answers section on the board, and work through the first word as an example.

Set for pairwork. Feed back, building up the table in the Answers section on the board.

Answers

Model answers:

Stress	Sound	Part of speech	Type	Main meaning in banking
fi'nancial	/ʃ/	adj		concerning money
'giro	/dʒ/	n	C/U	a system of moving money from one bank to another
re'ceipt	/iː/	n	C	a piece of paper given to show something has been received or money has been paid
ne'gotiable	/ʃ/	adj		able to be transferred from one person to another or exchanged for cash
re'serve	/z/	n or v	C/U T	(n) money from profits not paid as dividends but kept in case of need
with'draw	/ɔː/	v	T	take money out of an account

Exercise G

Demonstrate how to do the exercise by giving a few definitions and asking students to tell you the word (without reading from the board or their books, if possible). Keep to banking rather than general English definitions and encourage students to do the same.

Exercise H

Work through the illustrations. Check that students understand what they show and the relationship to banking.

For reference, the illustrations show:

1 a chart showing fluctuations in the **bank base rate**
2 a bank **vault**
3 a **bank card** (**credit** or debit card)
4 a **bank draft** (a type of **cheque** usually signed by the issuing bank's manager)

Closure

Remind students that you can identify the part of speech of an unknown word by looking at the words before or after the word, i.e.,

● nouns often come before and after verbs, so if you know that X is a verb, the next content word before or after is probably a noun
● nouns often come immediately after articles
● verbs often come after names and pronouns
● adjectives come before nouns or after the verb *be*

Come back to this point when you are giving feedback on the reading texts in this unit.

Point out that dictionaries often use a small set of words that help define, e.g., *material, device, principle, system, situation, place, organization, document.* Give definitions using these words and ask students to identify what you are defining, e.g., *It's a system of moving money from one bank to another* (giro); *It's a place where money is made* (mint).

2.2 Reading

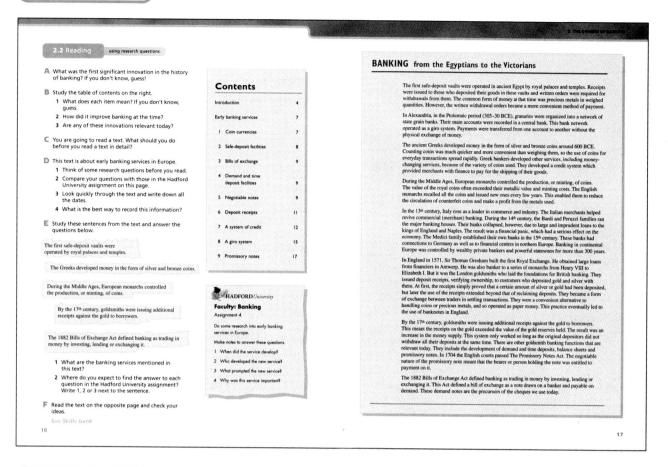

General note

Take in an English–English dictionary.

Read the *Skills bank* section on doing reading research at the end of the Course Book unit. Decide when, if at all, to refer students to it. The best time is probably at the very end of the lesson or the beginning of the next lesson, as a summary/revision. Alternatively, you could refer students to the *Skills bank* after Exercise C.

Lesson aims

- prepare for reading research
- use research questions to structure reading research

Introduction

1 Hold up an English–English dictionary and say a word from Lesson 1. Ask students where approximately they will find it in the dictionary – i.e., beginning, middle, two-thirds of the way through, etc. Follow their advice and read the word at the top left. Ask students if the target word will be before or after. Continue until you get to the right page. Repeat with several more words from Lesson 1.

2 Give definitions of some of the banking words from Lesson 1 for students to identify.

Exercise A

First check understanding of *innovation*. Ask students to think of any very recent innovations in banking.

Set Exercise A for general discussion. Point out that this refers to innovations before the 20th century.

Feed back, accepting all reasonable answers, e.g., money in the form of coins; money-changing services; a system of credit.

Exercise B

Refer students to the extract from a table of contents.

1/2 Give a couple of examples, e.g., safe-deposit facilities, negotiable notes. Set for pairwork. Have students guess the answers if they don't already know.

3 General discussion. Tell students there is no 'correct' answer. Be prepared to accept any answer you think is reasonable. Encourage debate. Answers will depend on the student; encourage them to justify their choice(s).

Answers

Possible answers:

Note: These are for your guidance only. Do not give them to the students at this pre-reading stage. At the end of the lesson you can return to these questions.

Innovation	Meaning	How it improved the existing service	Relevance today?
coin currencies	metal money	counting quicker than weighing; more transportable	yes (not precious metals), but paper and plastic money more useful
safe-deposit facilities	a strong room (vault)	kept valuables safer, stored away from own premises	yes – still used for same reasons
bills of exchange	written commitment from a bank to pay	more convenient than transporting large sums of money	yes – used in international trade for payments in foreign currency
1. demand and 2. time deposit facilities	money in a bank account that earns interest	1. gave flexibility for withdrawals 2. set a fixed date for withdrawals	yes
negotiable notes	transferable instrument, exchangeable for money	could be transferred from one person to another, or exchanged for money; very convenient	yes
deposit receipts	acknowledgement that something has been received	gave people security; acknowledged the deposit and the depositor	yes
a system of credit	a period of time allowed before debt has to be paid	allowed the borrower time before having to pay the debt incurred for goods or services	yes
a giro system	the electronic transfer of money from one account to another	quick and convenient – saved time (no need to physically make inter-bank transactions)	yes – very relevant
promissory notes	a document promising to pay an amount of money on a specific date	the person with the note could guarantee they would receive payment on a fixed date	yes – as banknotes in our currencies

Exercise C

Students may or may not be able to articulate preparation for reading. Elicit ideas. One thing they must identify – reading for a purpose. Point out that they should always be clear about the purpose of their reading. A series of questions to answer, or *research questions*, is one of the best purposes. Refer students to the *Skills bank* at this stage, if you wish.

Exercise D

1 Set for pairwork. Elicit some ideas, but do not confirm or correct.

2 Refer students to the Hadford University handout at the bottom of the page. Check comprehension, especially of the verb *prompted*. If students have come up with better research questions, write them on the board for consideration during the actual reading.

3/4 Class discussion on the different dates, their forms, their significance in the text and the best way to record the information (chronologically).

Exercise E

If students haven't mentioned topic sentences in Exercise C, introduce them for discussion, e.g., what they are, where you would expect to find them in a paragraph, and why. Point out that some topic sentences clearly announce what the paragraph will be about. Others may only give a hint of how it will develop. Give them time to read the topic sentences in this exercise.

1 Set for group discussion.

2 Remind students of the Hadford University research questions. Point out that they may match a research question to more than one topic sentence, and that some topic sentences may not relate to the

research questions (i.e., they don't have to write a number for each topic sentence). Set for pairwork.

Answers

Possible answers:

1 Safe-deposit vaults, coin currency, minting, receipts against gold, (banking)

2 The following is a reasonable prediction, although students may argue that each of the first four paragraphs potentially contains the answers to all four research questions.

The first safe-deposit vaults were operated by royal palaces and temples.	2
The Greeks developed money in the form of silver and bronze coins.	2
During the Middle Ages, European monarchs controlled the production, or minting, of coins.	1, 2
By the 17th century, goldsmiths were issuing additional receipts against the gold to borrowers.	1, 2
The 1882 Bills of Exchange Act defined banking as trading in money by investing, lending or exchanging it.	

Exercise F

Point out, if students have not already said this, that the topic sentences are normally the first sentences of each paragraph. Tell students to compare the contents of each paragraph with their predictions. Encourage them to take notes as they read.

If necessary, the reading can be set for homework.

Closure

1 Unless you have set the reading for homework, do some extra work on oral summarizing as a comprehension check after reading (*see Skills bank – Using topic sentences to summarize*). Students work in pairs. One student says a topic sentence and the other student summarizes the paragraph from memory in his/her own words, or if necessary reads the paragraph again and then summarizes it without looking.

2 You may also want to redo the text as a jigsaw – the text is reproduced in the additional resources section (Resource 2B) to facilitate this.

3 As a further activity after reading, remind students of the note-taking skills practised in Unit 1. Discuss appropriate note-taking forms for this text. They can then write notes on the text. Tell them to keep their notes, as they will be useful for the summary exercise in Lesson 3.

2.3 Extending skills

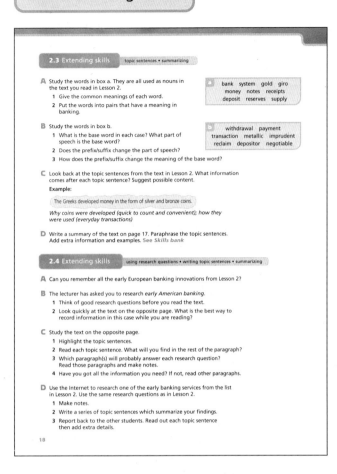

2.3 Extending skills — topic sentences • summarizing

A Study the words in box a. They are all used as nouns in the text you read in Lesson 2.
  1 Give the common meanings of each word.
  2 Put the words into pairs that have a meaning in banking.

a | bank system gold giro
money notes receipts
deposit reserves supply

B Study the words in box b.
  1 What is the base word in each case? What part of speech is the base word?
  2 Does the prefix/suffix change the part of speech?
  3 How does the prefix/suffix change the meaning of the base word?

b | withdrawal payment
transaction metallic imprudent
reclaim depositor negotiable

C Look back at the topic sentences from the text in Lesson 2. What information comes after each topic sentence? Suggest possible content.
  Example:

  The Greeks developed money in the form of silver and bronze coins.

  Why coins were developed (quick to count and convenient); how they were used (everyday transactions)

D Write a summary of the text on page 17. Paraphrase the topic sentences. Add extra information and examples. See *Skills bank*

2.4 Extending skills — using research questions • writing topic sentences • summarizing

A Can you remember all the early European banking innovations from Lesson 2?

B The lecturer has asked you to research *early American banking*.
  1 Think of good research questions before you read the text.
  2 Look quickly at the text on the opposite page. What is the best way to record information in this case while you are reading?

C Study the text on the opposite page.
  1 Highlight the topic sentences.
  2 Read each topic sentence. What will you find in the rest of the paragraph?
  3 Which paragraph(s) will probably answer each research question? Read those paragraphs and make notes.
  4 Have you got all the information you need? If not, read other paragraphs.

D Use the Internet to research one of the early banking services from the list in Lesson 2. Use the same research questions as in Lesson 2.
  1 Make notes.
  2 Write a series of topic sentences which summarize your findings.
  3 Report back to the other students. Read out each topic sentence then add extra details.

18

General note

Take in a set of English–English dictionaries.

Lesson aims

- produce good topic sentences and a summary text

Further practice in:

- vocabulary from Lesson 2

Introduction

Test students on the factual information in the text from the previous lesson, e.g., *What system did Greek bankers develop to help the merchants?* If a student says, accurately, *I didn't read about that. It wasn't relevant to my research*, accept it and praise the student.

Exercise A

1 Set for pairwork. Refer students back to the text if necessary. Feed back.

2 Give most of the students time to find the pairs. Point out they must use each word once only. Accept all reasonable collocations. Feed back orally, checking students understand the meaning of all the terms.

Answers

1 Answers depend on the students.

2 Possible answers (i.e., the most common collocations):
  money supply
  deposit receipts
  banknotes
  giro system
  gold reserves

Methodology note

Don't help students to find words in a text. It's a key reading skill to be able to pattern match, i.e., get a word in your mind's eye and then find it on the page.

Exercise B

Set for individual work and pairwork checking. Students can check these points in a dictionary. Feed back, taking apart the words and showing how the affixes can change the meaning.

Answers

Model answers:

Word	Base word	Affix and meaning
withdrawal (n)	withdraw (v)	*al* = verb → noun
payment (n)	pay (v)	*ment* = verb → noun
transaction (n)	transact (v)	*tion* = verb → noun
metallic (adj)	metal (n)	*ic* = noun → adjective
imprudent (adj)	prudent (adj)	*im* = not
reclaim (v)	claim (v)	*re* = again
depositor (n)	deposit (v)	*or* = verb → noun (person)
negotiable (adj)	negotiate (v)	*able* = can be

Exercise C

Ideally, display the topic sentences (or give them on a handout) so that students do not have to turn back to pages 16 and 17. Include all the topic sentences from the text, not just the ones on page 16. The topic sentences are reproduced in the additional resources section at the back of the Teacher's Book to facilitate this (Resource 2C). Work through the example, showing that you can deduce (or in this case to some extent remember) the contents of a paragraph from the topic sentence. Do another example orally. Set for pairwork.

Feed back, eliciting possible paragraph contents. Only correct ideas which are not based on the topic sentence. Allow students to check back with the text and self-mark.

Answers

Possible answers:

Topic sentence	Possible paragraph content	Supporting information/example(s)
The first safe-deposit vaults were operated by royal palaces and temples.	how exactly these vaults operated	receipts were issued; written orders required for withdrawals
In Alexandria, granaries were organized into a network of state grain banks.	how they operated	operated as a giro system
The Greeks developed money in the form of silver and bronze coins.	why/how coins were used	coins were quick to count and convenient; used for everyday transactions
During the Middle Ages, European monarchs controlled the production, or minting, of coins.	why/how they used coins	they issued new coins and made a profit on the metal and minting costs
In the 13th century, Italy rose as a leader in commerce and industry.	what effect this had on banking	revival of merchant banking; banking controlled by wealthy private bankers and statesmen
In England in 1571, Sir Thomas Gresham built the first Royal Exchange.	what effect this had on banking in Britain	laid foundations of British banking; led to use of banknotes
By the 17th century, goldsmiths were issuing additional receipts against the gold to borrowers.	what effect this had on banking	they were able to increase the money supply; development of demand and time deposits, balance sheets and promissory notes.
The 1882 Bills of Exchange Act defined banking as trading in money by investing, lending or exchanging it.	definition of banking, bankers, bills of exchange	demand notes led to use of cheques

Discourse note

In academic writing, topic sentences often consist of a general point. The sentences that follow then support the general statement in various ways, such as:

- giving a definition and/or a description
- giving examples
- giving lists of points (e.g., arguments or reasons)
- restating the topic sentence in a different way to help clarify it
- giving more information and detail on the topic sentence to clarify it

Often – but not always – the type of sentence is shown by a 'discourse marker' – e.g., *for example, first of all*, etc. This helps to signal to the reader how the writer sees the link between the sentences and is therefore a good clue as to the purpose of the sentences following the topic sentence.

Methodology note

There are two reasons for students to use their own words in written work (except when quoting and acknowledging sources):

1 The work involved in rewording information and ideas helps us to mentally process them and to retain them in memory.

2 Copying whole sentences from the work of other writers is plagiarism (unless the quotation is acknowledged). Universities disapprove of plagiarism and may mark down students who plagiarize. In the commercial world an accusation of plagiarism can cause legal problems, and in the academic world it can severely damage a teacher's reputation.

Exercise D

Refer students to the *Skills bank*. Set for individual work. If students took notes in Lesson 2, Exercise F, they should use these as the basis for this exercise. Encourage students to add extra information or examples to fill out the summary. They can start in class, while you monitor and assist, and finish for homework.

Closure

Tell students to define some of the banking words from the text on page 17. Alternatively, give definitions and tell students to identify the words.

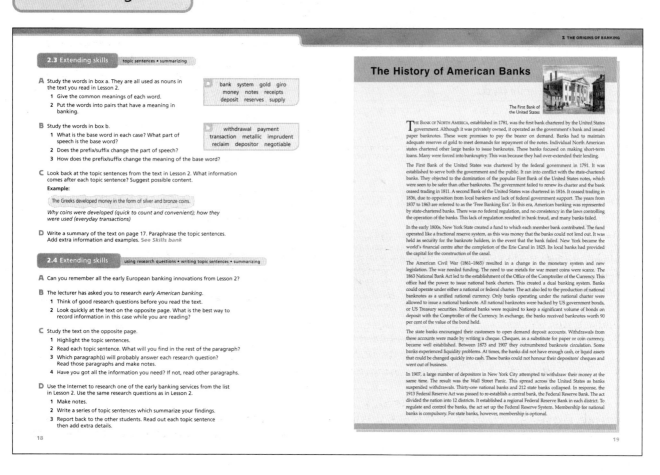

Lesson aims

- use research questions to structure reading research
- write topic sentences for a short research report/summary

Introduction

Give a word from the text in Lesson 2 which is part of a phrase. Ask students to try to complete the phrase. It's probably better if you give the first word in the phrase, but you might also try giving the second word at times or at the end of the exercise.

Possible phrases:

safe-deposit	*vault/facilities*
giro	*system*
money-changing	*services*
credit	*system*
merchant	*banking*
private	*banker*
money	*supply*
deposit	*receipts*
demand	*deposit*
time	*deposit*
balance	*sheet*
promissory	*note*
bill of	*exchange*

Exercise A

Group discussion. Build up the list on the board, students' books closed.

Answers

coin currencies
safe-deposit facilities
bills of exchange
demand and time deposit facilities
negotiable notes
deposit receipts
a system of credit
a giro system
promissory notes

Exercise B

1 Refer students to the title of the text – *The History of American Banks*. Tell them the focus is on North America after the declaration of independence in 1776. Remind students of the importance of research questions – reading for a purpose. Set for pairwork. Feed back orally.

2 Elicit the different kinds of notes you can use – see Unit 1 *Skills bank*. Remind students to think about the best kind of notes while they are reading.

Methodology note

It is good for students to get into the habit of thinking about the form of their notes before they read a text in detail. If they don't do this, they will tend to be drawn into narrative notes rather than notes which are specifically designed to help them answer their research questions.

Answers

1 Accept all responses. Build up the most appropriate questions on the board or OHP.

2 See Unit 1 *Skills bank*. Timeline/chronological notes would be appropriate here.

Exercise C

1 Remind students of the importance of topic sentences. Set for individual work and pairwork checking.

2 Encourage students not to read ahead. Perhaps you should ask students to cover the text and only reveal each topic sentence in turn, then discuss possible contents of the paragraph. Remind them that it is not a good idea to read every part of a text unless you have to. If you have an OHP or other visual display, you can tell students to shut their books and just display the topic sentences from the jigsaw text in the additional resources section (Resource 2D), or you can give them as a handout (Resource 2E).

3 Set the choice of paragraphs for pairwork. Students then read individually, make notes and compare them. Monitor and assist.

4 Give students time to read other paragraphs if they need to.

Discourse note

It is as well to be aware (though you may not feel it is appropriate to discuss with students at this point) that in real academic texts, the topic sentence may not be as obvious as in the texts in this unit. Sometimes there is not an explicit topic sentence, so that the overall topic of the paragraph must be inferred. Or the actual topic sentence for the paragraph can be near rather than at the beginning of the paragraph. Sometimes, also, the first sentence of a paragraph acts as a topic statement for a succession of paragraphs.

Answers

Possible answers:

1/2

Topic sentence	Possible paragraph content
The Bank of North America, established in 1781, was the first bank chartered by the United States government.	role of the Bank of North America; other banks?
The First Bank of the United States was chartered by the federal government in 1791.	role of the Bank of the United States; how different from Bank of North America
In the early 1800s, New York State created a fund to which each member bank contributed.	why this was done, and what the result was
The American Civil War (1861–1865) resulted in a change in the monetary system and new legislation.	why this happened, what the change was, what the result was
The state banks encouraged their customers to open demand deposit accounts.	why the state banks did this, and what the result was
In 1907, a large number of depositors in New York City attempted to withdraw their money at the same time.	why this happened, and what the result was

3 The appropriate paragraphs to read depend on the research questions you and your students decide on.

Exercise D

1 If it is possible to research on the Internet during the lesson, send students to the computers now. They can work in groups, according to the banking service they have chosen. If Internet access is not available, set the task for homework and feed back next lesson.

2 Set for individual work and group work checking.

3 The idea is that students, on the basis of the topic sentences, present their information to fellow students. Make sure students realize that they only have to write the topic sentences. They can add the details in orally. Encourage them to stick to information that is relevant to their research questions.

Closure

1 Students can use the information they gathered in Exercise D to write a full summary of their findings.

2 Get students to define some of the banking words from the text on page 19. Alternatively, give definitions of some of the words and get students to identify the words.

Extra activities

1 Work through the *Vocabulary bank* and *Skills bank* if you have not already done so, or as a revision of previous study.

2 Use the *Activity bank* (Teacher's Book additional resources section, Resource 2A).

   A Set the wordsearch for individual work (including homework) or pairwork.

   Answers

   B To review two-word phrases, give students a word from the text in Lesson 2 which is part of a phrase, e.g., *safe-deposit*. Ask students to try to complete the phrase. They may answer *box* or *vault* or *facilities*. Accept all answers as correct.

   Ask students to work in pairs or small groups. Remind them to use each word once only. Tell them there are different possibilities. Acknowledge all correct options.

   Answers

   Possible answers:
   bank fraud
   deposit account
   economic depression
   financial panic
   foreign ownership
   liquid assets
   national currency
   Accept foreign currency/national ownership as alternative pairings.

3 Ask students to work in small groups to research and feed back to the group on other banking achievements of the 20th century. The three research questions are the same as in Lesson 2.

   If students are going to do research on the Internet, suggest that they type in *History* then their topic to get some potential texts. Alternatively, you can do this research before the lesson and print off some pages for students to work from.

   Remind students that they can't possibly read everything they find, so they must use the topic sentences to decide if a paragraph is worth reading.

4 You can get students to practise their reading aloud – a skill which is not vital but is sometimes useful – by following this approach.

   Photocopy and cut up one of the jigsaw texts in the additional resources section (Resources 2B and 2D). Give topic sentences to Student A and the corresponding paragraph to Student B.

   Student A reads out a topic sentence.

   Student B finds the corresponding paragraph and reads it out.

   An alternative is to give Student A the topic sentences and Student B a set of sentences chosen from each paragraph (one sentence per paragraph). Student A reads out the topic sentences one by one. Student B decides which of his/her sentences is likely to appear in the same paragraph as the topic sentence. Both students have to agree that the paragraph sentence matches the topic sentence.

5 Have a competition to practise finding words in a monolingual dictionary. Each student or pair will need an English–English dictionary. Put students in teams with their dictionaries closed. Select a word from the Unit 2 key vocabulary list and instruct students to open their dictionaries and find the word. The first student to find the word is awarded a point for their team. Additional points can be awarded if the student can give the correct pronunciation and meaning.

3 BANKING INSTITUTIONS

Unit 3 looks at the different types of banking institutions and what services they provide. The first lecture looks at the different ways of categorizing banks – either in terms of who owns them (members or shareholders), or in terms of the services they provide (e.g., wholesale, retail or central). Investment banks are also examined in some detail. The second lecture looks at a number of different banks from different categories in the UK and explores the way their services cut across traditional boundaries.

Skills focus

🎧 Listening

- preparing for a lecture
- predicting lecture content
- making lecture notes
- using different information sources

Speaking

- reporting research findings
- formulating questions

Vocabulary focus

- stress patterns in multi-syllable words
- prefixes

Key vocabulary

building society	insurance	securities
central bank	investment bank	share capital
conglomerate	loan (n and v)	telephone banking
credit card	merchant bank	text message banking
dividend	mortgage	touch-screen share dealing
equity	mutual (n)	trade services
foreign investments	online banking	
fund (n and v)	personal loan	

3.1 Vocabulary

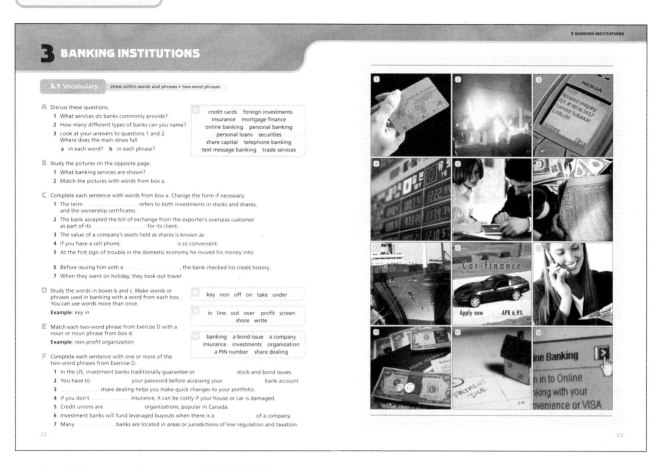

3 BANKING INSTITUTIONS

3.1 Vocabulary   stress within words and phrases • two-word phrases

A Discuss these questions.
1 What services do banks commonly provide?
2 How many different types of banks can you name?
3 Look at your answers to questions 1 and 2. Where does the main stress fall
   a in each word?   b in each phrase?

credit cards   foreign investments
insurance   mortgage finance
online banking   personal banking
personal loans   securities
share capital   telephone banking
text message banking   trade services

B Study the pictures on the opposite page.
1 What banking services are shown?
2 Match the pictures with words from box a.

C Complete each sentence with words from box a. Change the form if necessary.
1 The term _____ refers to both investments in stocks and shares, and the ownership certificates.
2 The bank accepted the bill of exchange from the exporter's overseas customer as part of its _____ for its client.
3 The value of a company's assets held as shares is known as _____
4 If you have a cell phone, _____ is so convenient.
5 At the first sign of trouble in the domestic economy he moved his money into _____
6 Before issuing him with a _____, the bank checked his credit history.
7 When they went on holiday, they took out travel _____

D Study the words in boxes b and c. Make words or phrases used in banking with a word from each box. You can use words more than once.
Example: *key in*

key non off on take under

in line out over profit screen
shore write

E Match each two-word phrase from Exercise D with a noun or noun phrase from box d.
Example: *non-profit organization*

banking   a bond issue   a company
insurance   investments   organization
a PIN number   share dealing

F Complete each sentence with one or more of the two-word phrases from Exercise D.
1 In the US, investment banks traditionally guarantee or _____ stock and bond issues.
2 You have to _____ your password before accessing your _____ bank account.
3 _____ share dealing helps you make quick changes to your portfolio.
4 If you don't _____ insurance, it can be costly if your house or car is damaged.
5 Credit unions are _____ organizations, popular in Canada.
6 Investment banks will fund leveraged buyouts when there is a _____ of a company.
7 Many _____ banks are located in areas or jurisdictions of low regulation and taxation.

22

23

General note

Read the *Vocabulary bank* at the end of the Course Book unit. Decide when, if at all, to refer your students to it. The best time is probably at the very end of the lesson or the beginning of the next lesson, as a summary/revision.

Dictionaries will be useful in this lesson.

Lesson aims

- gain a greater understanding of the importance of stress within words and phrases and some of the common patterns
- gain fluency in the target vocabulary

Introduction

Revise the vocabulary from the first two units. Check:

- meaning
- pronunciation
- spelling

Exercise A

1 Refer students to the first question. Elicit suggestions and list on the board.

2 Put students in pairs to discuss the second question. Tell students to make brief notes. Prompt if necessary, e.g., *What type of bank is HSBC?*

3 Check pronunciation of the words and phrases from questions 1 and 2, focusing on stress within words and in multi-syllable words.

Answers

Possible answers:

1 cheque accounts, savings accounts, loans, credit cards, electronic transfers

2 commercial bank, savings bank, national bank, retail bank, wholesale bank, merchant bank, central bank, international bank, investment bank

3 Answers depend on the words and phrases suggested by the students for questions 1 and 2. For example:

   a Main stress in single words: a'ccount, 'credit, elec'tronic, 'transfer, 'money, com'mercial, 'savings, 'national, 'retail, 'wholesale, 'merchant, 'central

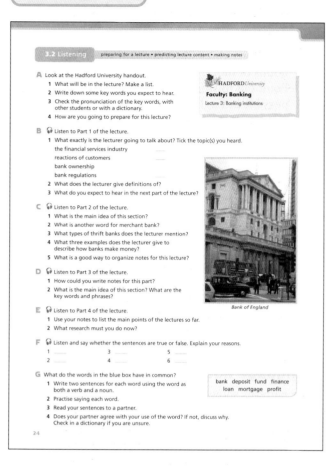

3.2 Listening preparing for a lecture • predicting lecture content • making notes

A Look at the Hadford University handout.
1 What will be in the lecture? Make a list.
2 Write down some key words you expect to hear.
3 Check the pronunciation of the key words, with other students or with a dictionary.
4 How are you going to prepare for this lecture?

B Listen to Part 1 of the lecture.
1 What exactly is the lecturer going to talk about? Tick the topic(s) you heard.
   the financial services industry
   reactions of customers
   bank ownership
   bank regulations
2 What does the lecturer give definitions of?
3 What do you expect to hear in the next part of the lecture?

C Listen to Part 2 of the lecture.
1 What is the main idea of this section?
2 What is another word for merchant bank?
3 What types of thrift banks does the lecturer mention?
4 What three examples does the lecturer give to describe how banks make money?
5 What is a good way to organize notes for this lecture?

D Listen to Part 3 of the lecture.
1 How could you write notes for this part?
2 What is the main idea of this section? What are the key words and phrases?

E Listen to Part 4 of the lecture.
1 Use your notes to list the main points of the lectures so far.
2 What research must you do now?

F Listen and say whether the sentences are true or false. Explain your reasons.
1 ___   3 ___   5 ___
2 ___   4 ___   6 ___

G What do the words in the blue box have in common?
1 Write two sentences for each word using the word as both a verb and a noun.
2 Practise saying each word.
3 Read your sentences to a partner.
4 Does your partner agree with your use of the word? If not, discuss why. Check in a dictionary if you are unsure.

HADFORD University
Faculty: Banking
Lecture 3: Banking institutions

Bank of England

bank deposit fund finance loan mortgage profit

24

Lesson aims

Further practice in:

- planning and preparing for a lecture
- predicting lecture content
- choosing the best form of notes
- making notes

Introduction

Review key vocabulary from this unit by:

- using flashcards
- categorizing the banking services from Lesson 1 according to whether they involve lending/borrowing, saving/investing, or other services
- playing the alphabet game in the Extra activities section at the end of this unit.

Exercise A

Refer students to the Hadford University handout. Write the title *Banking institutions* on the board.

1 Set for individual work. Elicit some ideas.

2 Set for pairwork. Brainstorm to elicit key words. Allow the class to decide whether a word should be included.

3 Set for pairwork with a dictionary. Feed back.

4 Elicit some points – the four Ps (Plan, Prepare, Predict, Produce). If necessary, refer students to Unit 1 *Skills bank* to review the preparation for a lecture. One way to help students to make provisional notes is to:

- brainstorm what they would include
- organize their topics into a logical sequence

Exercise B

1 Tell students they are only going to hear the introduction to the lecture. Ask what information they expect to get from the introduction (i.e. the outline of the lecture).

Give students time to read the choices of topics. Check that they understand the meaning and relevance. Remind them they will only hear the introduction once, as in a lecture. Play Part 1. Allow them to compare answers.

Feed back. Ask them to justify their choice by saying what they heard that related to it. Confirm the correct answer.

2 Elicit ideas. Confirm or correct.

3 Elicit ideas.

Answers

Possible answers:

1 bank ownership

2 commercial banks (profit-orientated banking institutions owned by shareholders); building societies (specialists in mortgage finance and savings accounts); mutuals/credit unions (institutions owned by their members); depositors (people who put money into accounts at the bank)

3 the types of services offered by different institutions (mentioned in the introductory paragraph but not fully discussed in the body of the talk).

Transcript 🎧 1.11

Part 1

OK. Is everybody here? Right, let's start.

In the first lecture, I mentioned that banks are part of the larger financial services industry. You will remember that banks, as a licensed institution, are a distinct category of financial institution. Today, we'll be looking at different types of banking institutions. We'll start by looking at the question of ownership, before looking in greater detail at the types of services offered by different institutions.

Banking institutions may be defined by their ownership. For example, commercial banks – joint stock banks – are owned by share (or stock) holders, who are either private investors or bank holding companies. The term *commercial bank* is used to distinguish it from an investment bank. Commercial banks provide loans to businesses. They also accept and manage deposits for businesses and individuals, and provide mortgage finance and loans. They aim to make a profit, which is paid out in the form of dividends to their shareholders, though sometimes it's retained to build capital or net worth.

Building societies are included here (or SLAs – that is, savings and loan associations in the US and Canada). They specialize in providing mortgage finance and deposit and savings accounts. Some building societies or SLAs are mutuals, or mutual savings banks. These are owned by depositors – that is, the people who put money into accounts in the bank – and run by an elected board of trustees. They're profit-orientated, but their objective is either to build capital, lower future loan rates or raise future deposit rates for deposit owners.

Credit unions, popular in Canada and the US, are cooperatives owned by their members. They don't operate for profit, but retain surplus funds to build capital. They provide their members with the same services as the retail banks. Typically, their members work for the same employer, but they can also be based on residence in the same geographical area.

🎧 Exercise C

Before playing Part 2, give students time to read questions 1–5. Tell them to write only brief notes. The main task is to absorb the meaning.

Play Part 2. Give students time to answer questions 1–5. Allow them to compare their answers. Feed back.

Answers

Possible answers:

1 Types of bank and the services they provide.
2 Investment bank.
3 Credit unions, savings and loan associations.
4 They charge interest on loans; they borrow money and recycle it for better returns; they charge fees for their services.
5 Answers depend on the students. A diagram is useful for classification of information.

Transcript 🎧 1.12

Part 2

Other classifications of banking institutions are possible. In the first lecture I made a broad distinction between wholesale, retail and central (or government) banks. The distinction between retail and wholesale banks has to do with the services they provide. Wholesale banks focus mainly on business-to-business banking services. Their clients are the merchant banks, or investment banks as they are known in the US, and other financial institutions.

Building societies, savings and loans, savings and retail banks are sometimes called depository (or deposit-taking) institutions. Retail banks provide individual services for the mass market. These include savings and cheque accounts, mortgages, personal loans, debit and credit cards, and so on. There is nothing inherently different about savings banks. In the UK some savings banks offer online services only. Savings and loan associations or credit unions are sometimes referred to as thrift banks in the US.

However, even if they're non-profit operations, banks need to cover their costs. And there are a variety of ways in which banks make money. The most common methods, as you know, are that they charge interest on loans. They finance these loans with their deposits. Although depositors earn interest on their money, it is re-lent by the bank at a higher rate. Banks operate on fractionalized deposits: that is, only a fraction of the total deposits in the bank is required, by law, to be kept in reserve. Banks also borrow money – for example, from other financial institutions – at a discount rate, and recycle it for better returns. Finally, banks charge fees for their services: cheque fees, ATM fees, and so on.

🎧 Exercise D

Set for individual work and pairwork checking. Play Part 3. Tell students to take notes. Allow students to compare their definitions. Don't, at this stage, confirm the answers.

Answers

Possible answers:

1 A diagram or spidergram is good for definitions.
2 The services provided by investment, or merchant, banks.
   Key phrases: international finance, dealing with multinational corporations, act as an intermediary, facilitate mergers and corporate reorganizations, act as a broker, underwrite IPOs, fund LBOs, entrepreneurial, retail or insurance services, asset management.

Transcript 🎧 1.13

Part 3

An institution can be defined as an organization that is both large and important. A web search for the top banking institutions is dominated by the Wall Street investment banks, the large American banks. These merchant banks, as they are known in the UK, operate for profit ... big profit! In terms of banking, the merchant or investment banks are perceived as extremely important, and capable of generating huge profits or indeed, losses. Sometimes referred to as money market or money centre banks, they have a global presence, and their knowledge of international finance makes them the specialists in dealing with multinational corporations.

In the UK, merchant banks traditionally provide finance to companies to enable them to increase the share capital of their subsidiary companies. They act as an intermediary between an issuer of securities and the investing public, they facilitate mergers and corporate reorganizations, and act as a broker for institutional clients. In the US, corporate banking, brokering, or underwriting private local US banks are part of their services.

When a company decides to go public and sell stock, investment banks underwrite IPOs – initial public offerings. They also fund LBOs. This term, leveraged buyout, refers to the takeover of a company whereby the company assets are the security for the money lent by the bank.

The traditional trading banks have a very conservative image. They loan money and make investments to businesses to buy, sell and merge. However, the merchant or investment banks are very entrepreneurial. For example, they have moved into areas traditionally dominated by insurance companies and share brokers. In fact, merchant or investment banking may not even be the largest part of their revenue stream. For some, that may now be their retail or insurance services, although asset management is still an important sector.

🎧 Exercise E

Tell students that this is the last part of the lecture. What do they expect to hear? Confirm that it is a summary. Play Part 4.

1 Students should check their notes and definitions as they listen. After the summary has finished, they should correct and complete their notes. Guide them to the correct answer: that is, the correct meaning, not necessarily the words given here.
2 Elicit ideas. Then set the research for students to work on in pairs or individually. They will need to report back in Lesson 3.

Answers

1 Possible answers:

Main ideas
Banking institutions may be classified according to i) their ownership; ii) the services they provide.
If classified by ownership they fall into two groups: i) owned by their members (e.g., mutuals); ii) owned by shareholders/stockholders (commercial and investment banks).
If classified by services provided, they can be classified as i) wholesale, ii) retail, or iii) central (or government) banks. Wholesale banks focus on businesses and other banks. Retail banks focus on the mass market.
Investment banks are capable of generating huge profits or losses. They are global, entrepreneurial banks. Today, multinational banking conglomerates consist of all types of banks providing a wide range of services.
All banks must cover their costs. Banks make money through charging interest, borrowing money to lend on for better returns, and by charging fees on services.

2 Students should research banks in UK and the services they provide.

Transcript 🎧 1.14

Part 4

So, to summarize, banking institutions can be defined according to their ownership, or by the services they offer.

If they're defined by ownership, they fall into two basic categories: those owned by their members, such as cooperatives and building societies, and those owned by shareholders, or stock holders as they're called in the US. Cooperatives aim to build capital and improve interest rates for their members. Banks owned by shareholders operate for profit which is paid in the form of dividends to the shareholders.

If they're defined by their services, they can be broadly categorized into three major groups. These are wholesale banks, offering corporate banking, brokering or underwriting services; retail banks, providing services for the mass market; and central or government banks.

The term *commercial* is used to make a distinction between a commercial and an investment bank, which focuses on capital markets and large multinational corporations. However, since these two genres no longer have to be separate organizations, the term *commercial bank* is often used to refer to bank activities which focus mainly on companies. Investment banks include the multinational conglomerates whose subsidiary companies all provide very different banking products and services. For example, one American conglomerate, Citigroup, is involved in commercial and retail lending, owns a merchant bank, an investment bank and a private bank. It also has subsidiaries which offer offshore banking services.

Finally, whatever the type of institution, all banks must cover their operating costs or else they will fail over time.

OK, that's it for today. Next time we'll do a brief survey of the services offered by some of the banks operating in the UK. Don't forget to do a bit of research on that before you come. Thank you.

🎧 Exercise F

These sentences are about the ideas in the lecture. Set for pairwork. Say or play the sentences. Give time for students to discuss and then respond. Students must justify their answers. Advise them to beware of statements containing absolutes such as *always, never, all*. These are rarely true.

Answers

Model answers:

1 false	Building societies are not investment banks; their core business is savings, loans and mortgages.
2 false	Cooperatives are owned by their members.
3 true	
4 false	Investment banks are profit-orientated.
5 false	Some banks are very entrepreneurial.
6 true	This is an inference; students may argue that we don't know from the lecture whether this statement is true or false.

Transcript 🎧 1.15

1 Building societies are a type of investment bank.
2 Cooperatives are a type of banking institution owned by different banking groups.
3 By law, banks are required to keep in reserve only a fraction of their total deposits.
4 Investment banks are not profit-orientated.
5 Banks are never entrepreneurial.
6 In the past, banks were not involved in insurance or share market services.

Exercise G

Refer students to the words in the box and ask the question. The key similarity, apart from all being to do with money, is that they can all be both nouns and verbs.

1 Set for individual work and pairwork checking.
2 Check pronunciation (e.g., silent *t* in *mortgage*). Check stress.
3/4 Set for pairwork. Monitor, check, and correct students' answers.

Language note

Some people may feel that it is unnecessary to make a verb from *loan* since we already have the perfectly adequate *lend*. However, *loan* as a verb tends now to be used when the thing lent is money, and when it is lent by an institution rather than an individual.

Closure

This is a version of the game 'Whispers'. Write the correct sentences from Exercise F on strips of paper and place them in a box on a desk, well away from the seated students.

Set for pairwork. Student A is the 'runner' and Student B the 'writer'. On your command the Student As go to the box and select one sentence. They read the sentence, memorize it, then return to their partner. Student B writes down the sentence as dictated by Student A.

Repeat the activity until all the sentences have been read. Compare what has been written with the original sentence. Review common problems, e.g., pronunciation, word order, etc., as necessary. The first pair with all sentences written correctly is the winner.

Note: Students will need their lecture notes from Lesson 2 in the next lesson.

Table 1: Top ten banking groups in the world ranked by assets (2004)

Rank 2004	Institution	Total assets (US$ bn.)
1	UBS	1,533
2	Citigroup	1,484
3	Mizuho Financial Group	1,296
4	HSBC Holdings	1,277
5	Crédit Agricole	1,243
6	BNP Paribas	1,234
7	JPMorgan Chase & Co.	1,157
8	Deutsche Bank	1,144
9	Royal Bank of Scotland	1,119
10	Bank of America	1,110

Source: Wikipedia

questions to get the missing information. Refer them to the *Skills bank* if you wish for language they can use in the pairwork.

Pairs then compare notes and decide what other information would be useful and where they could get it from. For example, definitions of the key words might be useful, from a specialist dictionary or an encyclopedia. In the feedback, write a list of research sources on the board, at least including dictionaries, encyclopedias, specialist reference books and the Internet.

Point out that dictionaries are good for definitions, although you may need to go to a specialist dictionary for a banking definition of a word. Otherwise, try an encyclopedia, because words are often defined in entries when they are first used. You could also try Google's 'define' feature, i.e., type *define: underwrite* but remember you will get definitions from all disciplines not just your own, so you need to scan to check the relevant one.

Exercise A

Point out the importance of stressed syllables in words – see *Language note*.

In this exercise, students will hear each word with the stressed syllable emphasized, and the rest of the syllables underspoken.

Play the recording, pausing after the first few to check that students understand the task. Feed back, perhaps playing the recording again for each word before checking. Ideally, mark up a large poster or OHT of the words.

Language note

In English, speakers emphasize the stressed syllable in a multi-syllable word. Sometimes listeners may not even hear the unstressed syllables. Vowels, in any case, often change to schwa or a reduced form in unstressed syllables. Therefore it is essential that students can recognize key words from the stressed syllable alone when they hear them in context.

General note

Read the *Skills bank* at the end of the Course Book unit. Decide when, if at all, to refer students to it. The best time is probably at the beginning of this lesson or the end of the next lesson, as a summary/revision.

Lesson aim

This lesson is the first in a series about writing an assignment or giving a presentation based on research. The principal aim of this lesson is to introduce students to sources of information.

Introduction

1 Tell students to ask you questions about the information in the lecture in Lesson 2 as if you were the lecturer. Refer them to the *Skills bank* for typical language if you wish.

2 Put students in pairs. Student A must ask Student B about the information in the lecture in Lesson 2 to help him/her complete the notes from the lecture. Then they reverse roles. Go round, helping students to identify gaps in their notes and to think of good

Answers

broking	8
capital	2
commission	13
conglomerate	7
dividends	1
insurance	3
integration	11
investors	5
leveraged	10
management	9
mortgages	12
profitable	6
subsidiaries	4

Transcript 🎧 1.16

1 'dividends
2 'capital
3 in'surance
4 sub'sidiaries
5 in'vestors
6 'profitable
7 con'glomerate
8 'broking
9 'management
10 'leveraged
11 inte'gration
12 'mortgages
13 com'mission

Exercise B

Erase the words or turn off the OHP. Ask students to guess or remember where the stressed syllable is on each word. Tell them to mark their idea with a light vertical stroke in pencil. Elicit and drill. Refer students to the *Vocabulary bank* at this stage if you wish.

Answers

See transcript for Exercise A.

Exercise C

Set for pair or group work. Go round and assist/correct.

Exercise D

Set for group work. Refer students back to Lesson 1, but tell them also to include other services they know. Encourage them to use the language from the *Skills bank* to get information from others.

Feed back, building up the table on the board. The more services the students can name, the better. Get students to justify their answers. Answers depend on whether you are looking at the services from a client's perspective or from a bank's perspective. Accept anything reasonable.

Answers

Possible answers:

The table may include items from Lesson 1 Exercise B, plus students' own suggestions, e.g.,
Borrowing: overdrafts, short- or long-term loans
Saving: equity funds, savings accounts
General services: current accounts, money transfers, foreign exchange

Exercise E

Refer students to the research questions and the table with 2004 figures (students should try to find the most recent figures they can). Get them to define what category they will use to assess the 'top' banks, e.g., by their asset base, by their income, or by their capital. Discuss resources they will need and sources of information. Discuss the most appropriate form of note-taking.

Set for individual work. If students have access in class to reference material, allow them to at least start the activity in class. Otherwise, set the task for homework. Before the feedback to partner stage, refer students to the *Skills bank – Reporting information to other people.*

Closure

Dictate sentences with words from Exercise A in context for students to identify the words again.

3.4 Extending skills

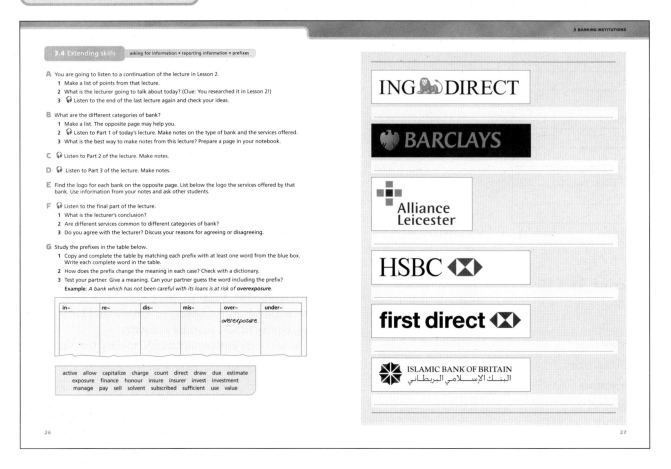

3.4 Extending skills | asking for information • reporting information • prefixes

A You are going to listen to a continuation of the lecture in Lesson 2.
  1 Make a list of points from that lecture.
  2 What is the lecturer going to talk about today? (Clue: You researched it in Lesson 2!)
  3 🎧 Listen to the end of the last lecture again and check your ideas.

B What are the different categories of bank?
  1 Make a list. The opposite page may help you.
  2 🎧 Listen to Part 1 of today's lecture. Make notes on the type of bank and the services offered.
  3 What is the best way to make notes from this lecture? Prepare a page in your notebook.

C 🎧 Listen to Part 2 of the lecture. Make notes.

D 🎧 Listen to Part 3 of the lecture. Make notes.

E Find the logo for each bank on the opposite page. List below the logo the services offered by that bank. Use information from your notes and ask other students.

F 🎧 Listen to the final part of the lecture.
  1 What is the lecturer's conclusion?
  2 Are different services common to different categories of bank?
  3 Do you agree with the lecturer? Discuss your reasons for agreeing or disagreeing.

G Study the prefixes in the table below.
  1 Copy and complete the table by matching each prefix with at least one word from the blue box. Write each complete word in the table.
  2 How does the prefix change the meaning in each case? Check with a dictionary.
  3 Test your partner. Give a meaning. Can your partner guess the word including the prefix?
     Example: A bank which has not been careful with its loans is at risk of **overexposure**.

in~	re~	dis~	mis~	over~	under~
				overexposure	

active allow capitalize charge count direct draw due estimate
exposure finance honour insure insurer invest investment
manage pay sell solvent subscribed sufficient use value

26

27

Lesson aims

- ask for information to complete notes
- extending knowledge of words which contain prefixes

Further practice in:

- choosing the best form of notes
- making notes

Introduction

Elicit as much information from the lecture in Lesson 2 as possible. If necessary, prompt students by reading parts of the transcript and pausing for students to complete in their own words.

🎧 Exercise A

Remind students of the language involved in asking for information from other people – see *Skills bank*. Drill some of the sentences if you wish.

1/2 Set for pairwork.

3 Play Part 4 of the lecture from Lesson 2 to enable students to check their answers. Elicit information from the students' research. Do not confirm or correct at this stage except pronunciation mistakes on key words.

Transcript 🎧 1.14
Part 4

So, to summarize, banking institutions can be defined according to their ownership, or by the services they offer.

If they're defined by ownership, they fall into two basic categories: those owned by their members, such as cooperatives and building societies, and those owned by shareholders, or stock holders as they're called in the US. Cooperatives aim to build capital and improve interest rates for their members. Banks owned by shareholders operate for profit which is paid in the form of dividends to the shareholders.

If they're defined by their services, they can be broadly categorized into three major groups. These are wholesale banks, offering corporate banking, brokering or underwriting services; retail banks, providing services for the mass market; and central or government banks.

The term *commercial* is used to make a distinction between a commercial and an investment bank, which focuses on capital markets and large multinational corporations. However, since these two genres no longer have to be separate organizations, the term *commercial bank* is often used to refer to bank activities which focus mainly on companies. Investment banks include the multinational conglomerates whose subsidiary companies all provide very different banking products and services. For example, one American conglomerate, Citigroup, is involved in commercial and retail lending, owns a merchant bank, an investment bank and a private bank. It also has subsidiaries which offer offshore banking services.

Finally, whatever the type of institution, all banks must cover their operating costs or else they will fail over time.

OK, that's it for today. Next time we'll do a brief survey of the services offered by some of the banks operating in the UK. Don't forget to do a bit of research on that before you come. Thank you.

Answers

Model answers:

1 Answers depend on the students. Accept anything reasonable.

2/3 The services offered by some banks operating in the UK.

🎧 Exercise B

Refer students to the different banks on the right-hand page of the Course Book.

1 Ask students to make the list. Do not confirm or correct at this stage.

2 Play Part 1. Ask students to make notes. Feed back orally.

3 Set for pairwork discussion then individual work. Feed back.

Answers

1/2 Answers depend on the students.

3 The best way is probably a three-column table for comparison of data. Ask students to write the names of the banks in the left-hand column. In the second column they can list the type of bank, and in the third column the services. Don't tell them the ones they can't remember. It would be quite normal in a lecture that they couldn't write all of them down.

Transcript 🎧 1.17

Part 1

In the last lecture we talked about banking institutions. We categorized them by their ownership and the services they offer. I mentioned that the large banking institutions engage in multiple activities and gave, as an example, one of

the American conglomerates. Since we have time, I thought it might be useful to check out some of the websites of banks that operate in Britain and see what services they offer. Let's look first at the bank that promotes itself as the world's leading direct savings bank, ING Direct. What services do you think they offer? … You're right; they're mainly a savings bank. You can open an account with them over the telephone and access your accounts with them online. They also offer home insurance.

How do the services offered by the Alliance and Leicester, a commercial bank, differ? Well, to start with, this was previously a building society. That should give you a clue. I said at the start that building societies are included in the commercial bank category, and they specialize in providing mortgage finance, as well as deposit and savings accounts. As a visit to their website reveals, the Alliance and Leicester has a retail banking site providing current accounts, loans, mortgages, savings and credit card services, and a commercial banking site with services including money transmission, financing and investing. Next I'll discuss Barclays Bank.

🎧 Exercise C

Play Part 2 of the lecture. Students should recognize the rhetorical structure and add to their table. Tell them to note the type of bank and as many of the services as they can.

Transcript 🎧 1.18

Part 2

Barclays promotes itself as a global financial service provider. In other words, it's another conglomerate. Its UK services include current accounts, savings and investments, loans, mortgages, insurance and credit cards. It offers both personal and business banking.

HSBC is one of the largest banking conglomerates and its shares are listed in the FTSE100 in London. It has personal, business and corporate divisions and provides services including current accounts, savings and investments, finance, payments, credit cards, loans, mortgages, insurance, and international services. Its corporate division includes corporate and institutional, global markets payments and cash management, private equity, securities and trade services.

🎧 Exercise D

Set for pairwork. Play Part 3 of the lecture. As before, remind students to note the type of bank and as many of the services as they can.

Transcript 🎧 1.19

Part 3

Finally, a brief look at two very different banks: first direct Internet savings bank, and the Islamic Bank of Britain. We'll start with first direct. As you can see, it offers a variety of services, from current and savings accounts, mortgages, loans, insurance, credit cards, to text message banking and touch-screen share dealing via the Internet.

The Islamic Bank of Britain provides retail banking services to individuals and small businesses in accordance with Islamic shariah principles. The personal services it provides include current accounts plus savings and home-buying accounts.

Exercise E

Set for individual work initially. When students have completed as much as they can, tell them to ask other students for any missing information.

Answers

Model answers:

Bank	Type	Services
ING Direct	savings bank	savings accounts, home insurance
Alliance and Leicester	retail and commercial bank	mortgages, deposit/savings/current accounts, loans, credit cards (retail); money transmission, financing, investing (commercial)
Barclays	retail and commercial bank	current account/savings/investment accounts, loans, mortgages, insurance, credit cards
HSBC	retail and commercial bank	current/savings/investment accounts, finance, payments, credit cards, loans, mortgages, insurance, international services; global markets payments and cash management, private equity, securities and trade services
first direct	Internet savings bank	current/savings accounts, mortgages, loans, insurance, credit cards, text message banking, touch-screen share dealing
Islamic Bank of Britain	retail bank	current/savings accounts, home-buying accounts

🎧 Exercise F

1/2 Play Part 4 of the lecture. Feed back orally.

3 Set for group work. Divide students into three groups: 1 agree, 2 disagree, 3 not sure. Students justify their reasons.

Redivide groups to include students from each of the groups. Students debate and justify their stance and try to persuade other students to accept their argument.

To conclude the exercise, ask for a show of hands of students who changed their original stance. Elicit reasons why.

Transcript 🎧 1.20

Part 4

Well, I think that what this exercise has confirmed for us is ... is that today, it is the integrated bank model that prevails. As we have seen, banking institutions engage in multiple activities and will, I think, continue to diversify in the future.

Answers

Model answers:

The lecturer concludes that banks tend to offer a range of services that cross category boundaries – and that this trend will continue.

Notes:

1 All the banks mentioned offer Internet banking even if it is not specified on their website.

2 The focus is only on the UK operations of these banks. Focusing on the international banks would result in the answers being mostly *investment* banks. As an extension to this exercise you may like to compare the UK services and the international services of Barclays and HSBC, for example.

Exercise G

Set for pairwork. Monitor and assist. Feed back, writing the words on the board as the students correctly identify them. Accept any reasonable alternatives. Check pronunciation and stress patterns.

Answers

Possible answers:

1

in~	re~	dis~	mis~	over~	under~
inactive	recount	disallow	miscount	overactive	undercapitalize
indirect	redirect	discharge	misdirect	overcharge	undercharge
insolvent	redraw	discount	misestimate	overdraw	underestimate
insufficient	reestimate	dishonour	mismanage	overdue	underexposure
	refinance	disinvest	missell	overestimate	underfinance
	reinsure	disinvestment	misuse	overexposure	underinsure
	reinsurer			overpay	underinvest
	reinvest			oversell	underpay
	repay			oversubscribed	undersubscribed
	resell			overuse	underuse
	reuse			overvalue	undervalue

2

Prefix	Meaning
in	not
re	again
dis	not
mis	do wrong
over	excessively
under	insufficiently

Methodology note

End all listening lessons by referring students to the transcripts so they can read the text while the aural memory is still clear. You could set this as standard homework after a listening lesson. You can also get students to highlight key sections and underline key sentences.

Closure

Dictate to students a random selection of core words from Exercise G . Students have to write the word with an appropriate prefix. Review with the whole class. Accept anything reasonable.

4 COMPUTERS IN BANKING

The theme of this unit is computers. Two aspects of the use of computers relevant to banking students are addressed: their use in the banking industry and their use in education. Lessons 1, 3 and 4 guide students to a more efficient use of the Internet and computers in research. Lesson 2 looks at the computerization of banking.

Students will need access to a computer with an Internet connection for some exercises. Check that all students have used the Internet. If any haven't, sit them beside someone who has, to guide them.

Skills focus

Reading

- identifying topic development within a paragraph
- using the Internet effectively
- evaluating Internet search results

Writing

- reporting research findings

Vocabulary focus

- computer jargon
- abbreviations and acronyms
- discourse and stance markers
- verb and noun suffixes

Key vocabulary

access (n and v)	input (n and v)	password
browse	integral	search (n and v)
compatible	integrate	search engine
computerize	interface (n)	search results
data	interlink (v)	software
database	key in	specification
document	keyword	transaction
e-banking	log in/log on	transfer (n and v)
electronic media	log off	username/ID
hardware	menu	
hyperlink	output (n and v)	

ICT abbreviations

CAD	DVD	ISP	PDF	USB
CAL	HTML	LCD	ROM	WAN
CAM	HTTP	PIN	URL	WWW

Banking abbreviations

ACH (automated clearing house)

ATM (automated teller machine)

CDI (customer data integration)

CHAPS (clearing house automated payment system)

CHIPS (clearing house interbank payments system)

EFT (electronic funds transfer)

ODFI (originating depository financial institution)

RDFI (receiving depository financial institution)

RTGS (real-time gross settlement)

SWIFT (Society for Worldwide Interbank Financial Telecommunication)

4.1 Vocabulary

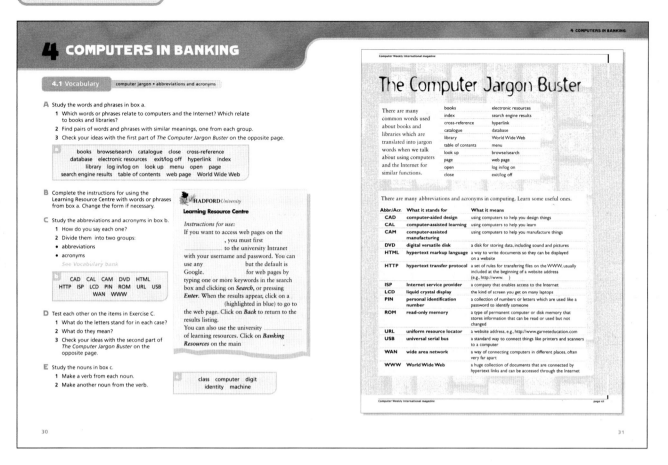

General note

If possible, hold this lesson in a room where there is a computer, or bring in a computer.

Read the *Vocabulary bank* at the end of the Course Book unit. Decide when, if at all, to refer your students to it. The best point is probably Exercise C, or at the very end of the lesson or the beginning of the next lesson, as a summary/revision.

Lesson aim

- gain fluency in the meaning, pronunciation and spelling of key computing terms, acronyms and abbreviations

Introduction

Familiarize students with computer terminology using some or all of the following activities.

1 Using a computer or a picture of a computer as a starting point, elicit the some or all of the following:

PC	laptop	hand-held computer
monitor	screen	desktop
icon	keyboard	keys

mouse	hard disk	CPU (central
floppy disk	program	processing unit)
slot	CD	DVD
USB port	accessory	printer
CD burner	Internet	scanner
e-mail	database	

2 Ask students to suggest verbs used in computing. Elicit some or all of the following. A good way to do this is to open a program such as Word (in English) and look at the words and symbols on the toolbars.

switch on	press	paste
start up	open	enter
shut down	close	delete
log on/log off	exit	insert
click	save	highlight
double-click	select	undo
hold	copy	

3 Ask students whether they normally use the library or the Internet to find information. Elicit the advantages and disadvantages of both. (There is so much emphasis on using computers nowadays, students often forget that there is a lot of information readily to hand in the library.)

Answers

Possible answers:

Library

+	–
easy to look things up in a dictionary or an encyclopedia	books can be out of date
you can find information in your own language	the book may not be in the library when you want it
information is usually correct	most books can't be accessed from home (though this is now starting to change)

Internet

+	–
a lot of information from different sources	difficult to find the right keywords
information is usually more up-to-date than books	difficult to know which results are the best
can be accessed from home	information is often not correct
you can quickly and easily get copies of books or journal articles not in your library	you may have to pay for the books/articles/information

Exercise A

Ask students to study the words in the blue box and elicit that they all relate to research.

Set for pairwork. Tell students to decide and justify the groups/pairs they choose. If necessary, give an example: *index, search engine results.*

To help students understand what a database is, refer to ones they are familiar with in your college, e.g., student records, exam results, library catalogues, etc.

Answers

Model answers:

Common word or phrase for books and libraries	Word or phrase for Internet and electronic information
books	electronic resources
index	search engine results
cross-reference	hyperlink
catalogue	database
library	World Wide Web
table of contents	menu
look up	browse/search
page	web page
open	log in/log on
close	exit/log off

Exercise B

Set for individual work and pairwork checking. Ensure that students read all the text and have a general understanding of it before they insert the missing words.

Feed back by reading the paragraph or by using an OHT or other visual display. Discuss alternative ideas and decide whether they are acceptable. Verify whether errors are due to using new words or to misunderstanding the text.

Answers

Model answers:

If you want to access web pages on the World Wide Web, you must first log in to the university Intranet with your username and password. You can use any search engine but the default is Google. Browse/Search for web pages by typing one or more keywords in the search box and clicking on *Search*, or pressing *Enter*. When the results appear, click on a hyperlink (highlighted in blue) to go to the web page. Click on *Back* to return to the results listing.

You can also use the university database of learning resources. Click on *Banking Resources* on the main menu.

Exercise C

Set for pairwork. Feed back, eliciting ideas on pronunciation and confirming or correcting. Build up the two lists on the board. Establish that one group are acronyms, i.e., they can be pronounced as words: PIN = /pɪn/ The other group are abbreviations, i.e., they are pronounced as letters: HTTP = H-T-T-P. Drill all the abbreviations and acronyms. Make sure students can say letter names and vowel sounds correctly. Elicit that words with normal consonant/vowel patterns are *normally* pronounced as a word and those with unusual patterns are *normally* pronounced with single letters. Refer to the *Vocabulary bank* at this stage if you wish.

Methodology note

Don't discuss the meaning at this point. This is covered in the next activity.

Answers

1/2 Some words are acronyms, i.e., they can be pronounced as words: PIN = /pɪn/.

The others are abbreviations, i.e., they are pronounced as letters: HTTP = H-T-T-P.

acronyms: CAD /kæd/, CAL /kæl/, CAM /kæm/, PIN /pɪn/, ROM /rɒm/, WAN /wæn/

abbreviations: DVD, HTML, HTTP, ISP, LCD, URL (not pronounced /ɜːl/), USB, WWW

Exercise D

1 Introduce the verb *stand for*. Elicit examples of common abbreviations and ask what they stand for. Set for pairwork. Tell students to pick out the ones they already know first. Next, they pick out the ones they are familiar with but don't know what they stand for – and guess.

2 Elicit the meanings without reference to the *Jargon Buster* if possible.

3 Refer students to the *Jargon Buster* to verify their answers. As a follow-up, elicit other common abbreviations from IT or banking.

Language note

If students don't use acronyms or initial abbreviations in their language, a discussion about the reasons for using them is useful. They will then know how to find the meaning of new ones when they meet them. You might point out that abbreviations can sometimes be longer than the thing they abbreviate! For example, *World Wide Web* is three syllables, whereas *WWW* is six. It evolved because it is quicker to write, but it is longer, and harder, to say. It is also possible to mix acronyms with abbreviations: for example, JPEG – J /peg/. Point out that the field of ICT is developing at an incredible speed and new acronyms and abbreviations are constantly being created.

Exercise E

Set for individual work and pairwork checking. Feed back, highlighting the changes from noun form to verb in the case of *identity/identify* and *machine/mechanize*.

Answers

Model answers:

Noun 1	Verb	Noun 2
class	classify	classification
computer	computerize	computerization
digit	digitize	digitization
identity	identify	identification
machine	mechanize	mechanization

Closure

Ask students whether they agree with the following statements.

1 Every college student must have a computer.

2 The college library uses a computer to help students find information.

3 College departments use computers to store research data.

4 Students can't do research without a computer.

5 College computers can access research data from other colleges and universities.

6 College computers can access research data from businesses and the media.

7 A personal computer can store information students think is important.

8 Computers can help us to talk with students from other colleges and universities.

9 Computers can help students access data from anywhere in the world.

10 A computer we can carry in our pocket can access worldwide data.

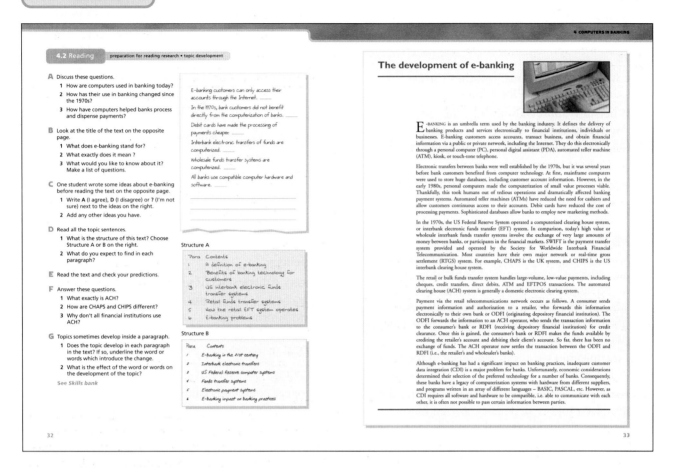

General note

Read the *Skills bank* at the end of the Course Book unit. Decide when, if at all, to refer students to it. The best time is probably at the very end of the lesson or the beginning of the next lesson, as a summary/revision.

Lesson aims

- prepare to read a text by looking at title, figures, topic sentences
- understand the purpose of discourse markers and stance markers in the development of a topic

Introduction

Ask students how, where and why they use computers. They should answer in some detail with examples. Encourage them to use the vocabulary, abbreviations and acronyms from Lesson 1.

Exercise A

Set for general discussion. Allow students to debate differences of opinion. Encourage them to give examples if they can.

Answers

Possible answers:

1 In all departments: to keep records, access accounts, transact business, obtain financial information, etc.

2 In the 1970s, mainframe computers were used within banks only. Now PCs provide customers with access to a greater range of services.

3 ATMs provide customers with access to their accounts 24 hours a day, 7 days a week; debit cards have reduced the cost of processing payments.

Exercise B

1 Write the title of the reading text on the board. Elicit the answer.

2 Set the question for general discussion. Encourage students to define e-banking or speculate on what it might involve.

3 Set for pairwork. Tell students to think of four or five questions with different *Wh~* question words:

What ...?	*How ...?*
Where ...?	*Who ...?*
When ...?	*Why ...?*

Answers

Possible answers:

1 Electronic banking.
2 The delivery of banking products and services to financial institutions, individuals or businesses electronically.
3 Possible questions:

What processes can be computerized?

Where do people use e-banking?

Why is e-banking used?

When did people start using it?

Who operates the computers?

How successful is e-banking?

Exercise C

1 Set for individual work and pairwork checking. Feed back, trying to get consensus on each point, but do not actually confirm or correct. Preface your remarks with phrases like: *So most of you think … You all believe …* Remind students to look back at these predictions while they are reading the text (Exercise E below).
2 Elicit some more ideas, but once again, do not confirm or correct. Draw students' attention to words like *only* and *all*. Point out that these words make statements very strong. The truth may actually be better expressed with a limiting word, e.g., *most/some/many*, or with words which express possibility such as *may* or *seem*, or adverbs such as *sometimes, usually, often*.

Exercise D

Review paragraph structure – i.e., paragraphs usually begin with a topic sentence which makes a statement that is then expanded in the following sentences. Thus, topic sentences give an indication of the contents of the paragraph. You may wish to refer students to the *Skills bank* at this point.

1 Write the topic sentences from the text on an OHT, or use Resource 4B from the additional resources section. Students should use only the topic sentences for this exercise. Set for individual work and pairwork checking.
2 Set for pairwork. Tell students that close analysis of the topic sentences will help them. Feed back with the whole class. Point out any language features which led them to draw their conclusions.

Answers

Possible answers:

1 Text structure A.
2 Accept anything reasonable. Possible answers:

	Predicted content
Para 1	what e-banking is; how it operates
Para 2	details of how computer technology benefits customers, e.g., online/telephone access to accounts
Para 3	a history of US clearing systems; comparison with today?
Para 4	a description of the retail funds transfer system
Para 5	how retail funds transfers operate
Para 6	how CDI is a problem for banks

Exercise E

Set the reading. Students should make notes on the differences between their predictions and the text.

Answers

Possible answers:

Paragraph 1
Prediction: what e-banking is; how it operates
Actual: The prediction was correct.

Paragraph 2
Prediction: details of how computer technology benefits customers, e.g., online/telephone access to accounts
Actual: It starts by describing the usage of mainframes. The rest of the paragraph then describes the benefits of technology for banks.

Paragraph 3
Prediction: a history of US clearing systems; comparison with today?
Actual: It starts by defining the EFT system then describes today's computerized clearing house systems for large-value funds.

Paragraph 4
Prediction: a description of the retail funds transfer system
Actual: The prediction was correct.

Paragraph 5
Prediction: how retail funds transfers operate
Actual: The prediction was correct.

Paragraph 6
Prediction: how CDI is a problem for banks

Actual: The prediction was correct. The focus is on CDI and the reasons for the problems with CDI.

Note: In every paragraph the basic theme is the same. In paragraph 2, two aspects of the theme are addressed. Paragraph 4 serves as an introduction to paragraph 5.

Exercise F

1/2 Ask students to write answers to these questions.

3 Set for general discussion and feedback.

Answers

Possible answers:

1 ACH (automated clearing house) is a domestic retail funds transfer system that handles large volumes of relatively low-value payments, including cheques, credit transfers, direct debits, ATM and EFTPOS transactions.

2 CHAPS (clearing house automated payment system) is the UK system; CHIPS (clearing house interbank payments system) is the system used in the US.

3 Most banks and financial institutions are using incompatible computer products. It is very expensive to replace them with a single integrated system.

Exercise G

The purpose of this exercise is for students to try to identify the information structure of each paragraph and to see how a new step in the progression of ideas may be signalled by a rhetorical marker or phrase.

Refer also to the *Skills bank* at the end of this unit. Elicit more examples of discourse markers and stance markers.

Set for pairwork. Feed back. A good idea is to make an OHT or other visual display of the text and use a highlighter to indicate which are the relevant parts of the text. Students should notice that there is not a discernible topic development in every paragraph.

Answers

1/2 Possible answers:

Methodology note

It could be argued that words like *but, however,* and phrases like *on the other hand* do not fundamentally change the topic of a paragraph. Point this out if you wish. However, (change of topic?) they do bring in a concessive element where the reader of a topic sentence might assume that the whole paragraph would be (for example) positive.

Imagine a school report with the topic sentence: *John is an extremely able student* which then proceeded with a great deal of praise, but ended with the following: *Despite his many good qualities, however, John will have some difficulty in gaining high marks in his exams unless he concentrates more in class.* We could justifiably claim either that:

1 the whole paragraph is about John and his school work

or

2 the paragraph has two topics – John's positive aspects and his negative aspects.

Closure

1 Divide the class into groups. Write the six topic sentences on strips, or photocopy them from the additional resources section (Resource 4B). Make a copy for each group. Students must put them into the correct order.

Alternatively, divide the class into two teams. One team chooses a topic sentence and reads it aloud. The other team must give the information triggered by that topic sentence. Accept a prediction or the actual paragraph content. However, ask students which it is – prediction or actual.

	Discourse marker	Stance marker	Effect
Para 1	–	–	
Para 2	but		to show contrast
	At first		to highlight a specific time
	However		to show contrast (a change to a new technology and usage)
		Thankfully	to signal the writer's view that computerization has brought benefits
Para 3	In comparison		to show contrast/compare
Para 4	–	–	
Para 5	–	–	
Para 6	Although		to show contrast
		Unfortunately	to signal the writer's view that this is a problem for banks
	Consequently		to show a link (cause/effect) to the previous statement
	However, as		to qualify the previous statement – CDI cannot be the future for all banks

Language note

There is no universal logic to the structuring of information in a text. The order of information is language-specific. For example, oriental languages tend to have a topic sentence or paragraph summary at the end, not the beginning, of the paragraph. Or students whose first language is Arabic might structure a particular type of discourse in a different way from native English speakers. So it is important for students to see what a native speaker writer would use as a 'logical' ordering.

2 Refer students back to the sentences in Exercise C. Students should find it easier to comment on these now that they have read the text.

3 Focus on some of the vocabulary from the text, including:

automated
funds
personal computer
mainframe computer
settlement
transaction
clearance
software
hardware
compatible
computerize
data
database

4.3 Extending skills

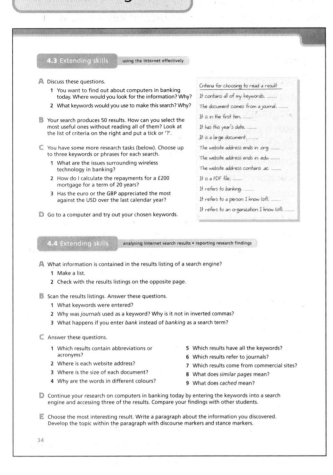

advice for using the Internet. Then, as a class, produce an accepted set of advice.

Key words to elicit: *search engine, keyword, website, web page, website address, search result, subject directory*

Note: Where the subject is a new one or a fairly general topic, it is a good idea to start first with a **subject directory** which evaluates sites related to the topic and collects them in one place. Some examples are: Academic Info; BUBL LINK; INFOMINE; The WWW Virtual Library.

Exercise A

Write *computers in banking* on the board.

1 Set for class discussion. Make sure students give reasons for their answers. Accept their answers at this stage.

2 Remind students that words in English often have more than one meaning, so care must be taken to get the desired result.

Answers

Possible answers:

1 In a current technical journal – very useful, as recent articles give the latest information.

On the Internet – good if the correct keywords are used and a careful selection of results is made.

In a textbook – useful if there is an up-to-date one, but books take time to publish, so even the latest may be out of date in these technologically fast-moving times.

2 In this list of possible keywords, the first four are obvious starting points; others are also possible.

latest/recent	
computers/computerization	very specific
technology	to the task
banking/e-banking (process)	

journal	journals give the latest information

this year	
current state	
(the year's date)	the time factor
nowadays	

EFT	
CHAPS	specific to the
CHIPS	technology
ACH	

General note

Students will need access to a computer with an Internet connection. If computers are not available during the lesson, this part of the lesson can be set for private study.

Lesson aim

- Learn or practise how to use the Internet effectively for research

Introduction

Brainstorm the uses of the Internet. Then brainstorm what the important factors are when using the Internet. These should include:

- the search engines students use and why
- how to choose *and write* keywords in their preferred search engine
- how they extract the information they want from the results

Put students in groups and ask them to compare how they normally use a computer to find information. Ask each group to produce a set of

Exercise B

Set for pairwork. Remind students of the research topic.

Feed back, encouraging students to give reasons for their decisions. Emphasize that we only know what *might* be useful at this stage.

Answers

Possible answers:

✓ It contains all of my keywords. *(but check that the meaning is the same)*

✓ The document comes from a journal. *(current information)*

? It is in the first ten. *(a web page can have codes attached to put it high in the list)*

✓ It has this year's date. *(current information)*

? It is a large document. *(size is no indication of quality)*

✓ The website address ends in .org *(because it is a non-profit organization)*

✓ The website address ends in .edu *(because it is an educational establishment)*

✓ The website address contains .ac *(because it is an educational establishment)*

? It is a PDF file. *(file type is no indication of quality)*

? It refers to banking. *(may not be relevant)*

✓ It refers to a person I know (of). *(reliable)*

✓ It refers to an organization I know (of). *(reliable)*

Language note

PDF stands for *portable document format*. PDF documents can be viewed and printed on most computers, without the need for each computer to have the same software, fonts, etc. They are created with Adobe Acrobat software.

Exercise C

Set for individual work and pairwork checking. Ask students to compare their choice of keywords with their partner, and justify their choice.

Answers

See Exercise D.

Exercise D

Students should try out different keywords to discover for themselves which give the best results.

Answers

Possible answers:

1 Lack of a human element; difficulties in supporting customers; inoperability among devices; the challenge of 'range', i.e., transferring data over long distances; physical differences among various applications; security.

2 A search including "banking" + "mortgage repayments" should bring up mortgage calculators. Group checking. Answers will depend on the interest rates.

3 Answer will depend on the year.

Closure

Tell students to think of their own questions for research, as in Exercise C, and find the best web page for the data by entering appropriate keywords.

Ask students to write their question on a piece of paper and sign it. Put all the questions in a box. Students pick out one of the questions at random and go online to find the best page of search results. From those results they can find the most useful web page. They should ask the questioner for verification.

2 The information is intended for the bank's shareholders and any other interested parties. It would be public information.

Exercise B

The purpose of this exercise is to introduce and build sets of antonyms used in banking and financial data, and their collocations.

Set for pairwork. Students should use their dictionaries if necessary to check the grammatical information. They should note other words with similar meanings. Point out that not all pairs in box a can be used with a word from box b.

Feed back with the whole class, building up the table in the Answers section on the board, and eliciting other related banking words, if relevant.

Answers

Model answers:

Part of speech	Word 1	Word 2	Related word
n	assets	liabilities	–
n	deficit	surplus*	accounts/revenue
adj	distributed	retained	profits
n	expenses	income	account
adj	intangible	tangible	assets
n	loss	profit	account
adj	operating	non-operating	revenue

*can also be an adjective

> ### Language note
>
> The amount earned from a company's principal activities (e.g., selling goods or providing services) is known as *revenue*.
>
> *Income* is sometimes used instead of the word *revenue*. However, in accounting terms, the word *income* means 'net of revenues and expenses.' Therefore, a bank's income from its operations is its revenue minus costs and operating expenses.

Exercise C

Refer students to the graph (Figure 1). Set for pairwork, or, with a fast class, do as high-speed oral. Accept all reasonable answers. During feedback, establish the meaning of the categories in the bar graph. Ask students the following questions and elicit appropriate answers (possible answers in brackets):

What assets do banks commonly have? (loans to clients; cash; fixed assets)

How many different types of bank income can you name? (interest; service fees; profit on investments)

How could you categorize the different types of expenses? (personnel; occupancy; general)

Answers

Model answers:

1 The data for 2007.
2 Dollars in millions.
3 Left = expenses.
4 Right = income.

Exercise D

First review the pronunciation of dates and numbers. For example:

- the number 1,234 is 'one thousand, two hundred and thirty-four' (American usage normally 'one thousand, two hundred thirty-four') unless discussing the year 1234, when it is 'twelve thirty-four'
- the forms for numeric dates differ between the US (mm/dd/yy) and Britain (dd/mm/yy)
- spoken convention for dates: 'The tenth of October, two thousand and seven'/'October the tenth, two thousand and seven' (American usage normally 'October tenth, two thousand seven')

Review the pronunciation and spelling of cardinal numbers (e.g., 18, 80) and ordinal numbers (e.g., *eighth* only one *t*; *twelfth f* not *v*, etc.).

Refer students to the numbers in box c. Say numbers at random and get students to point to the correct number, then check with a partner in each case. Elicit the numbers from the whole class, then individual students, and establish correct pronunciation.

Now refer students to Table 1. Discuss the questions with the whole class. Set for pairwork. Tell students to use calculators if required. Monitor as necessary to identify pronunciation difficulties. Establish correct stress and pronunciation of *per cent* – /pəˈsent/ – and *percentage*.

During feedback, ask students to say whether they think the table indicates a strong bank performance, and if so, how the increase in profits was generated.

Establish that net profit is the result after income tax is deducted from before-tax (or pre-tax) profit. The minus sign and underline indicate that interest expenses are deducted from interest income and the figures are underlined to show the result, which is net interest income.

Answers

Model answers:

1 The bank's net profit increased by $136 million. While total expenses increased by 3.7%, total income increased by 3.9%; therefore the increase in income generated the extra profit. This increase in

profit indicates that the bank is performing reasonably well

2

	2007 $m	2006 $m	% change
Interest income	18,560	17,780	4.4
Interest expenses	−11,890	−11,260	5.6
Net interest income	6,670	6,520	2.3
Other banking income	4,730	4,450	6.3
Total income	**11,400**	**10,970**	**3.9**
Personnel expenses	−3,210	−3,015	6.5
Occupancy expenses	−530	−480	10.4
General expenses	−2,815	−2,710	3.9
Provision for doubtful debts	−275	−380	−27.6
Total expenses	**−6,830**	**−6,585**	**3.7**
Before-tax profit	4,570	4,385	4.2
Income tax	-1,364	−1,315	3.7
Net profit	**3.206**	**3,070**	**4.4**

Language note

In English a comma is often used to separate thousands in numbers, and a full stop at the decimal point. This is the exact opposite to many countries, including Brazil, Holland, Indonesia, France.

When referring to the numeral '0', in British English 'zero', 'nought', or 'oh' are used. Americans use the term 'zero' most frequently.

Exercise E

Establish that when you are reporting changes, you need to say how something has changed (e.g., whether it has decreased or increased) and often how quickly or slowly it has changed. With the whole class, discuss language used for describing trends in performance. Elicit both verbs and adverbs. For example:

Go up	No change	Go down	Adverbs
rise	stay the same	fall	slightly
increase	remain at …	decrease	gradually
grow	doesn't change	decline	steadily
improve	is unchanged	worsen	significantly
		drop	sharply
			dramatically

Set the text completion for individual work and pairwork checking. Do one or two examples orally, then ask students to complete the remaining sentences. Feed back.

Answers

Model answers:

Table 1 shows changes <u>in</u> the bank's financial performance <u>for/in</u> the years 2006 and 2007. There was an increase <u>of</u> 4.4% <u>in</u> net profit <u>for/in</u> the year 2007.

While there was a <u>sharp rise</u> of 10.4% in occupancy-related expenses, the provision for doubtful debts <u>decreased/went down/declined/fell/dropped</u> <u>significantly/sharply</u> by 27.6%. Other banking income showed a/an <u>marked</u> <u>improvement/growth/rise/increase</u> of 6.3% from the previous year. Interest income also <u>improved/rose/went up/increased/grew slightly</u> to $18,560 m, a/an <u>increase/rise/growth</u> of 4.4%. However, personnel expenses also <u>rose/went up/increased/grew.</u>

As a follow-up, build up the table below on the board (leave on the board for Exercise F).

Ask students to make nouns from the verbs and adjectives from the adverbs. You could reproduce the table on an OHT or handout – leave the noun and adjective columns blank. The incomplete table is reproduced in the additional resources section (Resource 5B) to facilitate this.

Verbs	Nouns	Adverbs	Adjectives
rise	a rise	gradually	gradual
increase	an increase	sharply	sharp
grow	growth*	slightly	slight
improve	improvement	markedly	marked
fall	a fall	significantly	significant
decrease	a decrease	rapidly	rapid
drop	a drop	steeply	steep
decline	a decline	steadily	steady

*usually (but not always) uncountable in this sense.

Exercise F

Set for pairwork. Pairs then discuss their answers with another pair.

Note: There are no 'correct' answers for questions 2–5. Students should use their own background knowledge and experience. Accept anything reasonable.

Answers

Possible answers:

1 The doubtful debts provision was $105,000,000 lower in 2007 than in 2006.

2 The bank did not increase its lending rates to maintain its interest rate spread between its costs of funds and its lending rates. The possible reason was that the market was too competitive to allow for increased lending rates.

Answers

Possible answer:

The lecturer will discuss the statement of financial position. Firstly, she will discuss assets. Then she will look at liabilities. Finally, she will examine equity.

> ### Methodology note
>
> If students are new to the subject of finance in banking, they may only be able to make simple points about the tables and figures, as in the answer above.

🎧 Exercise B

Tell students they are only going to hear the introduction to the lecture. Give them time to read the topics. Check that they understand the meaning. Remind them they will only hear the introduction once, as in a lecture. Tell them to listen out for the signpost language on the board. They should number the topics from 1–5 in the order in which the lecturer will talk about them.

Play Part 1. Allow students to compare answers. Feed back. Establish that assets, liabilities and equity are included on the statement of financial *position*, not the statement of financial *performance*.

Ask students to say what signpost language they heard related to each topic. Confirm the correct answers.

Answers

Model answers:

assets – 2 (*I'll start with, …*)

equity – 4 (*After that, …*)

liabilities – 3 (*followed by …*)

statement of financial performance – 5 (*Finally, …*)

statement of financial position – 1 (*Firstly, …*)

Transcript 🎧 1.21

Part 1

Good morning, everyone. To start with, I'm going to talk about how we can assess the financial strength of a bank. What do we mean by 'strength'? How do we measure this?

Well, we can look at a comparative analysis; that is, how the particular bank compares with other banks, or how it compares with its own performance in previous years. In this lecture I'm going to focus on individual bank performance and … the bank we will be looking at is the ANW Bank. I'll use the financial accounts in the shareholders' report, which contains two tables of interest to us. These are the statement of financial performance, and the statement of financial

position. While both these documents provide different information on the bank's financial strength, the statement of financial position is arguably the document for understanding the state of the bank's finances.

The main discussion will be on the statement of financial position. Firstly, I'll define exactly what a statement of financial position is. Then I'll briefly go over the categories included in a statement of financial position. I'll start with assets, followed by liabilities. After that, I'll look at equity.

Finally, I'll talk briefly about the statement of financial performance. This shows the movements in income, expenditure and profit which have taken place since the end of the previous accounting period. In other words, it shows the trading results for 12 months.

Exercise C

Set for pairwork. Divide the topics up among the pairs so that each pair concentrates on one topic. Feed back. Accept all reasonable answers with good justifications.

Answers

Possible answers:

Statement of financial position: assets, liabilities, equity.

Statement of financial performance: income, expenditure, profit.

Assets: cash/liquid, loans, property, equipment.

Liabilities: borrowings, deposits, debts, income tax liabilities.

Equity: reserves, retained profits, contributed equity.

Exercise D

1 Set for individual work. Students can discuss the financial terms in pairs, but don't explain all the terms at this stage, as they will be explained in the lecture.

2/3 Elicit suggestions from the whole class. Refer students to the *Skills bank* in Unit 1 if necessary. As the lecture relates to classification and definitions, a diagram or spidergram would be a good way to record the information; numbered points would also be suitable. You could get the class to try different forms of note-taking, then discuss which form the students found most useful for this type of lecture.

🎧 Exercise E

Tell students to use their outline from Exercise D to take notes. Which topic(s) do they expect to hear in this section?

Play Part 2. Put students in pairs to compare their notes

and discuss the questions. Feed back. After checking answers to questions 2 and 3, build a complete set of notes on the board.

Answers

Model answers:

2 Statement of financial position; assets.

3 Loans and advances to bank customers.

Transcript 🎧 1.22

Part 2

A statement of financial position shows what the bank has in the categories of assets, liabilities and equity at a certain date. In other words, the book value of the bank at a certain point in time. Before we look at the figures, I'll briefly go over what each of these categories includes.

The basic equation is that what the company owns, including money owed to the bank, must equal what the bank owes to its creditors and shareholders. In other words, assets must balance with liabilities and capital. Capital, of course, is not an asset. It is owed to the shareholders and would be paid back to them if the bank closed down.

If you look at the handout, you will see that the bank's assets are made up, firstly, of 'Cash and liquid assets' – that is, for example, cheques in the process of collection, and demand securities. In other words, those assets that can readily be turned into cash.

Next we have 'Due from other financial institutions', which includes advances and loans made by the ANW Bank to other banks. This is not to be confused with 'Due to other financial institutions', which forms part of the bank's liabilities and includes advances and loans made to the ANW Bank by other banks.

Continuing with assets, we have 'Trading securities', which include negotiable financial instruments. Negotiable financial instruments are basically financial instruments that can be assigned to another purchaser at any time. What I mean is, for example, government bonds purchased by the bank.

Financial instruments held for the long term are included under 'Investments and securities'. Arguably, they could be included in a financial instruments category. It follows that the bank's shares in listed companies are included under 'Investments and securities'.

Actually, the largest type of assets held by a bank is normally loans and advances made to bank customers, which is the next category.

And finally, we have the fixed assets held by the bank. These are fundamentally the 'Property, plant and equipment' owned by the bank.

🎧 Exercise F

Ask students what they expect to hear about in the next part. Refer students to their outline again. Give them time to read the questions. Note that the final part of the lecture will be heard in Lesson 3, but there is no need to tell them this at this point.

Play Part 3. Set the questions for pairwork. Students should use their notes to help them answer the questions. When it becomes clear that the lecturer did not actually stick to the plan in the introduction, say that this happens very often in lectures. Lecturers are human! Although it is a good idea to prepare outline notes, students need to be ready to alter and amend these. Discuss how best to do this. One obvious way is to use a non-linear approach such as a mind map or spidergram, where new topics can easily be added.

Feed back. Note that there is no need to build a set of notes on the board at this point – this will be done in Lesson 3. Ask students if they can remember exactly what the lecturer said to indicate that she had lost her place.

Answers

Model answers:

1 Liabilities.

2 Balance dates.

3 Deposits and other borrowings from customers.

4 The different financial reporting requirements. (... *Where was I? Oh, yes.*)

5 Potential losses (e.g., bad debts – loans made to customers which are not repaid).

Transcript 🎧 1.23

Part 3

The largest group of liabilities is generally 'Deposits and other borrowings'. These represent deposits and other advances made by bank customers. 'Income tax liabilities' – well, that's pretty self-explanatory – and ... 'Bonds and notes', which are financial instruments issued by the bank to raise funds to lend to customers.

Now if you look at the handout, you'll see that in this example the date, March 31st 2007, is preceded by the words 'as at'. It shows the financial strength of the organization on that particular day. In our example, the statement of financial position presents a view of the ANW Bank's financial position at two points of time. The figures are presented for March 31st 2007 with comparative figures for the same date in the previous year, that is, 2006.

The words 'for the year ended ...' refer to the date which is the end of the financial year for an organization. In other words, its annual balance date. This is not to be confused with the end of the calendar year. Year end balance dates are commonly December 31st, March 31st, or June 30st, subject to the tax regime of the country concerned. The reporting format may vary between banks ... and also by country. While there are international accounting standards, each country can modify these for their own particular legal requirements. Now ... where was I? Oh yes, to return to the main point, a country could have quarterly, or six-monthly or annual reporting requirements.

... and now to go back to liabilities. Naturally, banks have to make financial provisions to provide for potential losses, such as, for example, the non-repayment of loans made to customers. 'Provisions' includes the provision made for future risk, whereas 'subordinated debt' includes loans to the bank that have a lower level of security. The 'Provisions' category is basically the financial allowances made by the bank to provide for potential losses and is necessary in order to give a true and fair view of the bank's financial position.

Exercise G

This gives further practice in identifying words and phrases used synonymously in a particular context. Set for individual work and pairwork checking.

Answers

Model answers:

1	analysis	examination
2	modify	change
3	provisions	allowances
4	requirements	regulations
5	self-explanatory	easy to understand
6	subject to	depending on

Closure

1 Check that students understand some of the concepts and vocabulary in the unit so far, including Lesson 1. If time, use the vocabulary review in the additional resources section (Resource 5C); for answers see the extra activities section for this unit.

2 Depending on the knowledge of the group, discuss how they think this bank is performing.

5.3 Extending skills

Facsimile of Course Book page 41:

5.3 Extending skills | note-taking symbols • stress within words • lecture language

A Look at a student's notes from the lecture in Lesson 2.
1 What do the symbols and abbreviations mean?
2 The notes contain some mistakes. Find and correct them.
3 Make the corrected notes into a spidergram.
4 What do you expect the next part of the lecture to be about?

Assess strength
Comparative analysis
- cf. other banks
- indiv. bank cf. prev. yrs.
1 State. fin. perf. • 12 mths.
2. .. .. position • @ certain date
what bank owns must • what bank owes
i.e. assets • liabilities • capital
2.1 Assets NB loans to cust. • largest liab.
2.2 Equity – largest • gen. deposits & other borrowings

B Listen to the final part of the lecture.
1 Complete your notes.
2 Check your notes with the handout in Lesson 2. Make changes as necessary.
3 Why does the lecturer have to stop?
4 What is the research task?

C Listen to some stressed syllables. Identify the word below in each case. Number each word.
Example: You hear: 1 pa /pæ/ You write:
accumulated ___   contributed ___   preceded ___
analysis ___   equation ___   regime ___
arguably ___   equity ___   retained ___
comparative /   generally ___   securities ___

D Study part of the lecture on the right.
1 Choose the best word or phrase in each case.
2 Listen and check your ideas.
3 Match words or phrases from the blue box with each word or phrase. There may be more than one option.
4 Think of other words or phrases with similar meanings.

generally   in essence   in fact
in other words   lastly   possibly
practically   probably
some people say   that is to say
therefore   usually

E Discuss the research task set by the lecturer.
1 What kind of information should you find?
2 What do you already know?
3 Where can you find more information?

Negotiable financial instruments are *basically / arguably* financial instruments that can be assigned to another purchaser at any time. *Therefore / What I mean is*, for example, government bonds purchased by the bank.
Financial instruments held for the long term are included under 'Investments and securities'. *Usually / Arguably*, they could be included in a financial instruments category. *It follows that / In other words*, the bank's shares in listed companies are included under 'Investments and securities'.
Actually / Naturally, the largest type of assets held by a bank is normally / *on the other hand* loans and advances made to bank customers, which is the next category.
And *in the end / finally*, we have the fixed assets held by the bank. These are fundamentally the 'Property, plant and equipment' owned by the bank.

41

Lesson aims

- use symbols in note-taking
- understand and use lecture language such as stance adverbials (*obviously, arguably*), restatement (*in other words ...*) and other commentary-type phrases

Further practice in:

- stress within words
- asking for information
- formulating polite questions

Introduction

1 As in Unit 3, encourage students to ask you questions about the information in the lecture in Lesson 2 as if you were the lecturer. Remind them about asking for information politely. If they can't remember how to do this, you could tell them to revise the *Skills bank* for Unit 3.

2 Put students in pairs. Student A must ask Student B about the information in the lecture in Lesson 2 to help him/her complete the notes from the lecture. Then they reverse roles. Again, they can revise language for this in the *Skills bank* for Unit 3.

Exercise A

1 Revise/introduce the idea of using symbols and abbreviations when making notes. Ask students to look at the example notes and find the symbols and abbreviated forms. Do they know what these mean? If not, they should try to guess. Point out that multi-syllable words are often reduced to their first and second syllables followed by a full stop (optional) to indicate it is an abbreviation (e.g., *prev. = previous*).

If you wish, you could expand the table in the Answers section below with more symbols and abbreviations that will be useful for the students. There is also a list at the back of the Course Book for students' reference.

2 Ask students to tell you what kind of notes these are (linear and numbered). Set the task for pairwork. Students will need to agree what the notes are saying and then make the corrections.

3 Set for individual work. Feed back with the whole class and build the spidergram in the Answers section (or students' preferred version) on the board.

4 Elicit suggestions.

Language note

Some abbreviations are universal and some are personal. People often develop their own personal system of symbols and abbreviations. For example, *m* for million is used by everyone but mths. is an example of a longer word abbreviated by the individual who wrote these notes.

Answers

Model answers:

1

Symbol/abbreviation	Meaning
cf.	compared to/compare
indiv.	individual
prev.	previous
yrs.	years
state.	statement
fin.	financial
perf.	performance
mths.	months
=	is, equals, is the same as
"	ditto
@	at
i.e.	that means, that is, in other words

Answers

Model answers:

1 Accept all reasonable definitions.

2/3/4

Table 1

Word	Banking meaning	Part of speech	Synonym
appreciate	increase in value	v	increase
basket	a group of commodities or currencies	n	group
capital	business assets, property and money	n	finance
reserves	funds retained	pl n	provisions*
stable	not moving up and down (e.g., interest rates)	adj	steady
stock	ownership in a company	n	shares

provisions are funds retained for a specific purpose, whereas *reserves* are retained for a more general purpose. In this regard *provisions* is not a true synonym.

Exercise B

Refer students to the table in the report extract on the right-hand page. Set for pairwork discussion. Monitor but don't assist.

Feed back with the whole class. Accept any reasonable answers.

Answers

Model answers:

1 The table shows the responsibilities of four central banks.
2 The European Union, the United Kingdom, the United States of America, Japan.
3 There is a common objective across all banks which is price stability.

Exercise C

Set for pairwork discussion. Tell students to refer to the table on the right-hand page for contextual clues. Monitor but don't assist.

Feed back with the whole class. Accept all reasonable answers. Discuss the extent to which the synonyms are true synonyms.

Answers

Model answers:
See table below.

Table 2

Word	Part of speech	Banking meaning	Synonym
mandate	n	authority to act	(area of) responsibility
stability	n	being steady, not moving up or down	steadiness
prejudice*	n	a bad/negative effect	harm, damage
maintenance	n	successfully keeping something in a particular state	holding, keeping
support	n	actions or money intended to help someone or something	help, aid
quantified	adj	showing the effect of something in figures	determined, measured
prioritization	n	making something the most important; putting in order of importance	preferred order/rank
qualitative	adj	measured subjectively (as opposed to quantitative = measured in numbers)	judgement-based
sound	adj	reliable, balanced	solid, steady
specification	n	detailed information	standard

*students should note that this is different from the usual meaning of *prejudice* (to make a hasty and often false judgement about something, not based on evidence)

Exercise D

Set for individual work and pairwork checking. Students should make antonyms for the words in the first column, not the base word.

Feed back with the whole class. Establish that the antonym of *stable* is *unstable* (compare with *stability/instability*).

Answers

Model answers:

Table 3

Word	Base word	Part of speech of base word	Antonym with prefix
stability	stable	adj	instability
quantified	quantify	v	unquantified
employment	employ	v	unemployment
sound	sound	adj	unsound

Exercise E

Set for individual work and pairwork checking. Feed back with the whole class. Ask students to justify their choices. If possible, don't give the correct answers until every student has responded.

Answers

Model answers:

1	false	Maintaining low inflation is one of three objectives of the Federal Reserve.
2	false	The Federal Reserve sets the inflation objective.
3	true	
4	true	(it is set by the Treasury, a government department)
5	false	The Bank of Japan oversees its own inflation policy.
6	true	

Exercise F

One aim of this exercise is to introduce or revise the students' use of the passive. (There are passives in question 1, items 2 and 3.) Another aim is to practise paraphrasing at sentence level (question 2).

1 Set for individual work and pairwork checking. Feed back with the whole class.

2 Set for individual work or for homework. Refer students to the *Vocabulary bank*. Encourage them to reorder the information and to change vocabulary and grammar as far as possible to create good paraphrases of the sentences.

Answers

Model answers:

1 1 The Bank of England's primary goal is <u>to maintain</u> (*maintain*) price stability.

   2 The Bank's objectives for price stability <u>are quantified</u> (*quantify*) by the Treasury.

   3 Support for its growth and employment objectives <u>is required</u> (*require*) by the government.

   4 The Bank of England's objectives of low inflation, and growth and employment <u>conflict</u> (*conflict*).

   Note: If students suggest *in conflict* (even though they are asked for a verb), point out the difference in stress between the noun and the verb: *'conflict/con'flict*.

2 Answers depend on the students.

Closure

Set the following question for students to make individual notes, then for pairwork discussion. Feed back with the whole class. Accept any reasonable answers.

Why might the Bank of England's objectives of low inflation and growth and employment conflict?

Possible answer: Some economists argue that when there is full employment, people have more money to spend. As a result there is an increase in the demand for, and purchase of, consumable items. Businesses grow to meet the demand for products. An increase in demand leads to an increase in prices. Consequently, it is argued that economic growth and full employment are incompatible with low inflation.

6.2 Reading

6.2 Reading   identifying subject-verb-object in long sentences • paraphrasing

A Discuss these questions.
1 Who are the owners of a central bank?
2 What are the main functions of a central bank?
3 Explain the term 'lender of last resort'.

B Look at the title, the introduction and the first sentence of each paragraph on the opposite page.
1 What will the text be about?
2 Using your ideas from this exercise and from Exercise A above, write some research questions.

The Bank of Japan, Tokyo

C Read the text. Does it answer your questions?

D Study the highlighted sentences in the text. Find and underline the subject, verb and object or complement in each sentence. See *Skills bank*

E Two students paraphrased a paragraph of the text.
1 Which paragraph is it?
2 Which paraphrase is better? Why?

Student A

The objective for most central banks is to carry out policies that result in a stable currency and economy.

By setting the official interest rate of their country, central banks hope to manage the inflation rate.

Inflation involves an increase in the price of a 'basket' of goods rather than an increase in just one product or service.

Student B

The majority of state banks have to execute the agreed financial goals of parliament.

A certain number of them fix the government interest rate.

This is seen as a means of controlling inflation (increasing costs on a range of products), and deflation.

F Read the text on the opposite page.
1 Select part of the text.
2 Paraphrase it in your own words without changing the meaning:
• use synonyms where possible
• change from active to passive voice as necessary
• use a replacement subject where possible
3 Exchange your paraphrase with another student or pair. Can you identify the part of the text they selected?
See *Vocabulary bank*
48

6 CENTRAL BANKS

The role of the central bank

A central bank (reserve bank or monetary authority) is created by government legislation. It normally has the legal right to create money. It can print more money to increase the supply, or exchange money for securities. It can sell securities to decrease the money supply. It is responsible for maintaining stability in the banking system of its country, or group of member states. In times of financial crisis, the central bank acts as 'lender of last resort' (i.e., extending credit when no one else will) to the banking sector. Some central banks, such as the Bank of England, are involved in coordinating, with solvent banks, 'lifeboat' rescues of banks in crisis.

The mandate of most central banks is to carry out their government's fiscal and monetary policy to ensure a stable economy and currency. Some central banks set their country's official interest rate. They do this to manage inflation (a rise in the price of a 'basket' of goods), as well as deflation. Central banks can influence money supply, interest rates, and foreign exchange rates. They may also manage the country's foreign exchange, gold reserves, plus the government's stock register.

Central bank structures and conditions vary significantly within and across nations. The European Central Bank (ECB) operates across several countries. The Federal Reserve Bank (Fed) operates across all states in the USA. Central banks are managed by a board of directors. The head of the central bank is usually a governor or president. All governments have some influence over their central banks. In the USA, the chairman of the Federal Reserve Bank is appointed by the president. However, his or her appointment must be confirmed by Congress. In some countries, the key monetary policy decisions are made by committees or individuals, independent of the political appointee. The Monetary Policy Committee of the Bank of England, for example, is dominated by representatives of private corporations.

In most countries, a central bank carries out supervision and regulation of the banking industry. Some central banks still require trading banks to maintain a certain amount of their deposits as reserves. However, most central banks address credit risk by requiring trading banks to meet certain capital requirements. These requirements (called capital adequacy ratios) require banks to hold a percentage of their assets as capital. The Basel Capital Accord's current guideline is 8% for international banks. This means that when a bank reaches its lending limit, 92% of assets, it must raise additional capital if it wishes to continue to increase its lending.

Central banks may also provide financial services such as transfer of funds, banknotes and coins or foreign currency. The Bank of Japan, for example, is a central bank that is actively engaged in financial transactions with other financial institutions. In this role, the central bank is known as the 'bank of banks'. In some countries, this may be the responsibility of a government department such as the ministry of finance.

Most central banks are state-owned. However, many economists view government intervention in the monetary policy of the country as undesirable. Advocates of an independent central bank argue that the power to create money, and the power to spend it (e.g., funding government budgets), should be separate. Independence, it is argued, creates a more credible monetary policy. Consequently, the financial market reacts more in line with the direction indicated by the central bank. It is also argued that political interference or pressure may lead to 'boom and bust' economic cycles as governments attempt to manipulate the economy before an election for short-term political gain. This may result in higher employment and consumer spending, but lead to higher inflation in the long term. During the 1990s, many countries, influenced by research correlating central bank independence with low and stable inflation, increased central bank independence. Critics of this trend say independence can weaken the central bank's public accountability. They argue that central bank independence needs to be balanced with accountability to the public and their elected representatives.
49

General note

Read the *Skills bank* at the end of the Course Book unit. Decide when, if at all, to refer students to it. The best time is probably at the very end of the lesson or the beginning of the next lesson, as a summary/revision.

Lesson aims

● identify the kernel SVC/O of a long sentence

Further practice in:

● research questions
● topic sentences
● paraphrasing

Introduction

Remind the class about techniques when using written texts for research. Ask:

What is it a good idea to do:

● *before reading?* (think of research questions)
● *while you are reading?* (look for topic sentences)
● *after reading?* (check answers to the research questions)

What words in a text signal the development of a topic in a new direction? (markers showing contrast such as *but, however, at the same time, on the other hand,* etc.).

If you wish, refer students to Unit 4 *Skills bank.*

Exercise A

Set for general discussion. Allow students to debate differences of opinion. Encourage them to give examples if they can. Do not correct or give information at this point, as these topics will be dealt with in the text.

Exercise B

Set for pairwork discussion. Monitor students' written research questions for spelling and grammar errors. You might like to select some students to write their questions on the board. Depending on your students, edit spelling, grammar, and sentence structure with the whole class. Do not elaborate further at this point, as more information will be found in the text.

Possible research questions might be:

How can central banks ensure a stable economy and currency?

What are the significant differences in central bank structures?

Feed back with the whole class. Accept all reasonable answers.

Exercise C

Set the reading for individual work and pairwork checking.

Exercise D

Draw a table with the headings from the Answers section on the board. If you wish, students can also draw a similar table in their notebooks. Explain that in academic writing, sentences can seem very complex. This is often not so much because the sentence structure is highly complex in itself but that the subjects and objects/complements may consist of clauses or complex noun phrases. Often the verb is quite simple. But in order to fully understand a text, the grammar of a sentence must be understood. Subject+verb+object or complement is the basic sentence structure of English. Students need to be able to locate the subjects, main verbs and their objects or complements.

Elicit from the students the subject, main verb and object for the first sentence. Ask students for the *head word* of each subject, main verb and object (underlined in the table in the Answers section). Write them in the table on the board. Point out that the head word isn't always very informative, but that is why it has to be modified with adjectives before or phrases after it.

Add the leading prepositional/adverbial phrase (if any), pointing out that this part contains information which is extra to the main part of the sentence. The sentence can be understood quite easily without it. Point out that the prepositional/adverbial phrase sometimes goes at the beginning of the sentence for emphasis.

Set the remainder of the exercise for individual work followed by pairwork checking. Finally, feed back with the whole class.

You may wish to refer students to the *Skills bank* at this stage.

Answers

Model answers:
See table below.

Exercise E

Refer students to the two sets of notes (Student A and Student B).

Set for individual work and pairwork checking. Make sure that students identify the original phrases in the text first (paragraph 2) before looking at the paraphrases in detail.

Feed back with the whole class. A good way to demonstrate how Student A's text contains too many words from the original is to use an OHT or other visual medium and highlight the common words in colour. (A table giving the sentences plus commentary is included in the additional resources section – Resource 6B.) Check that students are able to say which parts of the paraphrase match with the original, and which structures have been used.

Answers

1 Paragraph 2.
2 Student B's paraphrase is better, because it uses fewer of the words from the original text.

Language note

It is important that students understand that when paraphrasing, it is not sufficient to change a word here and there and leave most of the words and the basic sentence structure unchanged. This approach is known as 'patch-writing' and is considered to be plagiarism. It is also important when paraphrasing not to change the meaning of the original – also quite hard to do.

Prepositional/ adverbial phrase	Subject	Verb	Object/complement	Prepositional/ adverbial phrase(s)
	The <u>mandate</u> of most central banks	is <u>to carry out</u>	their government's fiscal and monetary <u>policy</u>	to ensure a stable economy and currency.
	Central bank <u>structures and conditions</u>	<u>vary</u>		within and across nations; significantly
In most countries,	a <u>central bank</u>	<u>carries out</u>	<u>supervision and regulation</u> of the banking industry.	
	<u>Central banks</u> may also	<u>provide</u>	financial <u>services</u>	such as transfer of funds, banknotes and coins or foreign currency.
However,	many <u>economists</u>	<u>view</u>	government <u>intervention</u> in the monetary policy of the country	as undesirable.

Exercise F

Refer students to the *Vocabulary bank* at this stage. Review paraphrasing skills with the whole class before starting this exercise.

Divide the text into parts. For example, each paragraph can be divided into different sections (though of course you should not use paragraph 2); give each section to different students to work on. Alternatively, you could choose one part of the text for all students to work on.

You can set this as pairwork to be done in class or as individual work for homework. If students are doing the work in class in groups or pairs, a good way to provide feedback is to get them to write their paraphrase on an OHT or other visual medium. Show each paraphrase (or a selection) to the class and ask for comments. Say what is good about the work. Point out where there are errors and ask for suggestions on how to improve it. Make any corrections on the OHT or other visual medium with a different colour.

Closure

Divide the class into two teams. Write the topic sentences from the reading text on strips, or photocopy them from the additional resources section (Resource 6C). One team chooses a topic sentence and reads it aloud. The other team must give the information triggered by that topic sentence. Accept only the actual paragraph content.

6.3 Extending skills

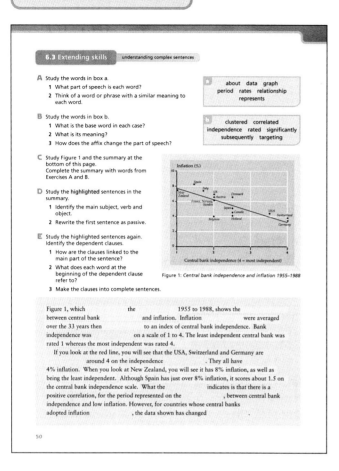

Lesson aims

- study sentence structure in more detail
- identify the main information in:

    an active sentence

    a passive sentence

    a complex sentence with participles

    a complex sentence with embedded clauses

Introduction

Ask students to see how many phrases or compound nouns they can make with the words *bank* and *banking*. Tell students to brainstorm a list in pairs. Feed back with the whole class.

Possible answers: *bank balance, bank card, banking hours, banknote, banker, bank account, bankrupt, bankroll, Internet banking,* etc.

Exercise A

Ask students to study the words in the box. Set for pairwork. Tell students *not* to use their dictionaries to begin with but to use what they know to guess meanings and parts of speech. If necessary, they should use dictionaries when checking after they have completed the task. Deal with any common problems with the whole class.

Answers

Model answers:

Word	Part of speech	Similar meaning
about	adverb	approximately, around
data	n (U/pl)*	information
graph	n (C)	chart
period	n (C)	time, time frame, length of time
rates	pl n	figures, amount
relationship	n (C)	connection, correlation
represents	v (T)	shows, depicts

**data* is the plural of *datum*, and as such can be used with a plural verb (*the data are being collected*); it is, however, increasingly used as a singular uncountable noun (*the data is being collected*)

Exercise B

Set for pairwork. Feedback with the whole class. Elicit answers and build up the table in the Answers section on the board. Note that not all the base words have meanings specific to banking. Tell students to explain the meaning in banking terms as far as possible.

Answers

Model answers:
See table on next page.

Word	Base and meaning	Effect of affix
clustered	cluster (v, I) – gather together in a group	~ed = past simple ending
correlated	correlate (v, T/I) – when two or more things have a connection or influence each other	~ed = past simple ending
independence	depend (v, I) – rely on something or someone	in~ = forms a new word with the opposite meaning to the original ~ence = changes a verb to a noun
rated	rate (v, T) – give value to	~ed = past simple ending
significantly	significant (adj) – important or noticeable	~ly = changes an adjective to an adverb
subsequently	subsequent (adj) – happening later or after something	~ly = changes an adjective to an adverb
targeting	1. target (n, C) – a focus or aim 2. target (v, T) – direct or focus on something or someone	2. ~ing = forms the present participle

Exercise C

Set for individual work and pairwork checking. Students can make use of all the words they have discussed in Exercises A and B (i.e., they can use synonyms as well as the words in the boxes).

Feed back with the whole class. Establish that the passive voice is used to describe how the information was selected for the bar chart (paragraph 1). In paragraph 2, while the period shown is 1955 to 1988 (i.e., in the past), we use the present tense, as we are describing the information as it appears now, in the present time.

Answers

Model answers:

Figure 1, which <u>represents</u> the <u>period</u> 1955 to 1988, shows the <u>relationship/correlation</u> between central bank <u>independence</u> and inflation. Inflation <u>rates/figures</u> were averaged over the 33 years then <u>correlated/related</u> to an index of central bank independence. Bank independence was <u>rated</u> on a scale of 1 to 4. The least independent central bank was rated 1 whereas the most independent was rated 4.

If you look at the red line, you will see that the USA, Switzerland and Germany are <u>clustered</u> around 4 on the independence scale. They all have <u>about/around</u> 4% inflation. When you look at New Zealand, you will see that it has 8% inflation, as well as being the least independent. Although Spain has just over 8% inflation, it scores about 1.5 on the central bank independence scale. What the <u>data/graph</u> indicates is that there is a positive correlation, for the period represented on the <u>graph/chart</u>, between central bank independence and low inflation. However, for countries whose central banks <u>subsequently</u> adopted inflation <u>targeting</u>, the data shown has changed <u>significantly</u>.

Exercise D

1 Start this exercise with the whole class. Copy (or elicit and write) the first highlighted sentence onto the board:

Figure 1, which represents the period 1955 to 1988, shows the relationship between central bank independence and inflation.

Copy the table headings from the Answers section onto the board. Ask students to put the parts of the first sentence into the correct column of the table. Complete the example with the students. Tell them that when they look at the 'Other verbs' column they may well find several, and should number each verb and subject/object/complement section separately. Point out that the order of each part of the sentence is not reflected in the table: the table is just a way to analyse the sentences.

Set the rest of the highlighted sentences for individual work and pairwork checking. Feed back with the whole class. Draw their attention to the 'main' parts of the sentence: it is very important in reading that they should be able to identify these. Notice also that the main parts can stand on their own and make complete sentences.

2 With the whole class, review the main points on the use of the passive voice. (Decide whether you do this before or after students have completed the question.) Establish that the passive is used to focus on the cause and effect of an action. It is often used in academic writing when describing pictorial information, e.g., a diagram that accompanies the text.

Set for individual work and pairwork checking.

Answers

Model answers:

1 See table on next page.

Main subject	Main verb	Main object/complement	Other verbs + their subjects + objects/complements	Adverbial phrases
Figure 1	shows	the <u>relationship</u> (between central bank independence and inflation)	<u>which</u> represents the period 1955 to 1988	
Inflation rates	were averaged		<u>then</u> correlated to an index (of central bank independence)	over the 33 years
The least independent central bank	was rated	1	<u>whereas</u> the most independent was rated 4	
New Zealand	has	(8%) <u>inflation</u>	you will see; <u>as well as</u> being the least independent	When you look at New Zealand
Spain	scores	(about) <u>1.5</u>% (on the central bank independence scale	<u>although</u> it has just over 8% inflation	

*underlined text = means by which dependent clause is joined to main clause

2   The relationship between central bank independence and inflation is shown in Figure 1 (,which represents the period 1955 to 1988).

Exercise E

This exercise involves looking carefully at the dependent clauses in the highlighted sentences.

1   Say that these clauses have special ways to link them to the main part of the sentence. Do this exercise with the whole class, using an OHT or other visual medium of the table in Exercise D, and a highlighter pen to mark the relevant words. (A version of the table without underlining is included in the additional resources section – Resource 6D.) Go through the clauses asking students what words or other ways are used to link the clauses to the main part of the sentence.

2   Set for individual work and pairwork checking. Students should look at each sentence and identify the antecedents of the relative pronouns. You could ask them to use a highlighter pen or to draw circles and arrows linking the words.

3   Students must be able to get the basic or kernel meaning of the clause. Take the first sentence as an example and write it on the board. Point out that the relative pronouns and other ways of linking these clauses to the main clause will need to be changed or got rid of. Students should aim to write something that makes good sense as a complete sentence. Set the remaining clauses for individual work. Feed back with whole class. Accept anything that makes good sense.

Answers

Model answers:

1   See table in Exercise D. The first sentence uses a relative clause. The other sentences use conjunctions.

2   *which* (pronoun) = refers to Figure 1

then = indicates the next stage in the process

whereas = contrast with rating 1

as well as = additional information to that about inflation

although = contrast with New Zealand, i.e., Spain has higher inflation and more central bank independence

3   Possible answers:

Figure 1 represents the period 1955–1988.

Correlated information on inflation and central bank independence is shown in the graph.

In contrast, the most independent central bank was ranked 4.

New Zealand is also the least independent.

Spain has just over 8% inflation.

Language note

A dependent clause contains a verb and a subject and is a secondary part of a sentence. It is dependent because it 'depends' on the main clause. A main clause can stand by itself as a complete sentence in its own right (usually). A dependent clause always goes with a main clause and cannot stand by itself as a sentence in its own right.

Dependent clauses are typically joined to main clauses with certain types of words: for example, relative pronouns (e.g., *who*, *which*, etc.), linking adverbials (e.g., *if*, *when*, *before*, *although*, *whereas*, etc.); words associated with reporting speech (e.g., *that*, a *Wh~* word such as *what* or *why*) and so on.

Some dependent clauses are non-finite, that is, they don't have a 'full verb' but a participle form (e.g., *having finish<u>ed</u>, open<u>ing</u>*) and the subject may not be stated.

For more on this, see a good grammar reference book.

Closure

Write the following underlined beginnings and endings of words on the board or dictate them. Ask students to give the (or a) complete word.

(analy)<u>sis</u>

<u>bas</u>(ket)

<u>cap</u>(ital)

<u>correl</u>(ation/ate)

<u>fi</u>(nance)

(in)<u>dex</u>

(man)<u>date</u>

(portfo)<u>lio</u>

(re)<u>serves</u>

6.4 Extending skills

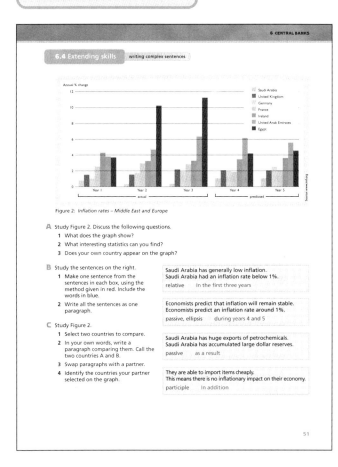

6.4 Extending skills writing complex sentences

Annual % change

☐ Saudi Arabia
■ United Kingdom
☐ Germany
☐ France
■ Ireland
☐ United Arab Emirates
■ Egypt

Year 1   Year 2   Year 3   Year 4   Year 5
actual   predicted

Figure 2: *Inflation rates – Middle East and Europe*

A Study Figure 2. Discuss the following questions.
1 What does the graph show?
2 What interesting statistics can you find?
3 Does your own country appear on the graph?

B Study the sentences on the right.
1 Make one sentence from the sentences in each box, using the method given in red. Include the words in blue.
2 Write all the sentences as one paragraph.

Saudi Arabia has generally low inflation.
Saudi Arabia had an inflation rate below 1%.
relative   In the first three years

Economists predict that inflation will remain stable.
Economists predict an inflation rate around 1%.
passive, ellipsis   during years 4 and 5

C Study Figure 2.
1 Select two countries to compare.
2 In your own words, write a paragraph comparing them. Call the two countries A and B.
3 Swap paragraphs with a partner.
4 Identify the countries your partner selected on the graph.

Saudi Arabia has huge exports of petrochemicals.
Saudi Arabia has accumulated large dollar reserves.
passive   as a result

They are able to import items cheaply.
This means there is no inflationary impact on their economy.
participle   In addition

51

Lesson aims

- write complex sentences:
  with passives
  joining with participles
  embedding clauses
  adding prepositional phrases

Further practice in:

- interpreting information in bar charts

Introduction

Revise words describing graphs (from Unit 5). Draw a line graph on the board. The line should rise and fall, sharply and gradually, have a peak and a point where it levels off. Point to each part of the line and ask students to give you the appropriate verb and adverb. Alternatively, draw your own line graph and describe it. Students should try to draw an identical line graph from your description while you are talking.

Exercise A

Set for pairwork then class discussion.

Answers

Model answers:

1 The graph shows inflation rates for seven European and Middle Eastern countries over a period of five years.

2/3 Answers depend on the students.

Exercise B

Set for individual work and pairwork checking. If necessary, do the first box with the whole class. Make sure students understand that they should write the four sentences as a continuous paragraph.

Feed back with the whole class. Accept any answers that make good sense. Point out where the phrases in blue act as linkers between the sentences to make a continuous paragraph.

Answers

Possible answer:

In the first three years, Saudi Arabia, which has generally low inflation, had a rate below 1%. It is predicted that inflation in the country during years 4 and 5 will remain stable, at around 1%. Saudi Arabia has huge exports of petrochemicals and, as a result, large dollar reserves have been accumulated. In addition, they are able to import items cheaply, which means there is no inflationary impact on their economy.

Exercise C

Set for individual work and pairwork checking. Alternatively, check paragraphs as a whole class activity. Select students at random to read their paragraph; the class identifies the country.

Refer to the extra activities section for an extension of this exercise.

Closure

Give students some very simple three- or four-word SVO/C sentences from the unit (or make some yourself) and ask them to add as many phrases and clauses as they can to make a long complex sentence. Who can make the longest sentence?

For example:
Central banks contain inflation.

→ *In many countries, central banks, which are … contain inflation by … and … which results in …*

7 INTERNATIONAL BANKING

In this unit, the focus is on the means of financing international trade. The first listening extract, from a lecture, looks at the different payment methods used in international trade, including letters of credit, documentary collection, cash with order and cash on delivery. It also examines some of the advantages and disadvantages associated with each method. The second listening extract is from a seminar in which students discuss the best payment methods for a company exporting to a range of customers in different countries.

Skills focus

🎧 Listening

- understanding speaker emphasis

Speaking

- asking for clarification
- responding to queries and requests for clarification

Vocabulary focus

- compound nouns
- fixed phrases from banking
- fixed phrases from academic English
- common lecture language

Key vocabulary

See also the list of fixed phrases from academic English in the Vocabulary bank (Course Book page 60).

authorize	document (n)	open account terms
bill of exchange	documentary collection	order (n and v)
buyer	export (n and v)	payment terms
cash on delivery	exporter	pre-shipment
cash with order	formalities	profit margin
credit (n and v)	fraud	receipt
credit rating	goods	regulation
creditworthy	importer	risk (n and v)
currency fluctuations	letter of credit	security
default (n and v)	liability	shipment
delivery	merchandise	terms

7.1 Vocabulary

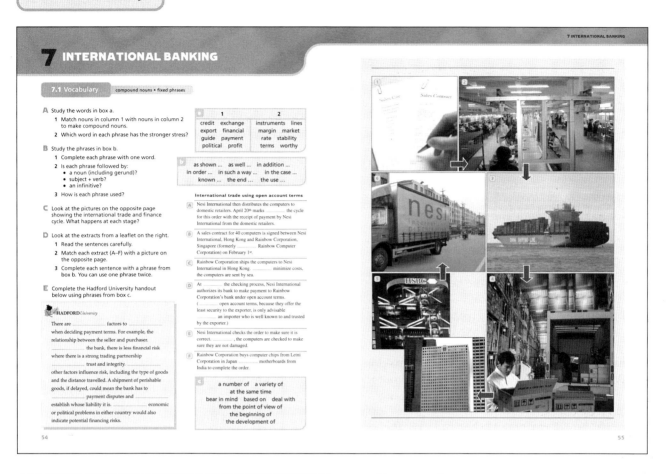

General note

Read the *Vocabulary bank* at the end of the Course Book unit. Decide when, if at all, to refer your students to it. The best time is probably at the very end of the lesson or the beginning of the next lesson, as a summary/revision.

Lesson aims

- understand and use some general academic fixed phrases
- understand and use fixed phrases and compound nouns from the discipline

Introduction

1 Revise some noun phrases (noun + noun, adjective + noun) from previous units. Give students two or three minutes to make word stars with a base word, trying to find as many possible combinations as they can (preferably without having to look at dictionaries).

For example:

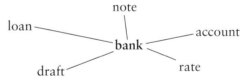

The central word could be either the first or second word of the phrase (bank rate/investment bank). Other base words which could be used are *money*, *loan*, *account*. If they are stuck for ideas, tell them to look back at previous units.

2 Introduce the topic of the lesson by looking at the pictures on the opposite page. Discuss what students know about international trade. How are banks involved?

Exercise A

Set for individual work and pairwork checking. Feed back with the whole class, making sure that the stress pattern is correct (the main stress is shown in the Answers section). Ask students to suggest other fixed phrases which could be made using the words in column 2, e.g., *domestic market*.

Answers

Model answers:

'creditworthy

ex'change rate

'export market

financial 'instruments

'guidelines

'payment terms

political sta'bility

'profit margin

Exercise B

1/2 Set for individual work and pairwork checking. Feed back with the whole class, building the first three columns of the table in the Answers section on the board.

3 Add the fourth column with the heading 'Use to …'. Give an example of the kind of thing you are looking for, i.e., a phrase which can describe why you would choose to use this fixed phrase. Elicit suggestions from the students to complete the table, supplying the information yourself if students don't know the answer. If students are not sure about the meaning of some of the phrases, give them some example sentences and tell them that you will look further at how they are used shortly. Leave the table on the board, as you will return to it.

Answers

Model answers:

Phrase	Followed by …		Use to …
as shown	in/by	noun/gerund	indicate a diagram or table
as well	as	noun/gerund	add information
in addition	to	noun/gerund	add information
in order	to/ that	infinitive	give the purpose for doing something
in such a way	that*	subject + verb	give the result of doing something
in the case	of	noun/gerund	refer to something
known	as	noun	give the special name for something
the end	of	noun	refer to the end of something
the use	of	noun	refer to the use of something

*as to is also possible after *in such a way*, although in this exercise, one word is required

Exercise C

Set for pairwork. Students should try to identify what each picture represents. One pair can describe each picture to the whole class. On the board, build up as many key words to describe the process as students can

come up with. If students don't know some important words, tell them they will meet them shortly.

Answers

Answers depend on the students.

Exercise D

Explain that the information from the leaflet *International trade using open account terms* goes with the pictures they have just discussed. Each picture has one piece of text (A–F). Note: both these companies are imaginary.

1 Set for individual work. Tell students to check words they can't guess in the dictionary. They should not pay attention to the spaces at this point.

2 Set for pairwork. Feed back with the whole class. Add any key words which might have been useful in Exercise C to the board.

3 Set for individual work. Refer back to the table in Exercise B, which will help students to choose the correct phrase. Feed back with the whole class.

Answers

Model answers:

Picture	Extract
1	**B** A sales contract for 40 computers is signed between Nesi International, Hong Kong and Rainbow Corporation, Singapore (formerly known as Rainbow Computer Corporation) on February 1st.
2	**F** Rainbow Corporation buys computer chips from Letni Corporation in Japan as well as motherboards from India to complete the order.
3	**C** Rainbow Corporation ships the computers to Nesi International in Hong Kong. In order to minimize costs, the computers are sent by sea.
4	**E** Nesi International checks the order to make sure it is correct. In addition, the computers are checked to make sure they are not damaged.
5	**D** At the end of the checking process, Nesi International authorizes its bank to make payment to Rainbow Corporation's bank under open account terms. (The use of open account terms, because they offer the least security to the exporter, is only advisable in the case of an importer who is well known to and trusted by the exporter.)
6	**A** Nesi International then distributes the computers to domestic retailers. April 20th marks the end of the cycle for this order with the receipt of payment by Nesi International from the domestic retailers.

If you wish, ask students to return to the table used in Exercise B and write one sentence for each of the fixed phrases to show their meaning. If you can put this into the context of an international trade process which students are very familiar with, such as an order for televisions (or computers as in the example), so much the better.

Exercise E

Set for individual work and pairwork checking. Students should use their dictionaries if they are not sure of the meaning of the phrases. Note that some phrases can be used for the same thing – it is a good idea to use a different word to avoid repetition. Feed back with the whole group.

Answers

Model answers:

There are <u>a number of</u> factors to <u>bear in mind</u> when deciding payment terms. For example, the relationship between the seller and purchaser. <u>From the point of view of</u> the bank, there is less financial risk where there is a strong trading partnership <u>based on</u> trust and integrity. <u>A variety of</u> other factors influence risk, including the type of goods and the distance travelled. A shipment of perishable goods, if delayed, could mean the bank has to <u>deal with</u> payment disputes and <u>at the same time</u> establish whose liability it is. <u>The development of</u> economic or political problems in either country would also indicate potential financing risks.

Closure

Tell students to cover the text and then describe the typical main stages of an international trade transaction.

🎧 Exercise E

1 Tell students that in the next part of the lecture they will hear the phrases in Exercise D. They know now what *type* of information is likely to follow. Now they must try to hear what *actual* information is given. If you wish, photocopy the table in the additional resources section (Resource 7D) for students to write their answers on.

Do the first one as an example. Play the first sentence and stop after *'optimal' source of finance.* Ask students: *What is the important concept?* (Answer: *the notion of an 'optimal' source.*)

Play the rest of the recording, pausing briefly at the points indicated by a // to allow students to make notes. Put students in pairs to check their answers.

Feed back with the whole class, asking questions based on the words in the 'Followed by ...' column. For example:

After phrase number 2, what is the word or phrase that is explained?

After phrase number 4, what is the example that is given?

2 Refer back to students' questions in Exercise A. Discuss with the whole class whether they heard any answers to their questions.

Transcript 🎧 1.31
Part 3

Now, an important concept in selecting finance is the notion of an 'optimal' source of finance. What do I mean by 'optimal' source? Banks, when considering finance options and terms, take into consideration the stage or stages in the transaction at which finance is required. Finance is usually required by either or both of the parties at two distinct stages: either at the pre-shipment stage or the post-shipment stage. The bank also looks at who assumes responsibility for the goods at what stage in the transaction. //

In financial terms, there is a direct relationship between the risks involved and the terms and costs of finance. Say, for example, the bank considers that there is a high risk for the exporter of payment default, then it would advise the exporter to try to obtain cash with the order. // In this way, the exporter is provided with pre-shipment finance to process and ship the goods. //

Another factor is the length of time finance is required – short, medium, or long-term. A letter of credit involves completing a lot of documentation and may be too costly when finance is required for a short period on a small order.

Answers

Model answers:

	Fixed phrase	Followed by ...	Actual information (suggested answers)
1	An important concept (is) ...	a new idea or topic that the lecturer wants to discuss	'optimal' source of finance
2	What do I mean by ...?	an explanation of a word or phrase	explanation of 'optimal' source of finance
3	In financial terms, ...	a general idea put into a financial context	the relationship between risks involved and terms/costs of finance
4	Say ...	an imaginary example	an example of a situation where the bank would advise cash with order
5	In this way ...	a concluding comment giving a result of something	the exporter is provided with pre-shipment finance
6	Looking at it another way, ...	a different way to think about the topic	it is may be the best option where there is an established trading relationship
7	As you can see, ...	a comment about something visual (e.g., a diagram or lecture slide) OR a fact that has just been demonstrated	obtaining the optimal payment terms involves many factors
8	The point is ...	a key statement or idea	no one method is optimal for all situations

2 Answers depend on students' questions.

The difference between a letter of credit and documentary collection is that, although documentary collection may be less expensive, the banks don't guarantee payment. It is less secure but, looking at it another way, it could be the best option for both exporter and importer if they have an established trading relationship. // As you can see, then, obtaining optimal payment terms involves many factors. The point is that no one method is going to be optimal for all companies and all situations.

🎧 Exercise F

The purpose of this question is to look at how information tends to be structured in sentences. It requires very close attention to the listening text. Before playing the recording, allow students time to read through the sentences. In pairs, tell them to discuss which sentence (**a** or **b**) they think follows the numbered sentences.

Play Part 4. Students should choose sentence **a** or **b**, then discuss why **a** or **b** was the sentence they heard.

Feed back with the whole class. Deal with sentences 1 and 2 first. Tell students that all the sentences are correct, but sentence **a** 'sounds better' when it comes after the first sentence. This is because of the way that sentences go together and the way in which information is organized in a sentence. Draw the table below on the board. Show how the underlined words in the second sentence have been mentioned in the first sentence. In the second sentence the underlined words are 'old' or 'given' information. When sentences follow each other in a conversation (or a piece of writing), usually the 'given' information comes in the first part of a sentence.

Now look at sentences 3 and 4. These are different. The normal choice would be the **a** sentences. However, here the speaker wanted to emphasize the idea of 'what happens' and 'what's different'. So a *Wh~* cleft sentence structure is used, which changes the usual order of information. Show this on the table as below. This 'fronting' of information has the effect of special focus for emphasis.

Answers

Model answers:

First sentence	Second sentence		
		Given information	New information
1 The payment form most beneficial to the exporter is <u>cash with order</u>.		**a** With <u>this type of payment</u>, …	… the importer pays for the goods pre-shipment.
2 A <u>letter of credit</u> is the most common form of payment used in international trade.		**a** In <u>this situation</u>, …	… the importer raises the letter of credit at the request of the exporter.
3 <u>Documentary collection</u> offers less security than a letter of credit.	normal order	**a** In <u>this case</u> …	… a bill of exchange is raised by the exporter and signed by the importer.
	special focus	**b** <u>What happens here is</u> …	… the exporter's bank receives payment, or a bill of exchange, against the shipping documents.
4 <u>Cash on delivery</u> terms are used only when the exporter is confident that there is no risk involved.	normal order	**a** Under <u>these terms</u> …	… the exporter ships the goods and sends the commercial documents directly to the buyer.
	special focus	**b** What's <u>different</u> to the previous options is that …	… the exporter ships the goods and sends the commercial documents directly to the buyer .

Language note

In English, important information can be placed at the beginning or at the end of a sentence. There are two types of important information. The first part of the sentence contains the topic and the second part contains some kind of information or comment about the topic. Usually the comment is the more syntactically complicated part of the sentence.

Once a piece of text or a piece of conversation (i.e., a piece of discourse) has gone beyond the first sentence, a 'given'/'new' principle operates. Information which is 'given', in other words that has already been mentioned, goes at the beginning of the sentence.

Normally speaking, information which is new goes at the end of the sentence. So in the second sentence of a piece of discourse, an aspect of the comment from the previous sentence may become the topic. The topic, if it has already been mentioned in the previous sentence, is also 'given'. 'Given' information normally goes at the beginning of the sentence. Of course, the given information may not be referred to with exactly the same words in the second sentence. Other ways to refer to the given information include reference words (*it, he, she, this, that, these, those*, etc.) or vocabulary items with similar meanings.

This topic is covered in the *Skills bank* in the Course Book Unit E.

Transcript 🎧 1.32

Part 4

Now ... let's see ... oh dear, I see we're running short of time ... but perhaps I should just say something about the basic mechanism of each of the four financing options mentioned.

The payment form most beneficial to the exporter is cash with order. With this type of payment, the importer pays for the goods pre-shipment. After the exporter's bank receives the payment, the exporter sends the documents, then ships the goods to the importer. The importer may need to raise short- to medium-term finance to cover the period between payment and receipt and sale of the goods. As the bank cannot take security over the goods, since ownership of them varies depending on the agreement, it usually takes a security in the form of a debenture over the assets of the importer's company.

A letter of credit is the most common form of payment used in international trade. In this situation, the importer raises the letter of credit at the request of the exporter. First the importer's bank issues a document stating a commitment to pay the seller, on behalf of the buyer, a specified amount under precisely defined conditions and on a specific date. This commitment is irrevocable. Then the exporter has to submit the title document to the goods, plus other documents, to the importer's bank. After the goods are shipped, provided the documents have been received, the importer's bank makes payment on the due date.

Documentary collection offers less security than a letter of credit. What happens here is the exporter's bank receives payment, or a bill of exchange, against the shipping documents. First, an exporter sends the title documents (including the bill of exchange) through its bank to the buyer's bank. After acceptance or payment of the bill of exchange by the importer, the exporter instructs the bank to release the goods to the importer. The importer has the right to take ownership of the shipment after obtaining the title documents.

Cash on delivery terms are used only when the exporter is confident that there is no risk involved. What's different to the previous options is that the exporter ships the goods and sends the commercial documents directly to the buyer. Only after satisfactory receipt of the goods by the importer does the exporter receive payment. This method offers the least security for the exporter, who is completely dependent on the buyer to make payment. Because the exporter is paid after delivery and the exchange rate may have changed, the exporter may want to take a foreign exchange contract on the transaction. Under such an arrangement an agreed exchange rate is fixed so that the exporter is guaranteed a certain price even if exchange rates change.

Subject note

With cash on delivery and cash with order the bank's role is as a facilitator for the payment only. In the case of letter of credit and documentary collection, the bank's role is more significant, as it acts as an agent for the parties.

Exercise G

Set for pairwork discussion. Note that the lecture has not yet finished. The last part will be heard in Lesson 3. Feed back with the whole class. Accept all reasonable answers.

Answers

Possible answers:

The lecturer starts by introducing the lecture topics but doesn't clearly follow them.

The lecturer is running out of time.

The lecturer has not had time to talk about advantages and disadvantages of the different financing options in much detail.

The lecturer has not had time to talk about the role of banks in much detail.

Closure

Make some statements about what you're going to do after the class and ask students to transform them into *Wh~* cleft sentences. For example:

I'm going to have a coffee after the class.

→ *What you're going to do after the class is have a coffee.*

I might go to a film tonight.

→ *What you might do tonight is go to a film.*

Put students in pairs to practise.

🎧 Exercise D

Tell students they will hear the final part of the lecture. On this occasion, they only have to find the main idea and the research tasks. Play Part 5. Feed back. Note that the two answers are similar.

Answers

Model answers:

1 The main factors influencing terms of payment.
2 They must research the factors influencing financing options.

Transcript 🎧 1.35

Part 5

I'm going to finish with some comments on the main factors influencing the terms of payment. Now, the fact of the matter is, it's a highly complex task to decide on the optimal financing terms. Payment terms have to take into account a wide variety of different factors – not to mention the fact that some of these factors are totally outside the control of the company. The reason for this is that there is no method for predicting, for example, currency fluctuations, after the order has been placed. In other words, changes in the exchange rates between the countries. You've probably heard of the Asian currency crisis. It was in the late 1990s that there was a rapid depreciation of Asian currencies. It was Mohamad Mahathir, the Malaysian prime minister at the time, who placed restrictions on US dollar payments to all foreign organizations. All organizations trading with Malaysian companies had to accept payments in the Malaysian currency. You can imagine the consequences for foreign trading companies. Plus there's the fact that significant economic instability can lead to political instability. Let's take Indonesia as an example. It can be argued that the Asian financial crisis was a contributing factor in the overthrow of the Suharto government.

OK. Where was I ? Oh, yes ... The advantage of having a variety of payment options is that some are more suited to a particular trading situation than others. Let me put it another way ... in any decision regarding payment terms there are a number of criteria that have to be considered, including, for example, the risks involved, the size of the order and the nature of the merchandise; the distance between buyer and seller; etcetera.

Oh, I almost forgot to mention your research tasks. OK, well, I've briefly mentioned some of the factors influencing financing options. However, I'd like you to do some further research on this. One important aspect is the relationship between the exporter and importer. Also, what's very important for the whole transaction is the size of the order and the component costs. So I'd also like you to find out the main criteria that need to be borne in mind by bankers when assisting a company to decide on financing options for various overseas trading ventures.

Exercise E

Set for pairwork. Feed back with the whole class. Ask for other phrases which have similar meanings, particularly from Lesson 3, and also from Unit 5. Build the table in the Answers section on the board. Accept any suitable words or phrases for the third column.

Answers

See table on the opposite page.

> ### Language note
>
> The phrases in Exercise E are appropriate in speaking. Many are not suitable for written language, for which different phrases should be used. After completing Exercises C and E, students can be referred to the *Vocabulary bank* and the *Skills bank* for consolidation.

Exercise F

Set the initial preparation for individual work. Students should think about how they can use the phrases they have looked at, and the ways of giving special focus/emphasis. (Note: They should not write out exactly what they are going to say in complete sentences and then read!)

Put students in pairs to give their oral summaries to each other, preferably pairing students who have chosen different sections to summarize.

Go around the class noting any problems or especially good examples of language use. You may wish to choose one or two individuals to give their summary to the whole class.

With the whole class, feed back any language or other difficulties which you noticed.

Exercise G

1 Set for pairwork. Suggest simple activities like making a cup of tea or a sandwich or writing an essay. Students should first list all the different processes and then decide how to order them and which processes overlap. They should draw their flowchart.

2 Put the pairs in groups of four to present their charts to each other.

Use	Fixed phrase	Other phrases
to introduce a new topic	You've probably heard of ...	Now, an important concept is ...
to make a major point	The fact of the matter is, ...	Actually, ... In fact, ... The point is that ...
to add points	I almost forgot to mention ... Not to mention the fact that ... Plus there's the fact that ...	also, and, too
to finish a list	etcetera	and so on
to give an example	Let's take ...	For example, ... Let's look at an example of this. For instance, ...
to restate	Let me put it another way. In other words, ...	What I mean is ... That is to say, ... By that I mean ... To put it another way, ...

Closure

Work on the stress and intonation patterns of the phrases in the box (Exercise E). If you wish, students can write sentences using the phrases in context. These do not necessarily need to be related to banking.

7.4 Extending skills

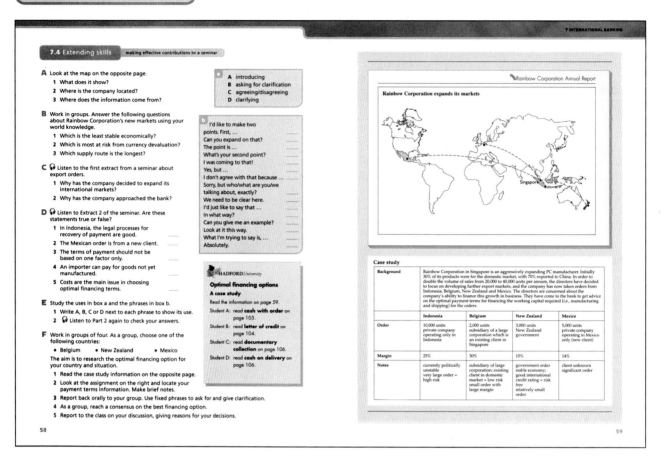

Lesson aims

- make effective contributions to a seminar:

  using pre-organizers – *I'd like to make two points;
  I don't agree with that because …*

  responding to queries by clarifying – *What I'm
  trying to say is … ; What I meant was …*

Introduction

Revise phrases from the previous lessons. Give a word
or phrase and ask students to give one with a similar
meaning. Ask for phrases from the previous lesson
which can be used to:

- introduce a new topic
- make a major point
- add a point
- finish a list
- give an example

Exercise A

Set for pairwork discussion. Feed back. Accept all
reasonable answers.

Answers

Possible answers:

1 It shows Rainbow Corporation's new markets.

2 Singapore.

3 The information comes from Rainbow
   Corporation's annual report.

Exercise B

Introduce the exercise with the whole class. Elicit/write
on the board the following country characteristics to
consider when looking at international trade:

- political stability
- economic stability
- uncertain legal processes for recovery of payment
- international credit rating
- travelling distance for the products
- quality of life
- cost of living

Set for small group discussion. Ask students to discuss
and then *describe* and *evaluate* the characteristics of
each country (i.e., Belgium, Indonesia, Mexico and
New Zealand) according to the above characteristics.

Feed back. Accept all reasonable answers. Do not comment or correct at this stage.

Answers

Answers depend on the students.

🎧 Exercise C

Allow students time to read the two questions. Play Part 1 once only. Check answers in pairs. Feed back with the whole class.

Answers

Model answers:

1 The company director wants to double the volume of sales from 20,000 to 40,000 units per annum.

2 To get advice on the optimal payment terms for financing the orders.

Transcript 🎧 1.36

Extract 1

Now, as we know, it is very important for companies to obtain optimal payment terms for their export orders. I asked you to look at the case of Rainbow Corporation, a Singapore personal computer manufacturer which has decided to significantly expand its export markets. Rainbow Corporation already has an export market in China. However, the company director has decided to double the volume of sales from 20,000 to 40,000 units per annum. The company has now taken orders from Indonesia, Belgium, New Zealand and Mexico. It has come to the bank to get advice on the optimal payment terms for financing the orders. I would like you to give your rationale for the terms you recommend in each situation.

🎧 Exercise D

Allow students time to read the questions. Play the recording straight through once while they mark the answers true or false. Check in pairs and/or as a whole class. Check any unknown vocabulary, such as *payment default, variable costs*.

Answers

Model answers:

1	false	In Indonesia the legal processes for recovery of payment are 'uncertain', i.e., not good.
2	true	The Mexican order is from a new client.
3	true	Payment terms must be based on a number of factors.
4	true	This occurs under cash with order terms which are recommended only when the importer has confidence in the exporter.
5	false	There are many factors; other factors mentioned previously are importer/exporter relationship, country economic and political stability, currency fluctuations, size of the order, etc.

Transcript 🎧 1.37

Extract 2

Note: the underlining relates to Exercise E.

JACK: Well, I'll start with Indonesia. I'd like to make two points. First, I think there's a high risk of payment default on this order.

LEILA: Can you expand on that, Jack?

JACK: Sure, Leila. Indonesia is a country where the legal processes for recovery of payment are uncertain.

LEILA: So?

JACK: So the point is that in this case the exporter should ask for cash with the order.

LECTURER: OK. So, what's your second point, Jack?

JACK: I was coming to that! My second point is that this is an order from a private company operating only in Indonesia.

LEILA: Yes, but that's true for Mexico, too. Even more so, I'd say, as the Mexican order is from a new client. So I think the risk of default is higher.

MAJED: Well, I don't agree with that, Leila, because we don't know if the Indonesian client is new or not.

EVIE: Sorry, but what are we talking about, exactly? I think before we decide on the payment terms we need to take into account other factors such as the order size.

LEILA: Yes, we need to be clear here. I think payment terms must be based on a number of factors. I'd just like to say that according to what I've read, the Indonesian order is the best example of one where cash with order terms would be best.

EVIE: In what way?

LEILA: Well when you look at the size of the order, you'll see that it will require a large number of imported components, I mean the chips and so on, so this is the best method for financing the working capital required for the order.

MAJED: I don't understand why you don't recommend a letter of credit, because it's the most common method of financing international trade. How can you get an importer to pay for goods not yet manufactured? <u>Can you give me an example</u>, Leila?

LEILA: OK. <u>Look at it this way</u>. A letter of credit facility involves a lot of documentation and consequently extra costs in bank charges. If the importer has the funds, has confidence in the exporter and wants to secure the order with the minimum amount of administration, then cash with order terms probably seems like the best option. There may also be foreign exchange benefits.

JACK: I don't get that. Foreign exchange benefits for whom?

LEILA: For the importer. <u>What I'm trying to say is that</u> in this case, as Indonesia is more likely to be subject to currency fluctuations than Singapore, the importer might benefit from paying in advance for the order if the Indonesian currency is predicted to depreciate.

MAJED: So everybody wins! In this situation cash with order is the best option.

LECTURER: <u>Absolutely</u>. In making a decision on financing international trade, companies have to think about their fixed and variable costs, as well as the revenue they're likely to get from a particular order. OK, that's it for today. I'd like you to look at the best financing options for the Belgium, New Zealand and Mexico orders for next time. Make sure you consider all the options and can justify your choices.

🎧 Exercise E

Check the meaning of 'introducing' phrases. This means a phrase you use before your main statement to show that you are going to say something. It may also signal how much you are going to say, or how important you think what you are going to say is.

Set for individual work and pairwork checking.

Play Part 2 from Exercise D a second time. Ask students to tell you to stop when they hear each phrase (underlined in the transcript above). Check what kind of phrase they think it is. Get students to repeat the phrase to copy the intonation.

If you wish, ask students to suggest other phrases that could be used in the same way.

Answers

Model answers:

I'd like to make two points. First, …	A
Can you expand on that?	B
The point is …	D
What's your second point?	B
I was coming to that!	D
Yes, but …	C
I don't agree with that because …	C
Sorry, but who/what are you/we talking about, exactly?	B
We need to be clear here.	D
I'd just like to say that …	A
In what way?	B
Can you give me an example?	B
Look at it this way.	D
What I'm trying to say is, …	D
Absolutely.	C

Exercise F

With the whole class, revise asking for information. Remind students of the questions used by the lecturer in Lesson 3. Remind students also about reporting information (see Unit 3 *Skills bank*).

If possible, divide students into three groups, one group for each country. Within each group, set individual students to work on one of the financing options presented. When everyone is ready they should feed back to their group, giving an oral report on the information. It's important that they do not simply read aloud the information, but use it to inform their listeners.

Remind students about agreeing and disagreeing, and about good and bad ways to contribute to seminar discussions (refer to Unit 5 if necessary).

Alternatively, the research activity can be done as a 'wall dictation' as follows. Use Resources 7E and 7F in the additional resources section. Make copies of the information (these can be enlarged) and pin the sheets on the classroom walls. Each student should leave his/her seat and go to the wall to find the information he/she needs. Students should not write anything down: instead they should read and try to remember the information. Then they return to their group and tell them the information. If they forget something they can go back to the wall to have another look.

Circulate, encouraging students to ask for clarification and to use the appropriate phrases when giving clarification. Note where students are having difficulty with language and where things are going well. When everyone has finished, feed back to the class on points you have noticed while listening in to the discussions.

While representatives of the groups are presenting their group decisions to the class, you should occasionally interrupt with a wrong interpretation so that students are forced to clarify their statements. Or you could ask for clarification.

Answers

Possible answers:

Belgium: documentary collection.

New Zealand: documentary collection or cash on delivery.

Mexico: letter of credit.

Closure

Put a table on the board and ask students to supply the missing nouns/verbs/adjectives (omit the words in italics). For example:

Noun	Verb	Adjective
contribution	contribute	–
finance	finance	*financial*
fluctuation	*fluctuate*	–
profit	*profit*	*profitable*
receipt	receive	–
regulation	regulate	*regulatory*
stability	–	stable

1 Work through the *Vocabulary bank* and *Skills bank* if you have not already done so, or as a revision of previous study.

2 Use the *Activity bank* (Teacher's Book additional resources section, Resources 7A–C).

   A Set the crossword (7A) for individual work (including homework) or pairwork.

   Answers

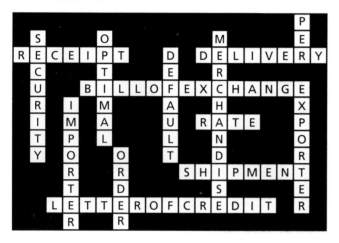

   B Put students in pairs to play 'word battleships'. The idea behind this game is that each word represents a battleship, which is 'sunk' when all the letters of the word have been located; the aim of the game is to be the first to sink all the ships.

   Give Resource 7B to Student A; give Resource 7C to Student B. Make sure they can't see each other's information. Students take turns to ask about individual squares, e.g., *Is there a letter in (1C)?* The other student answers either *No* or *Yes, it's (F).* They mark their empty grid accordingly – either putting a letter or a cross in each square. If a student finds a letter, he/she can continue asking until he/she gets a negative answer (i.e., an 'empty' square). Students continue asking one question each until one of them thinks they have found a word, when they can say *Is the word … ?* The first student to find all their words is the winner.

The words for each category are:

Student A:

- three words for money: *cash, currency, finance*
- two verbs meaning 'to assess the risk' and ending in ~ate: *calculate, evaluate*
- four words which can be nouns or verbs, meaning: 'loss of value' (*fall*); 'buying and selling' (*trade*); 'an official offer to purchase' (*order*); 'provision of something that is needed' (*supply*)

Student B:

- two nouns which refer to a business commitment: *agreement, contract*
- three plural nouns which refer to purchases for export: *goods, items, products*
- two nouns which refer to a financial commitment: *security, guarantee*
- two plural nouns meaning items required to complete the assembly of a product: *components, parts*

8 OFFSHORE BANKING

This unit looks at what offshore banking is and how its services differ from those provided by onshore banks. The reading text examines some of the key features of offshore banks: their location in low tax jurisdictions, their goal of providing high returns on investment, their relationship to larger onshore banks, and the balance of offering client privacy with the need to prevent criminal or terrorist associations.

Skills focus

Reading
- understanding dependent clauses with passives

Writing
- paraphrasing
- expanding notes into complex sentences
- recognizing different essay types/structures:
  descriptive
  analytical
  comparison/evaluation
  argument
- writing essay plans
- writing essays

Vocabulary focus
- synonyms
- nouns from verbs
- definitions
- common 'direction' verbs in essay titles (*discuss*, *analyse*, *evaluate*, etc.)

Key vocabulary

access (n and v)	licence (n and v) (US license)	residence
anonymity	location	resident
asset	money laundering	restriction
authorities (pl n)	non-resident	retain
controls (pl n)	offshore	return (n)
declaration	onshore	screening
declare	over-the-counter	tax evasion
disclosure	privacy	tax haven
illegal	registration	taxation
jurisdiction	regulation	
legislation		

8.1 Vocabulary

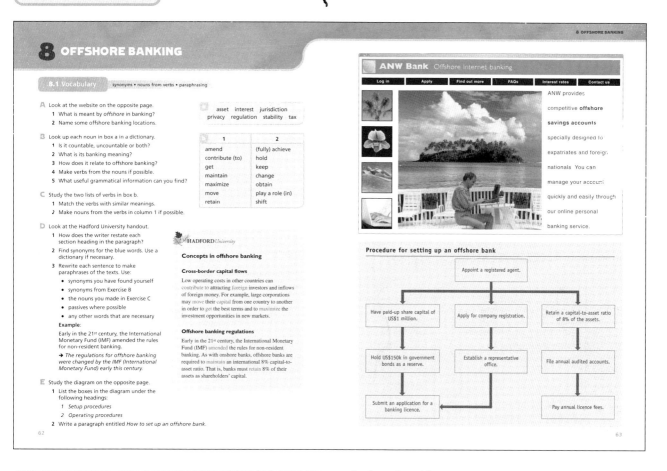

General note

Read the *Vocabulary bank* at the end of the Course Book unit. Decide when, if at all, to refer students to it. The best time is probably at the very end of the lesson or the beginning of the next lesson, as a summary/revision.

Lesson aims

- extend knowledge of synonyms and word sets (enables paraphrasing at word level)
- make nouns and noun phrases from verbs (enables paraphrasing at sentence level)

Further practice in paraphrasing at sentence level with:

- passives
- synonymous phrases
- negatives
- replacement subjects

Introduction

Revise ways of paraphrasing sentences. Write the following sentences from Unit 6 on the board and ask students to say what changes have been made to the paraphrased sentences.

Original sentence: *The mandate of most central banks is to carry out their government's fiscal and monetary policy to ensure a stable economy and currency.*

Paraphrase: *In order to maintain favourable economic conditions and stable exchange rates, the majority of state banks have to execute the agreed financial goals of parliament.*

(answer: change in word order, passive to active, use of synonyms)

Original sentence: *Some central banks set their country's official interest rate.*

Paraphrase: *In some countries, the central bank is responsible for fixing the rate of borrowing.*

(answer: change in word order, use of synonyms, plural becomes singular)

Exercise A

Set for pairwork discussion. Feed back with whole class. Accept all reasonable answers but do not correct and discuss at this stage.

Answers

Possible answers:

1 'Offshore' refers to a centre (including banks, companies, trusts), located outside the depositor's/user's country of residence. The majority of the account holder's transactions are carried out electronically.

2 Offshore banking locations include the Bahamas, Barbados, Belize, Bermuda, the British Virgin Islands, the Cayman Islands, the Channel Islands (Jersey and Guernsey), the Cook Islands, Cyprus, Dominica, Gibraltar, Hong Kong, the Isle of Man, Panama, Saint Kitts and Nevis, the Seychelles, Singapore, Switzerland, and the Turks and Caicos Islands. Of these, Switzerland and the Cayman Islands are the most important. Many offshore banks are located in small island nations.

Exercise B

Set for pairwork. You may wish to divide the work up between different pairs. For question 3, encourage students to identify the offshore dimension of each term. For question 4 (useful grammatical information) tell students to look out for words that can have the same form when used as a noun or verb, nouns that can be only singular or only plural, nouns that change their meaning when used as U or C, adjectives, etc.

Feed back with the whole class, building up the table in the Answers section on the board.

Answers

Model answers:

Word C/U	Banking meaning	Offshore aspect	Verb	Useful grammatical information
asset (C)	something of monetary value belonging to a person or company	an offshore asset is difficult for domestic jurisdictions to access and is protected from invasive bureaucracy, lawsuits and seizure		usually used in the plural in a banking context
interest (U)	money earned from deposits in a bank or paid on a loan	investment interest rates are generally more favourable, and there is no legal requirement for offshore banks to report interest on investments to other authorities	not used in a banking context	uncountable, so has no plural form in this context; is not used with the indefinite article
jurisdiction (C/U)	legal power or authority in a specific situation or location countable meaning: a state or country which exercises a set of legal powers	the term *tax haven* is associated with jurisdictions of low or no taxation		the countable form refers to a state or a country
privacy (U)	keeping personal/financial matters secret	under secrecy provisions in offshore legislation, banks and companies operating an offshore facility maintain their clients' privacy and anonymity	*privatize* is used to describe the sale of a nationalized industry to private owners	uncountable, so has no plural form; not used with the indefinite article adj = private
regulation (C/U)	government rules or controls	the absence of exchange control regulations facilitates the flow of currency for transfers and investment purposes	regulate	regulator (n) = the person responsible for administering regulations adj = regulatory
stability (U)	steady or unchanging position	the political and economic stability of an offshore jurisdiction is important to investors	stabilize	uncountable, so has no plural form; is not used with the indefinite article adj = stable/unstable
tax (C/U)	government levy on income earned	offshore financial centres either do not deduct tax or it is very low	tax	taxation (n) = the act of taxing an individual or business adj = taxable

Exercise C

Set for individual work and pairwork checking. Feed back with the whole class, discussing whether the verbs are exact synonyms, and if not, what the differences in meaning are.

Answers

Model answers:

Verb 1	Noun	Verb 2
amend	amendment	change
contribute (to)	contribution	play a role (in)
get	–	obtain
maintain	maintenance	keep
maximize	maximum	(fully) achieve
move	move	shift
retain	retention	hold

Exercise D

This is an exercise in paraphrasing based on word- and sentence-level techniques. As well as finding their own synonyms from memory and using the synonyms already discussed in Exercises B and C, students will use noun phrases in place of verb phrases as a technique in paraphrasing. Students should also make passive sentences wherever they can.

1   Set for individual work. Feed back with the whole class.

2   Set for individual work and pairwork checking.

3   Set for pairwork; pairs then check with other pairs. Alternatively, tell some students to write their answers on an OHT or other visual medium for discussion by the whole class.

Answers

Model answers:

1   *Cross-border capital flows* – move … capital from one country to another

    Offshore banking regulations – the rules for non-resident banking

2   Possible synonyms (including synonyms from Exercises B and C):

    Cross-border capital flows
    Low operating costs in other countries can (*contribute to*) <u>play a role in</u> attracting (*foreign*) <u>overseas</u> investors and inflows of foreign money. For example, large corporations may (*move*) <u>shift</u> their (*capital*) <u>funds</u> from one country to another in order to (*get*) <u>obtain</u> the best terms and to (*maximize*) <u>fully achieve</u> the investment opportunities in new markets.

    Offshore banking regulations
    Early in the 21st century, the International Monetary Fund (IMF) (*amended*) <u>changed</u> the rules

for non-resident banking. As with onshore banks, offshore banks are required to (*maintain*) <u>keep</u> an international 8% capital-to-asset ratio. That is, banks must (*retain*) <u>hold</u> 8% of their assets as shareholders' capital.

3   Possible paraphrases:

    Cross-border capital flows
    If overheads in an offshore location are low, this can play a role in attracting overseas investment. This may encourage multinational companies to shift funds to different locations with the aim of obtaining optimal terms and the highest returns in new markets.

    Offshore banking regulations
    The regulations for offshore banking were changed by the IMF (International Monetary Fund) early this century. Offshore banks must keep an international capital adequacy ratio of 8%, the same as onshore banks. In other words, 8% of their assets must be held as shareholders' capital.

Exercise E

Set for individual work and pairwork checking. Check that students understand the banking terminology in the diagram.

Answers

Possible answers:

1   Setup procedures:
    appoint a registered agent
    have paid-up share capital of US$1 million
    hold US$150k in government bonds as a reserve
    submit an application for a banking licence
    apply for company registration
    establish a representative office.

    Operating procedures:
    retain a capital-to-asset ratio of 8 % of the assets
    file annual audited accounts
    pay annual licence fees

2   To set up an offshore bank, first appoint a registered agent, who must register the company name and apply for a licence to operate the bank. Before applying for an offshore banking licence you must have paid-up share capital of US$1 million, and hold a reserve in government bonds of US$150,000. You then need to establish a representative office. Once you have your licence, registration and premises you are ready to open for business. During the whole term of your operation you must pay an annual licence fee and file audited accounts annually. You must comply with the IMF rules and retain a capital-to-asset ratio of 8% of the bank's assets.

Closure

Ask students to work in pairs or small groups to discuss the advantages and disadvantages of offshore banking. Is it getting easier to bank offshore? Explain why, or why not.

8.2 Reading

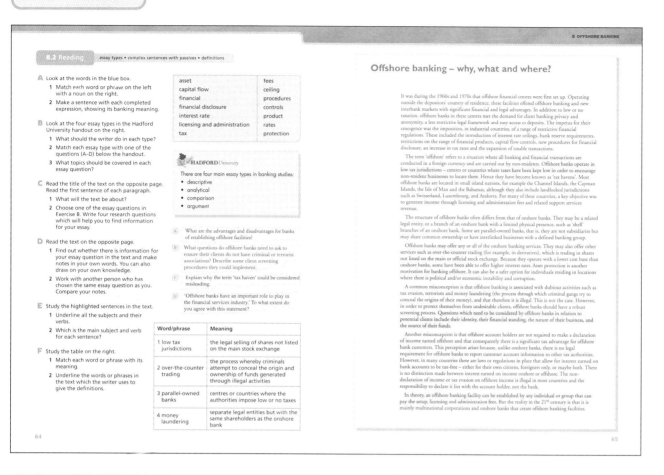

General note

Read the *Skills bank* at the end of the Course Book unit. Decide when, if at all, to refer students to it. The best time is probably at the very end of the lesson or the beginning of the next lesson, as a summary/revision.

Lesson aims

- understand essay types
- interpret essay titles
- find the main information in a passive clause
- understand internal definitions (see *Vocabulary bank*)

Further practice in:

- reading research
- finding the kernel of a long sentence

Introduction

1 With the whole class, discuss how to use written texts as sources of information when writing an answer for an essay question. Ask students:

  1 *How can you choose useful sources?* (to get an idea of whether a text might be useful, survey the text, i.e., look at the title, look at the beginning and the end and the first line of each paragraph; in other words, skim-read to get an approximate idea of the text's contents)

  2 *If you decide that a text is going to be useful, what is it a good idea to do …*

    ■ *… before reading?* (think of questions related to the essay question to which you would like to find some answers)

    ■ *… while reading?* (identify useful parts of the text; make notes in your own words)

    ■ *… after reading?* (check answers to the questions)

2 Revise concepts from Lesson 1 of this unit. Ask students to suggest services offered by offshore banks and to explain why they are not provided by onshore banks.

Exercise A

Set the two questions for pairwork discussion with whole class feedback. Accept any reasonable variations, e.g., *financial controls*.

Answers

Model answers:

1

asset	protection
capital flow	controls
financial	product
financial disclosure	procedures
interest rate	ceiling
licensing and administration	fees
tax	rates

2 Answers depend on the students.

Exercise B

1 Discuss this question with the whole class. Build up the table in the Answers section on the board.

2 Set for pairwork. Feed back with the whole class. Ask the class to identify the key words in each title which tell you what type of writing it is.

3 Set for pairwork. Feed back using the second table in the Answers section, discussing with the whole class which topics will need to be included in each essay. Add the notes in the third column.

Answers

Possible answers:

1 See table 1 below.

2/3 See table 2/3 below.
   Key words are underlined.

1

Essay types	What the writer should do
Descriptive	describe or summarize key ideas/key events/key points. Give the plain facts. Could involve writing about: a narrative description (a history of something); a process (how something happens); key ideas in a theory; main points of an article (answers the question *What ...?* or *Describe ...*)
Analytical	try to analyse (= go behind the plain facts) or explain something or give reasons for a situation; may also question accepted ideas and assumptions (answers the question *Why/How ...?*)
Comparison	compare two or more aspects/ideas/things/people, etc. usually also evaluate, i.e., say which is better/bigger, etc.
Argument	give an opinion and support the opinion with evidence/reasons, etc.; may also give opposing opinions (= counter arguments) and show how they are wrong

2/3

Type of writing	Question	Topics
Descriptive	B <u>What questions</u> do offshore banks need to ask to ensure their clients do not have criminal or terrorist associations? <u>Describe</u> some client screening procedures they could implement.	• client screening: what is it? Why is it important? • how to evaluate clients: questions/procedures • how effective these may be
Analytical	C <u>Explain why</u> the term *tax haven* could be considered misleading.	• tax haven: what is it? • are the reasons for the term valid? • if not, why not?
Comparison	A What are <u>the advantages and disadvantages</u> for banks of establishing offshore facilities?	• offshore banking: what is it? • examples of advantages for the banks • examples of disadvantages • do the advantages outweigh the disadvantages? If so, why? If not, why not?
Argument	D 'Offshore banks have an important role to play in the financial services industry.' <u>To what extent do you agree</u> with this statement?	• financial services industry: what is it? OR offshore banks: what are they? • what role do offshore banks have in the industry? • is their role important? To whom? How important?

Exercise C

1 Set for individual work. Feed back with the whole class. Accept all reasonable answers.

2 If necessary, remind students of the purpose of research questions and do one or two examples as a class. Set for individual work and pairwork checking. Feed back, getting good research questions for each essay topic on the board.

Answers

Possible answers:

1 The title of the text suggests that the text will look at the reasons for offshore banking, then describe it, then say where it is located.

Paragraph 1 will explain the background of offshore banking.

Paragraph 2 will give a definition of offshore banking.

Paragraph 3 will discuss the structure of offshore banks.

Paragraph 4 will compare services offered by offshore banks and onshore banks.

Paragraph 5 will discuss a common misconception (that offshore banking is not legal).

Paragraph 6 will discuss another common misconception (that with offshore banking you can legally avoid tax).

Paragraph 7 will discuss who can set up an offshore bank.

2 Answers depend on the students.

Exercise D

Set for individual work then pairwork comparison/checking. If you wish, students can make notes under the headings in the 'Topics' column of the table in the Answers section of Exercise B. Encourage students to make notes in their own words.

Answers

Possible notes:

A *What are the advantages and disadvantages for banks of establishing offshore facilities?*

- offshore = banking by non-residents carried out in a foreign currency
- advantages: less regulation; lower taxes; lower costs; attracts customers wanting privacy and anonymity; less exposure to unfavourable exchange rates; attracts high net-worth clients, therefore better revenue stream

- disadvantages: remote location; risk of being exposed to money laundering; financing terrorism, etc.; pressure for increased fiscal transparency; risk that countries with onshore banks revise their legislation to make offshore banking less attractive

B *What questions do offshore banks need to ask to ensure their clients do not have criminal or terrorist associations? Describe some client screening procedures they could implement.*

- client screening: carrying out procedures that ensure the banks 'know their client' to protect themselves from undesirable clients
- check client identity, financial status, source of their funds, nature of their business
- obtain evidence of information given in answer to the questions

C *Explain why the term 'tax haven' could be considered misleading.*

- tax haven: implies client pays very low or no taxes
- most offshore banks do not impose taxes themselves
- for the clients, interest earned could be taxable in their home jurisdiction (it is their responsibility to declare it)

D *'Offshore banks have an important role to play in the financial services industry.' To what extent do you agree with this statement?*

- financial services industry = broad term including banking, insurance, and all services relating to finance
- offshore banks can be viewed as providing an alternative (more favourable) option, particularly for residents in weak or controlled economies
- give private citizens and companies privacy
- it could be argued that given the demand for their services they have an important role in the industry in fulfilling a need not currently provided by onshore banks; more importantly, they create business opportunities for host countries

	Joining word	Subject	Verb	Object/complement
1		offshore <u>banks</u>	operate	in low tax <u>jurisdictions</u>
	where	taxes	have been kept	low
	in order to		encourage	non-resident <u>businesses</u>
	to		locate	there
2		**questions**	include	their <u>identity</u>, their financial <u>standing</u>, the <u>nature</u> of their business, and the <u>source</u> of their funds
	which		need to be considered	by offshore banks
3		**an offshore banking facility**	can be established	by any <u>individual</u> or <u>group</u>
	that		can pay	the setup, licensing and administration <u>fees</u>

* The underlined noun is the head word of the noun phrase.

Exercise E

Set for individual work and pairwork checking. Students could copy out the three sentences in their notebooks and then underline all the verbs and subjects.

Feed back with the whole class, building up the table in the Answers section on the board. Point out that each sentence has two verbs, which means that each sentence has two *clauses*. This means that the sentences are complex. (A simple sentence has only one main verb and subject.) To enable students to identify which is the 'main' part of the sentence (in bold in the table above), ask how the two clauses are 'joined' and add the joining words (shown in the first column). The main part of the sentence is linked to the *dependent* part with these words.

Check understanding of the passives in each case by asking how each clause and sentence could be rephrased with an active verb, e.g.,

1 Offshore banks operate in low tax jurisdictions – centres or countries where the government has kept taxes low in order to encourage non-resident businesses to locate there.

2 Questions which offshore banks need to consider in relation to potential clients include their identity, their financial standing, the nature of their business, and the source of their funds.

3 In theory, any individual or group that can pay the setup, licensing and administration fees can establish an offshore banking facility.

Answers

Possible answers:
See table above.

Language note

The choice of whether to use an active or a passive construction often depends on how the writer wants to structure the information. Refer to Unit 7 *Skills bank* for a note on information structure.

Exercise F

Set for individual work and pairwork checking. In question 2, tell students to look for the actual words used and the punctuation, grammatical and vocabulary devices which are used to indicate meanings.

Feed back with the whole class, pointing out the structures given in the third column of the table for question 2 in the Answers section.

Answers

Model answers:
1 See table below.

Word/phrase	Meaning
1 low tax jurisdiction	centres or countries where the authorities impose low or no taxes
2 over-the-counter trading	the legal selling of shares not listed on the main stock exchange
3 parallel-owned banks	separate legal entities but with the same shareholders as the onshore bank
4 money laundering	the process whereby criminals attempt to conceal the origin and ownership of funds generated through illegal activities

2

Word/phrase	Actual words giving the meaning	Punctuation/vocab/structure
1 low tax jurisdictions	... – centres or countries where taxes have been kept low	word/phrase followed by a dash + elided relative (*which are*) + noun phrase
2 over-the-counter trading	... , which is trading in shares not listed on the main or official stock exchange.	word/phrase followed by comma + *which is*
3 parallel-owned banks	... , that is, they are not subsidiaries but may share common ownership or have interlinked businesses with a defined banking group.	word/phrase followed by comma + *that is* + comma
4 money laundering	... (the process through which criminal gangs try to conceal the origins of their money)	word/phrase followed by explanation in brackets

Closure

Ask students to make up their own definitions of banking terms from this and earlier units, using the phrases and punctuation devices practised in Exercise F.

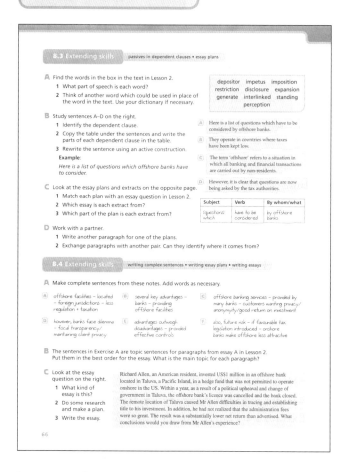

8.4 Extending skills

Offshore banks maintain an 8% capital-to-asset ratio.
Low operating costs attract overseas investors.

Exercise A

Set for individual work and pairwork checking.
Remind students that they should try to make sentences
in a good 'academic' style. Also remind them to use
passives where necessary/possible, and to look out for
ways of making dependent clauses, such as using
relative pronouns, linking words, etc. They will also
need to pay attention to making correct verb tenses.

Feed back with the whole class.

Answers

Possible answers:

A   Offshore facilities are located in foreign
jurisdictions with less regulation and taxation.

B   There are several key advantages for banks in
providing offshore facilities.

C   Offshore banking services are provided by many
banks to customers wanting privacy, anonymity
and a good return on their investment.

D   However, offshore banks face a dilemma between
fiscal transparency and maintaining client financial
privacy.

E   However, the advantages of an offshore facility
outweigh the disadvantages, provided there are
effective controls.

F   There is also the risk that, if favourable tax
legislation is introduced in the future, onshore
banks will make offshore banking less attractive.

Exercise B

Set for individual work. Feed back with the whole
class. Point out how this comparison essay is organized
by discussing all the advantages first and then all the
disadvantages. (See *Skills bank* for an alternative
approach to comparison.)

If you wish, you could take this exercise further, asking
students to build on the topic sentences by suggesting
what ideas could follow the topic sentence in each
paragraph. For this they will need to refer to ideas in
the text. Note that the disadvantages of setting up an
offshore banking facility are not discussed at length in
the text in Lesson 2, so ideas for this paragraph would
need to be researched further. A web search is a good
place to start for this. Revise the skills in Unit 4, e.g.,
'search words' and how to identify promising sites.

Lesson aims

- expand notes into complex sentences
- make an essay plan
- write an essay

Further practice in:

- writing topic sentences
- expanding a topic sentence into a paragraph
- writing complex sentences with passives
- identifying required essay type

Introduction

Remind students about complex and compound
sentences – that is, sentences with more than one
clause. Remind students that academic texts typically
consist of sentences with several clauses. Give the
following simple sentences (or make your own) and ask
students to add some more clauses to them.

Taxes are low.

Offshore banks offer higher interest rates.

Asset protection is a motivation for banking offshore.

Any individual or group can set up an offshore bank.

136

Answers

Model answers:

Topic sentences	Paragraph topic
C Offshore banking services are provided by many banks to customers wanting privacy, anonymity and a good return on their investment.	introduction/purpose of offshore facilities
A Offshore facilities are located in foreign jurisdictions with less regulation and taxation.	definition of offshore facilities
B There are several key advantages for banks in providing offshore facilities.	advantages of offshore facilities
D However, offshore banks face a dilemma between fiscal transparency and maintaining client financial privacy.	disadvantages of offshore facilities
F There is also the risk that, if favourable tax legislation is introduced in the future, onshore banks will make offshore banking less attractive.	possible future risk to banks
E However, the advantages of an offshore facility outweigh the disadvantages, provided there are effective controls.	conclusion

Exercise C

Discuss question 1 with the whole class. Set the research and planning (question 2) for group work, and the writing for individual work (this could be done at home). Students can do web searches to find more information on establishing an offshore banking facility and possible problems. For example, so far 'due diligence' has not been discussed.

Answers

1 Model answer:

This essay is largely analytical, since it requires students to think critically about possible problems with a system that is promoted as being very advantageous for investors.

2 Possible essay plan:

- Introduction: reasons for offshore investment; aims of essay.
- Definition and description of the offshore investment (i.e., the reasons for the investment, perceptions of benefit of the investment).
- Aspects of investing offshore which can cause problems for the investor – investor needs to:
  - choose the jurisdiction the bank operates from with care, as it is responsible for granting the bank's licence
  - have confidence that the country is well organized and administered
  - assess the political and economic risk associated with an offshore banking jurisdiction

- assess the difficulties of investing in an offshore facility in a physically remote location
- fully understand all fees and charges associated with the investment
- get independent advice on the financial soundness of an offshore investment in hedge funds
- Conclusion: thorough checking is required before making the investment.

Closure

Ask students if they can remember a word from the unit …

	Possible example(s)
beginning with c	capital
beginning with i	instability
ending with y	economy
ending with s	facilities
with two syllables	offshore
with three syllables	resident
with four syllables	motivation
which is a verb	maximize
which is a countable noun	derivative
which is an adverb	illegally
which goes together with another word	tax haven
which is difficult to pronounce	anonymity (students' answers will vary)

Accept all reasonable answers.

Extra activities

1 Work through the *Vocabulary bank* and *Skills bank* if you have not already done so, or as a revision of previous study.

2 Use the *Activity bank* (Teacher's Book additional resources section, Resource 8A).

A Set the wordsearch for individual work (including homework) or pairwork.

Answers

B Set the spelling exercise for individual work and pairwork checking.

Answers

Jumbled word	Correct spelling
nfciilaan	financial
naxtaito	taxation
greatsoniul	regulations
ordersupce	procedures
dluanerngi	laundering
tmvesinnet	investment
estumpi	impetus
antacrsnoit	transaction
littinamulona	multinational

3 Check word stress by writing the following words on the board *without* stress markings. Students have to mark the stress and pronounce the words correctly.

ano'nymity

cor'ruption

disad'vantages

e'conomy

'impetus

juris'diction

'laundering

'maximize

multi'national

4 Remind students of how to give definitions (see Lesson 2). Then select five or six familiar items (e.g., iPod, laptop, sunglasses, pen, mobile phone) and ask students to think of definitions (e.g., it's something that you use to listen to music; you need these when it is sunny; etc.).

This can also be done the other way round by giving the definitions and asking students to guess the word; once they get the idea students can come up with items, questions and definitions themselves. Other forms for definitions can include:

This is a place where …

This is a company which …

If you want to buy a X, you need to go to …

Other categories which can be used to practise both the language of definition and general banking and cultural knowledge include:

● well-known bank or company names, also use global multinationals

● familiar places in the town or college where the students are studying

● famous people

● movies and TV programmes

An alternative is the Weakest Link TV quiz show format, e.g., *What 'A' is a well-known brand of computer?* (Apple)

9 BANKING IN DEVELOPING COUNTRIES

This unit looks at the way banking is structured in the developing world. The first lecture looks at the different definitions of developed and developing countries, including the World Bank's income-based categories. It also examines the role of multilateral banks in the developing world. The second lecture focuses on commercial banks and the impact of foreign ownership in the developing world.

Skills focus

🎧 Listening

- using the Cornell note-taking system
- recognizing digressions in lectures

Speaking

- making effective contributions to a seminar
- referring to other people's ideas in a seminar

Vocabulary focus

- fixed phrases from banking
- fixed phrases from academic English

Key vocabulary

See also the list of fixed phrases from academic English in the *Vocabulary bank* (Course Book page 76).

acquisition
consolidation
diversification
economic indicator
emerging market
financial liberalization
foreign direct investment (FDI)
foreign ownership
globalization
gross domestic product (GDP)
highly indebted poor country (HIPC)

host country
indebted
industrialization
industrialized
infrastructure
less developed country (LDC)
liquidation
merger
micro-credit
micro-finance
multilateral development bank (MDB)

multilateral finance institution (MFI)
newly industrialized country (NIC)
per capita income
privatization
privatize
restructuring
source country
sub-regional

9.1 Vocabulary

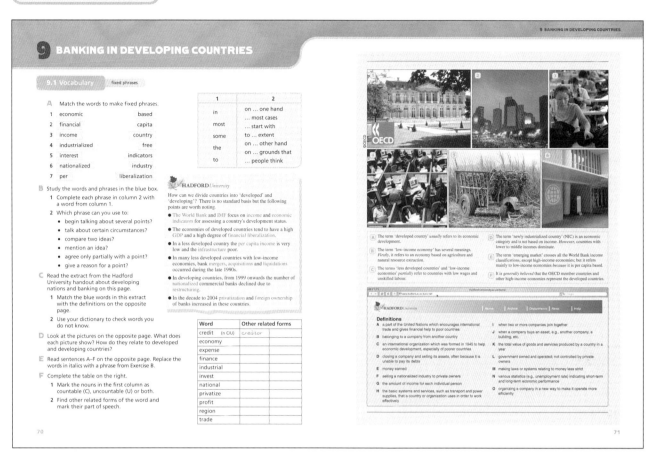

General note

Read the *Vocabulary bank* at the end of the Course Book unit. Decide when, if at all, to refer your students to it. The best time is probably at the very end of the lesson or the beginning of the next lesson, as a summary/revision.

Lesson aims

- understand and use some fixed phrases/compound nouns from banking studies
- understand and use some fixed phrases from academic English

Introduction

Introduce the topic for this unit.

1 Ask students to say what commercial banking is and arrive at a definition on the board, such as:

'Commercial banking is the type of banking done by most businesses and consumers, and includes retail banking where individual customers use local branches of larger commercial banks, for services such as savings and cheque accounts, mortgages, personal loans, debit cards, credit cards, etc.'

2 Ask students to write a definition of a developing country. They will check/revise this after the listening exercise in Lesson 2. A possible definition is:

'Developing countries are, in general, countries which are working towards greater economic growth through industrialization, but which have not achieved a significant degree of industrialization (relative to their populations), have a low level of economic diversification, low per capita income and high population growth.'

Accept all reasonable answers but do not confirm their definitions at this stage.

Exercise A

This gives revision of some compound noun phrases (noun+ noun) and adjective + noun phrases connected with banking.

Set for individual work or pairwork. Check that students are familiar with the meanings and that they can pronounce the compounds with the main stress on the correct word. Accept any reasonable alternatives which apply to the topic of banking.

Answers

Model answers:

1	economic	'indicators	statistics showing/indicating economic performance
2	financial	liberali'zation	less strict regulation of monetary systems
3	'income	based	in terms of money earned
4	industrialized	'country	country (political unit) having a lot of industry and factories
5	interest	'free	no interest to be paid (on a loan)
6	nationalized	'industry	government-controlled company
7	per	'capita	for each individual, e.g., per capita income = income for each individual

Exercise B

Set for individual work and pairwork checking. Point out that the words in column 1 can be used more than once, and that one of the bulleted functions has two phrases. Feed back with the whole class.

Answers

Model answers:

on the one hand	to compare two ideas
in most cases	to talk about certain circumstances
to start with	to begin talking about several points
to some extent	to agree only partially with a point
on the other hand	to compare two ideas
on the grounds that	to give a reason for a point
most people think	to mention an idea

Exercise C

This exercise gives some key terms relating to banking and development – and so is rather technical. The words will be used throughout the unit.

Tell students to read the handout extract first and ask them to discuss in pairs which of the blue words they know and which are new to them. Feed back with the whole class, to establish how much is known. Where students give correct explanations tell them they are right, and where they are wrong also tell them, but do not give the right answer at this point.

Set the exercise for individual work and pairwork checking. Feed back with the whole class, checking the meaning of other possibly unknown words.

If you wish, set students to work in pairs. One student should shut the book. The other student should say one of the words for Student B to explain. Then change over.

Answers

Model answers: see table below.

The World Bank	C	an international organization which was formed in 1945 to help economic development, especially of poorer countries
IMF (International Monetary Fund)	A	a part of the United Nations which encourages international trade and gives financial help to poor countries
income	E	money earned
economic indicators	N	various statistics (e.g., unemployment rate) indicating short-term and long-term economic performance
GDP (gross domestic product)	K	the total value of goods and services produced by a country in a year
financial liberalization	M	making laws or systems relating to money less strict
per capita income	G	the amount of income for each individual person
infrastructure	H	the basic systems and services, such as transport and power supplies, that a country or organization uses in order to work effectively
mergers	I	when two or more companies join together
acquisitions	J	when a company buys an asset, e.g., another company, a building, etc.
liquidations	D	closing a company and selling its assets, often because it is unable to pay its debts
nationalized	L	government owned and operated; not controlled by private owners
restructuring	O	organizing a company in a new way to make it operate more efficiently
privatization	F	selling a nationalized industry to private owners
foreign ownership	B	belonging to a company from another country

Exercise D

Set for pairwork discussion. Feed back with the whole class.

Answers

Model answers:

1 Organisation for Economic Co-operation and Development headquarters in Paris. OECD provides statistics about economic development to member and non-member countries.

2 Modern US city centre. This is the conventional example of a developed economy.

3 Young Chinese woman on a shoe factory production line. This illustrates low-cost industrial labour in a country moving away from an agricultural-based economy.

4 Modern office in India. This exemplifies a developing economy, with a growing information technology sector.

5 Old truck with a load of sugarcane. This is the conventional example of low-investment agriculture in a developing country.

6 The World Bank Group headquarters in New York. The World Bank lends development funds to developing countries.

Exercise E

Set for individual work. Tell students that in some cases it will be necessary to change the word order of the sentence. Check with the whole class, asking students to read out the quotation with the alternative phrase in place of the original words in italics.

Answers

Possible answers: see table below.

A	*usually*	*In most cases*, the term 'developed country' refers to its economic development.
B	*Firstly, …*	*To start with*, it refers to an economy based on agriculture and natural resource extraction.
C	*partially*	The terms 'less developed countries' and 'low-income economies' *to some extent* refer to countries …
D	*however, …*	*On the one hand*, the term 'newly industrialized country' (NIC) is an economic category and is not based on income; *on the other hand*, countries with lower to middle incomes dominate.
E	*because*	… but it refers mainly to low-income economies *on the grounds that* it is per capita based.
F	*It is generally believed*	*Most people think* that the OECD member countries …

Exercise F

Set for individual work. Tell students to use their dictionaries to check the meanings and grammatical categories of the words if they are not sure. Explain that some of the base words only have one other related form.

Feed back with the whole class, pointing out that most of the words have a particular use in this lesson. Check that students can pronounce all the words correctly, particularly those words where the stress shifts.

Answers

Model answers: see table below.

Word		Other related forms			
credit	n (C/U), v	creditor	n (C)		
economy	n, (C)	economic	adj	economically	adv
expense	n (C/U), v	expenditure	n (U)	expensive	adj
finance	n (C/U), v	financial	adj		
industrial	adj	industry	n (C/U)	industrialization	n (U)
invest	v	investor	n (C)	investment	n (C/U)
national	adj	nation	n (C)	nationalization	n (U)
privatize	v	privatization	n (U)	privatized	adj
profit	n (C/U), v	profitability	n (U)	profitable	adj
region	n (C)	regional	adj	regionalized	adj
trade	n (C/U)	trader	n (C)	trading	n (C)

Language note

1 With a good class, you can spend plenty of time on the issue of whether each noun is used as countable or uncountable or both, i.e., can the word be made plural, and if so, does that change the meaning? For example, *finance* = funding for a company/project; *finances* = general issues relating to income and expenditure.

2 Students will also find meanings and usages of many of these words and related forms which are not specific to banking and finance, e.g.,
  credit (v) = believe
  profit from (v) = benefit
  creditable = good (effort)
  economical = not costing a lot to run
  invest = give power to
Point out that this is quite normal in English. Many words used in banking have multiple meanings, some of which may have nothing to do with the specialist usage.

Closure

It is important that students are familiar with the terminology from this lesson. On the board write some terms from Exercises A and C and ask students to give a definition.

Or read out a definition and ask students to tell you the appropriate word or phrase. Check the pronunciation. This exercise can also be done as a dictation.

Alternatively, write the words and definitions on different cards and give a card to each student. The student then reads out the word or the definition and the rest of the class must produce the correct answer.

9.2 Listening

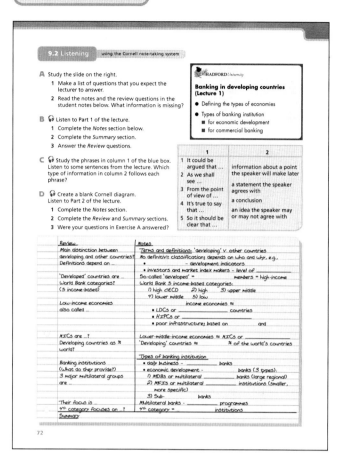

General note

Read the *Skills bank – Using the Cornell note-taking system* at the end of the Course Book unit. Decide when, if at all, to refer students to it. The best time is probably at the very end of the lesson or the beginning of the next lesson, as a summary/revision.

Lesson aims

- use the Cornell note-taking system

Further practice in:

- listening for an established purpose
- understanding fractured text
- recognition of fixed phrases and the type of information that comes next
- using abbreviations and symbols in note-taking

Introduction

1 Review key vocabulary from this unit. Write a selection of words from Lesson 1 on the board and ask students to put the words in groups, giving reasons for their decisions.

2 Revise note-taking symbols and abbreviations by using extra activity 4 at the end of this unit.

3 Introduce the elements of the Cornell note-taking system. Try to elicit some of the R words. Ask students to try to think of five words beginning with re- with six or seven letters that are good strategies to use when studying and taking notes. Write the words as follows on the board:

RE _ _ _ _ = record
RE _ _ _ _ = reduce
RE _ _ _ _ = recite
RE _ _ _ _ _ = reflect
RE _ _ _ _ = review

Discuss with the class what each word might mean when taking notes. Try to elicit the following, helping where needed.

record	Take notes during the lecture.
reduce	After the lecture, turn the notes into one- or two-word questions or 'cues' which help you remember the key information.
recite	Say the questions and answers aloud.
reflect	Decide on the best way to summarize the key information in the lecture.
review	Look again at the key words and the summary (and do this regularly).

Tell students that in this lesson they will be introduced to this system of note-taking – which can be used both for lectures, and also for reading and for revision for exams later. Do not say much more at this point; they will see how the system works as the lesson progresses.

Subject note

The Cornell system was developed by Walter Pauk at Cornell University, USA. (Pauk, W. and Owens, R. (2004). *How to study in college* (8th ed.). Boston: Houghton Mifflin.) Pauk advised students to use a large, loose-leaf notebook, with holes punched for filing. This is better than a bound notebook, because you can organize the notes in a file binder. You can also take out notes and rewrite them. Pauk's method is now called the Cornell system.

Pauk told students to divide up the page into three areas. The first area is a column 5 cm wide on the left side of the page. This is the cue area. The main part of the page is the note-taking area. At the bottom of the page is a row 8 cm high, which is the summary area. This basic grid, with information on what each section should contain, is reproduced in the additional resources section (Resource 9B).

The note-taking and learning process involves the Five Rs in the order listed in the introduction to this lesson (and in the *Skills Bank*). There are many references on the Internet for this system. Two useful ones at the time of writing are:
http:/www.yorku.ca/cdc/lsp/notesonline/note4.htm
http://www.clt.cornell.edu/campus/learn/LSC%20Re sources/cornellsystem.pdf

Exercise A

1 Set for pairwork discussion. Refer students to the lecture slide. Tell them to look at the title and bullet points, and for each bullet point to make questions which they expect the lecturer to answer. Do not explain any words from the slide or allow students to check in their dictionaries at this point, as the meanings of these words will be dealt with in the lecture.

   Feed back with the whole class, asking several students to read out their questions. Write some of the questions on the board if you wish.

2 Refer students to the notes at the bottom of the page. Tell them that this student has used the Cornell system to take notes but has not managed to complete everything and so has left some gaps. (Note that this is quite a normal occurrence in note-taking – details may need to be filled in later, for example by checking with other people.)

   Allow students time to read the gapped notes and identify information that is missing.

🎧 Exercise B

Make sure students have read question A2 and are ready to listen for the missing information.

Play Part 1, pausing after each major point if you wish. After the lecture has finished, allow students (if they are still writing) a minute to complete their note-taking.

Tell students to work in pairs to compare their answers to question 1, and to complete the summary in 2. Feed back with the whole class, using an OHT or other visual of the answers below if you wish. (The completed notes are reproduced in Resource 9C in the additional resources section to facilitate this.)

Now focus on the recite element of the Cornell system. Point out that here the student has completed the *Review* section. Cover up the *Notes* section of the answer and ask students if they can say anything about the first and second questions in the *Review* section. Then put students in pairs to test each other on the remaining notes.

Answers

Model answers:

1/2/3 See table on next page and Resource 9C.

Transcript 🎧 2.1

Part 1

Good morning, everyone. I'm going to talk to you this morning about banking in developing countries. However, before we can discuss the nature of their banking systems, we need to have an understanding of what we are referring to when we make the distinction between a developing country and other countries. Firstly, I'll identify the main terms used, then I'll briefly discuss the types of banking institution operating in developing countries.

Now to start with, there is no definitive classification nor is there an established convention for the designation of 'developing' countries or areas. As we shall see, it depends on the focus of the institution making the classification. Geographers tend to focus on development indicators. Investment information sources – for example, *The Economist* – or market index makers – for example, MSCI, Morgan Stanley Capital International – tend to focus on the level of economic development. MSCI makes the distinction between countries with *developed* markets, and those with *emerging markets*. The terms used may describe markets, regions or countries.

In terms of the so-called 'developed' countries, this generally includes the member countries of the OECD (that is, the Organisation for Economic Co-

Review	Notes
Main distinction between: developing + other countries?	<u>Terms and definitions</u>: 'developing' v. other countries
Definitions depend on …	No definitive classification; depends on who and why, e.g., ● <u>geographers</u> – development indicators ● investors and market index makers – level of <u>economic development</u>
'Developed' countries are …	So-called 'developed' = <u>OECD members</u> = high-income
World Bank categories? (5 income-based)	World Bank 5 income-based categories: 　1) high OECD　　2) high　　3) upper middle 　4) lower middle　　5) low
Low-income economies also called …	<u>Low</u>-income economies ● LDCs or <u>less developed</u> countries ● HIPCs or <u>highly indebted poor countries</u> ● poor infrastructure; based on <u>agriculture</u> and <u>natural resources</u>
NICs are … ?	Lower-middle-income economies ≈NICs or <u>newly industrialized countries</u>
Developing countries as % world?	'Developing' countries ≈ <u>82%</u> of the world's countries
Banking institutions (What do they provide?)	<u>Types of banking institution</u> ● daily business – <u>commercial</u> banks ● economic development – <u>multilateral</u> banks (3 types):
3 major multilateral groups are …	1) MDBs or multilateral <u>development</u> banks (large regional) 2) MFIs or multilateral <u>financial</u> institutions (smaller, more specific) 3) Sub-<u>regional</u> banks
Their focus is …	Multilateral banks – <u>macro</u> programmes
4th category focuses on … ?	4th category = <u>micro-finance</u> institutions

Summary
Developing countries can be roughly defined as those below the two 'high-income' World Bank categories – c. 82% of world's countries. Banking institutions in the developing world are divided into everyday commercial banks and multilateral banks which provide support for economic development.

operation and Development, which replaced the Organisation for European Economic Co-operation in 1961). Their economies are referred to by the World Bank and the IMF respectively as 'high-income' and 'advanced' economies. However, given that anomalies exist in the terminology used when determining any country's classification, the World Bank 1997 classification of nations by income makes a good starting point.

OK, so let's take a few moments to think about this classification. From the point of view of the World Bank, the world's countries can be classified into five income-based categories: 1) high-income OECD members, for example, Japan, Canada, France; 2) high-income non-OECD economies, for example, United Arab Emirates, Hong Kong,

Kuwait, Singapore; 3) upper middle-income economies, for example, Saudi Arabia, Argentina; 4) *lower* middle-income economies, for example, Turkey, Egypt; and 5) low-income economies, for example, Zimbabwe and Cambodia. As I mentioned earlier, both the terminology and the categorization of countries are continually changing, depending on the basis for the classification. Financial development and gross domestic product are often used as indicators. However, it's true to say that a major point of division can be identified between high-income countries, and the others.

So … to get back to the World Bank classifications. To start with, the World Bank classification of 'low-income economies' approximates to countries that are also classified as less developed countries (LDCs) and highly indebted poor countries (HIPCs). But as we shall see, these tend to have a different emphasis – I'll come back to this in a little while and tell you some of the similarities and differences.

Low-income economies are generally equated with a poor infrastructure and an economy based on agriculture and natural resource extraction. A country is classified as LDC if it is characterized by low income, unskilled human resources, and a low level of economic diversification, that is, it is predominantly an agriculturally based subsistence economy. The term HIPC was formalized by the World Bank and the IMF in 1996. This designation was based on a value of debt service to gross domestic product exceeding 80%, or a value of debt to exports exceeding 220%.

Lower-middle-income economies, the next category, can be loosely included in the group referred to in other data as NICs (that is, newly industrialized countries) – although the categorization of NICs is an economic as opposed to an income-based category.

To summarize so far … the definition of developing countries used in this lecture includes all the World Bank classifications except for the high-income categories (in other words, the high-income OECD members and the high-income economies). I think there are about 33 countries, that's approximately 18% of the world's countries, that fall into this high-income category. So it should be clear that what we're focusing on is the banking arrangements that exist for the other – approximately 82% – of the world's countries.

So, what sort of banking arrangements do we find in developing countries? It could be argued that banking structures in the developing countries are not that different from those of the high-income economies, with commercial banks providing about 90% of the total credit for everyday business activities. However, there are a number of international and regional institutions that provide financial support for economic development activities only in developing countries. These are the multilateral banks. As the term multilateral indicates, the membership of these banks may include other international banks and governments. Their contributions are pooled and then disbursed at the discretion of the agency.

Multilateral banks have been categorized by the World Bank into three major groups, based on their membership and mandate. The first group consists of international institutions, including the World Bank itself. They are large regional institutions known as the multilateral development banks (MDBs). This group includes the African Development Bank, the Asian Development Bank, the European Bank for Reconstruction and Development, and the Inter-American Development Bank. The membership of these MDBs is not exclusively limited to member countries of the developing region, but also includes some high-income country government donors. For example, the UK Department for International Development is a shareholder and contributor to the African, Asian, and Inter-American Development Banks as well as the European Bank for Reconstruction and Development.

The second major group in the World Bank category are described as multilateral financial institutions (MFIs). The distinction between MDBs and MFIs is that MFIs have a narrower membership structure and may focus on specific sectors or activities. Included in this category are the European Investment Bank, the Islamic Development Bank, the Nordic Investment Bank, plus organizations such as OPEC … do you all know what that stands for? No? Well, it means the Organization of the Petroleum Exporting Countries … As I was saying, MFIs also include the OPEC Fund for International Development, and the International Fund for Agricultural Development.

Thirdly, there is the group of institutions referred to as Sub-Regional Banks. This group includes the Central American Bank for Economic Integration, the East African Development Bank, and the West African Development Bank.

While the majority of the multilateral banks focus on what I call macro-programmes – that is, large loans that assist developing and aid-recipient countries – there is a fourth category of institutions that offer very small loans to populations ineligible for loans from traditional banks. They are the micro-finance institutions such as the Grameen Bank in Bangladesh. However, I will discuss multilateral banks and micro-finance institutions in more detail later …

🎧 Exercise C

Allow students time to read the phrases and the types of information, making sure that they understand any difficult words. Note that they are being asked not for the words that the speaker uses but the type of information the words represent.

Play the sentences one at a time, allowing time for students to identify the type of information which follows. Check answers after each sentence, making sure that students understand what the information actually is that follows.

Answers

Model answers:

	Fixed phrase	Type of information which follows	Actual words/information
1	It could be argued that …	an idea the speaker may or may not agree with	banking structures in the developing countries are not that different …
2	As we shall see, …	information about a point the speaker will make later	these tend to have a different emphasis
3	From the point of view of …	an idea the speaker may or my not agree with	the World Bank, the world's countries can be classified into five income-based categories
4	It's true to say that …	a statement the speaker agrees with	a major point of division can be identified between high-income countries, and the others
5	So it should be clear that …	a conclusion	what we're focusing on is the banking arrangements that exist for the other – approximately 82% – of the world's countries

Transcript 🎧 2.2

1 It could be argued that banking structures in the developing countries are not that different from those of the high-income economies …

2 But as we shall see, these tend to have a different emphasis – I'll come back to this in a little while and tell you some of the similarities and differences.

3 From the point of view of the World Bank, the world's countries can be classified into five income-based categories.

4 However, it's true to say that a major point of division can be identified between high-income countries, and the others.

5 So it should be clear that what we're focusing on is the banking arrangements that exist for the other – approximately 82% – of the world's countries.

🎧 Exercise D

1 Tell students to divide up a page of their notebooks into the three sections of the Cornell system. They should try to complete the *Notes* section as they listen. Warn them that they may not be able to complete their notes while listening so they should leave spaces which they can fill in later.

Play Part 2 straight through. Then put students in pairs to complete any gaps in their notes. Feed back with the whole class. Build up a set of notes.

2 Tell the students to work in pairs to complete the review questions and the summary. Feed back with the whole class.

3 Discuss with the class the extent to which their pre-questions in Exercise A have been answered.

Answers

Model answers:

Review	Notes

MDBs: 3 types of loans ... ?	<u>Investment in developing countries</u>
	
	1. MDBs
	
	    i) long-term loans @ market rates
	
	    ii) very long-term loans (or credits) @ concessional rates
	
	    iii) grant financing – technical and advisory services or project preparation, e.g., European Bank for Reconstruction and Development
	
	Also within World Bank:
	
	    ● IBRD – middle-income and creditworthy poor countries
	
	    ● International Development Association – ineligible countries (e.g., HIPCs)

MFIs: difference from MDB ... ?
 	
e.g., IDB ...
	2. MFIs
	
	Narrower membership; focus on specific sectors (e.g., EIB, IDB)
	
	Islamic Development Bank
	
	    ● can accept deposits and mobilize financial resources
	
	    ● members contribute to the Bank's capital ∴ participate in equity capital and grant loans
	
	    ● assists Muslim communities in non-member countries

Sub-regional banks:
difference from MDBs
and MFIs?
	3. Sub-regional banks
	
	Difference from MDBs and MFIs:
	
	    ● owned by borrowing members
	
	    ● focus on poverty and infrastructure issues

Micro-credit: main purpose ... ?	4. Micro-credit institutions
	
	    ● loans to very poor populations for small-scale work schemes
	
	    ● 'village banking'

Summary

Multilateral Development Banks tend to provide large long-term loans. Multinational financial institutions tend to focus on specific activities or sectors. Sub-regional banks are much more concerned with regional issues, including infrastructure and poverty. Micro-credit institutions provide loans to those ineligible for traditional banking services.

Transcript 🎧 2.3

Part 2

So, to get back to the topic ... let's look at the multilateral banks in more detail. Firstly, the multilateral development banks ... The financial support, provided by the World Bank and other MDBs, for investment in economic development activities in developing countries, happens in distinct ways – although these different ways are also connected.

Firstly, there are the long-term loans, with interest based on market rates. Because of the size of multilateral development banks (remember: they include more than two groups or countries), they are able to borrow on international capital markets to fund these loans. They then re-lend this money to borrowing programmes in developing countries. Secondly, there are the very long-term loans, with concessional rates, that is, interest well below market rates. These very long-term loans are referred to as 'credits' and are funded through direct contributions from governments in donor countries. A third form of financial support is grant financing. This financing is provided by some MDBs for technical and advisory services or project preparation. The investments, for example, of the European Bank for Reconstruction and Development – which was established when communism was collapsing in Central and Eastern Europe – mainly involve taking equity in private enterprises with commercial partners. But the bank is also able to mobilize domestic capital, due to its size and credibility.

The World Bank has its criteria of minimum credit requirements for the businesses or government agencies seeking a loan. The ability to repay is one of the criteria for receiving a loan. That is, they must be creditworthy. However, within the World Bank there are two institutions providing financial assistance to separate developing country sectors. The International Bank for Reconstruction and Development (IBRD) focuses on middle-income and creditworthy poor countries, whereas the International Development Association focuses on countries such as HIPCs (heavily indebted poor countries), which are ineligible for World Bank concessional, or below market rate, borrowing.

As I stated earlier, the multinational financial institutions have a narrower membership structure and may focus on specific sectors or activities. Let's focus on one example – the European Investment Bank. You don't need to take notes on this … Contrary to its name, the European Investment Bank, set up in 1958 by the Treaty of Rome, is *not* an investment bank. As a non-profit organization the EIB does not receive money from savings or current accounts. Nor does it receive funds from the European Union's budget – though the member states of the European Union do make contributions based on their economic position within the Union. Instead, the EIB is financed through borrowing on the financial markets. Bearing in mind that it has the backing of the European Union member states, you can understand that the EIB, like MDBs, can borrow very large amounts of capital on the world financial markets, at – I might add – very competitive terms. So its size and credibility enable the EIB to obtain loans which it in turn invests in projects that benefit the most disadvantaged regions. Generally, these projects would otherwise not get money – or would have to borrow it more expensively.

Let's move on now, to another MFI – the Islamic Development Bank (or IDB), which was formally opened in October 1975. Its purpose is to encourage economic and social development of member countries and Muslim communities. The bank is authorized to accept deposits and to mobilize financial resources. Members contribute to the bank's capital, which allows it to participate in equity capital and grant loans for productive projects and enterprises, as well as assisting Muslim communities in non-member countries. The IDB follows the principles of shariah, or Islamic jurisprudence. By the way, does anyone know what shariah-compatible practices include? Well, they aim to follow the principles of the Qur'an, which in

the common non-Islamic perspective are reflected in a prohibition of usury and the charging of interest. However, this is only one aspect of Islamic banking – we will look at this, and the other aspects, in more detail some other time.

Now, where was I? Oh, yes, I was talking about the multilateral finance institutions. If we turn now to the third group – the sub-regional banks. Sub-regional, of course, means the same as intra-regional; in other words, we are talking about a smaller part of a larger whole. The sub-regional banks differ from the other two categories in the following ways. The first significant difference is that they are typically owned by the borrowing members that make up their sub region. And the second major difference is that their focus is much more on poverty, infrastructure, and other key regional issues.

Finally, I would like to discuss a fourth category of institution. Whereas the previous three groups are all categorized as multilateral banks, this fourth category of institution exists in low-income economies in developing countries. Micro-credit projects provide very poor populations with loans for work schemes such as small weaving, irrigation or fishing projects to promote their economic self-development. In addition to loans, some micro-credit, or 'village banking' projects provide savings and other banking services.

So, what exactly have we looked at this morning? Well, to sum up, we need to understand the major differences between the multilateral institutions. Firstly, whereas multilateral development banks tend to look at large long-term loans to developing countries worldwide, multinational financial institutions tend to focus on specific activities or sectors. Sub-regional banks, on the other hand, are much more concerned with regional issues, including infrastructure and poverty. Furthermore, sub-regional banks are typically owned by the borrowing members of their sub region. In addition to the multilateral organizations, which operate at the macro level, there are the micro-credit institutions which provide loans for very poor populations ineligible for traditional banking services.

Closure

Play short sections from Part 2 of the lecture again. Stop the recording just before a word or phrase you want the students to produce and ask them what comes next in the lecture. For example:

Because of the size of multilateral development banks (remember: they include more than two groups or countries), they are able to …

The International Bank for Reconstruction and Development (IBRD) focuses on middle-income and creditworthy poor countries, whereas the International Development Association ...

So its size and credibility enable the EIB to obtain loans which ...

The sub-regional banks differ from the other two categories in the following ways ...

Alternatively, do this exercise by reading out parts of the transcript.

9.3 Extending skills

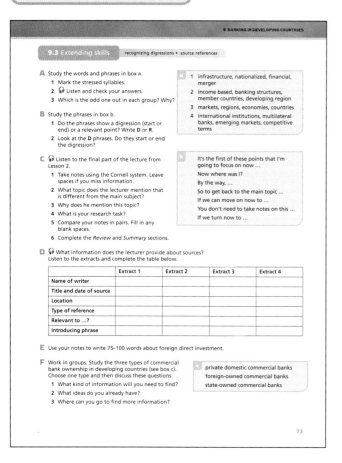

Lesson aims

- recognize digressions: start and end
- understand reference to other people's ideas: source, quotes, relevance

Further practice in:

- stress within words and phrases
- leaving space in notes for missing information – especially digressions

Introduction

Revise the lecture in Lesson 2 by asking students to use their Cornell notes. They should cover up the *Notes* section and use the *Review* and *Summary* sections to help recall the contents of the lecture. They could work in pairs to do this.

🎧 Exercise A

1 Set for individual work and pairwork checking. Students can underline the stressed syllables.

2 Play the recording for students to check their answers.

3 Set for individual work and pairwork checking. Tell students they need to identify the odd one out in terms of stress (not the meanings of the words). Feed back with the whole class, checking students' pronunciation, especially of the compound words, and elicit the odd ones out.

Answers

Model answers:

1/3 (odd one out in italics)

1 'infrastructure, 'nationalized, *fi'nancial* (stress is on second syllable), 'merger

2 'income based, 'banking structures, 'member countries, *developing 'region* (stress is on second word).

3 'markets, 'regions, *e'conomies* (stress is on second syllable), 'countries

4 *inter'national insti'tutions* (two equally stressed words), multilateral 'banks, emerging 'markets, competitive 'terms

Transcript 🎧 2.4

1 infrastructure, nationalized, financial, merger

2 income based, banking structures, member countries, developing region

3 markets, regions, economies, countries

4 international institutions, multilateral banks, emerging markets, competitive terms

Exercise B

Point out that the phases in the box are likely to relate to either a digression or a relevant point. Students' task is to identify which is more probable. Set for individual work and pairwork checking. Feed back with the whole class. Note that most of these phrases occurred in the lecture in Lesson 2. Some have occurred in previous units and one or two are new. Note also that the end of a digression is actually a transition back to the main point.

Answers

Model answers:

1/2 It's the first of these points that I'm going to focus on now ... R

Now, where was I? D (end)

By the way, ... D (start)

So to get back to the main topic ... D (end)

If we can move on now to ... R

You don't need to take notes on this ... D (start)

If we turn now to ... R

🎧 Exercise C

Refer students to the lecture slide in Lesson 2. Ask them what they already know about commercial bank ownership. What would they like to know?

Ask students to prepare a page to take notes using the Cornell system. Remind them that they may not get all the information. If they miss something, they should leave a space. They can fill it in after the lecture.

Let them read the questions through and tell them to listen out for the answers to questions 2, 3 and 4.

1 Play Part 3 straight through. Students should complete the *Notes* section.

2–4 Set for pairwork. Feed back with the whole class. Ask for suggestions for phrases to use to find out about the importance of digressions, e.g., *Why did the lecturer start talking about ...? I didn't understand the bit about ... Is it important?* and so on (see *Skills bank*).

5/6 Set for pairwork. Students compare their notes, complete any blank spaces and then write the *Review* and *Summary* sections.

Feed back with the whole class, building a set of notes on the board.

Answers

Possible answers:

1 See notes below.

2 The Cornell note-taking system.

3 It's important to know how to take good notes.

4 To find out about one type of commercial bank ownership in two developing countries.

5/6 See notes below.

Review	Notes
dev. country banking structures ...?	<u>Commercial banks – ownership</u>
banking crisis 80s/90s led to ...	post 1999 – mergers & acquisitions: ● improve efficiency ● eliminate weak banks ● more large banks/ more competitive industry
Latin America ? increase in foreign banks	1994–2004 country trends, e.g., Latin America, Cent. Europe – foreign-owned banks ↑ private dom. banks ↓
FDI = Foreign Direct Investment...? MIGA ...?	FDI ↑ due to globalization, trade, financial integration MIGA = established to promote FDI in dev. countries FDI re domestic banks = ↑ competition ↑ efficiency ↓ profitability
Benefits of privatization/ foreign ownership ...?	majority FDI from high-income countries. trend = FDI flows originating in developing countries (e.g., = approx. 5% of host country foreign-bank assets) certain characteristics attract FDI sources to host dev. country, e.g., ● share common lang; legal system; close proximity; economic integration
Summary Dev. country commercial banks similar to high-income country banks whether state, foreign or privately owned. Dev. countries attract FDI, mostly from high-income countries, though some FDI originating in developing countries occurs.	

Transcript 🎧 2.5

Part 3

OK, so moving on to look at banking structures in developing countries … to start with, I'd like to take a few moments to discuss the ownership of commercial banks.

The banking crisis in the 1980s and 1990s left many banking systems of emerging countries broken up. As Heffernan points out in *Modern Banking* (one of your core texts – the paperback edition was published in 2005) 126 banking crises were identified in developing market countries during this period. Consequently, during 1999 to 2004, there was a trend for bank consolidation, with the frequent occurrence of mergers, acquisitions and liquidations. In fact, mergers and acquisitions were seen by officials as a means of enlarging domestic banks, to make them more competitive with foreign banks … and a further important point, they were also a means of eliminating weak banks.

A study by the Bank for International Settlements showed that during the same period, across a number of developing country regions, the percentage of state-owned commercial banks declined, as governments in developing countries have been motivated to sell government-owned institutions to skilled investors.

Let's look in a bit more detail at some specific regions, beginning with Latin America. Here, private domestic bank ownership declined from 79% in 1994 to 47% in 2004, while, over the same period, foreign-owned banks increased from 6% in 1994 to 42% in 2004. There was a similar trend in Central Europe over the same period.

By the way, I see that some of you are using the Cornell note-taking system. That's very good. Do you all know about this? No? Right, well, if you want to know more about it, I suggest you look at *How to Study in College* by Walter Pauk, P-A-U-K, the 8th edition, published in 2004. It's very good, and it should be in the University Library.

So to get back to the main topic … Over the last decade the growth of globalization, trade, and financial integration have led to an increase in the number of foreign banks entering developing country regions via foreign direct investment (or FDI). A definition of foreign direct investment given in *thefreedictionary.com* on the Web is: 'long-term investment by a foreign direct investor in an enterprise resident in an economy other than that in which the foreign investor is based.'

The Multilateral Investment Guarantee Agency – which is part of the World Bank Group – was established to promote FDI by working with host governments in developing countries and investors in source countries. The agency provides guarantees to protect cross-border investment in developing member countries and also guarantees to protect investors. Mergers and acquisitions – including acquisitions involving the privatization of state enterprises – are a significant form of FDI.

There has been a large body of literature addressing the benefits and costs of privatization and foreign ownership of banks in developing countries. And there seems to be a consensus that foreign-bank participation generally increases competition, and makes the domestic banks more efficient – though it may affect their profitability. As Heffernan states: 'The foreign firm can bring in expertise and also train and educate the host country labour force …'; however, the extent to which FDI is beneficial to the host country also depends on the type of FDI.

While the majority of FDI is from high-income countries, there is also a trend for banks in developing countries to enter another developing country. One study found that 27% of all foreign banks in developing countries were owned by a bank from another developing country.

Developing-country foreign banks tend to operate intra-regionally and in developing countries that are unattractive to high-income country banks – on account of their small size, low income, and weak institutions. Although the source developing-country banks are not significant in terms of their assets (generally, they represent approximately 5% of foreign-bank assets in the host country), there is concern that they are disproportionately represented in low-income countries.

Certain characteristics in a particular host developing country may attract some source countries more than others. One obvious characteristic, for example, is that they share a common language. Whether the source is a high-income or another developing country, a common language reduces the cost of foreign direct banking for the source country. Other factors include a similar legal system, being in close proximity to each other, and economic integration.

Now, I think that's all I'm going to say for the moment on this topic. Are there any questions so far? No, good. As I said earlier, banking practices in developing countries and those in developed nations are similar, that is, commercial banks accept deposits and make loans. Banks may also finance government expenditure. However, many developing countries have common problems relating to their banking structure. For example, high operating costs (related to interest-rate ceilings), high inflation, and little competition.

9.4 Extending skills

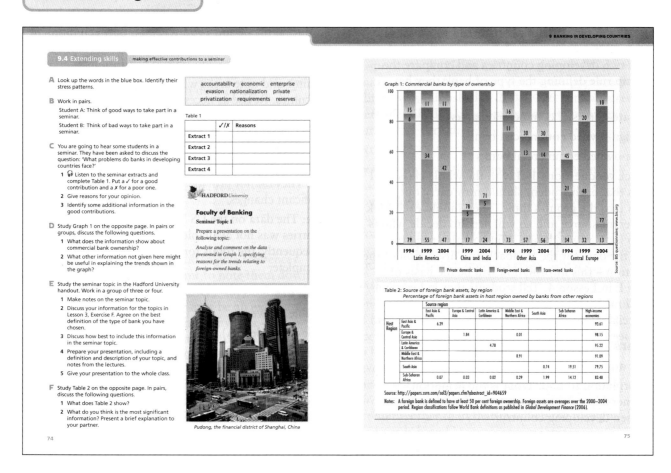

Lesson aims

- make effective contributions to a seminar

Further practice in:

- stress within words

Introduction

Use a few of the review cues from the Cornell notes in Lesson 3 for students to try to recall the ideas on foreign direct investment in the lecture. If students appear to be having difficulty remembering, ask them to look again at their own notes from Exercise C in Lesson 3.

Exercise A

Set for individual work and pairwork checking.

Answers

Model answers

Oo	'private
oO	re'serves
Ooo	'enterprise
oOo	e'vasion, re'quirements
ooOo	eco'nomic
oooOo	privati'zation, nationali'zation,
oooOoo	accounta'bility

Exercise B

This is revision from Unit 5. Set for individual work and pairwork checking. Feed back with the whole class. Give a time limit and see which pair can think of the most Do's and Don'ts in the time. Refer to Unit 5 Lesson 4 for suggestions if you need to.

Answers

Possible answers:

See table on next page.

Do's	Don'ts
ask politely for information	demand information from other students
try to use correct language	
speak clearly	mumble, whisper or shout
say when you agree with someone	get angry if someone disagrees with you
contribute to the discussion	sit quietly and say nothing
link correctly with previous speakers	
answer the question	make points that aren't relevant
be constructive	be negative
explain your point clearly	
listen carefully to what others say	start a side conversation
bring in other speakers	dominate the discussion
give specific examples to help explain a point	
paraphrase to check understanding	
use clear visuals	
prepare the topic beforehand	

🎧 Exercise C

Check that students understand the topic for the seminar discussion. Ask them what they might expect to hear. Complete questions 1–3 for each extract before moving on to the next. Work through these extracts one at a time.

1 Set for individual work.

2 First check that students have understood the extract as well as possible. Then ask for opinions from the whole class on the contribution.

3 Once everyone has a clear notion of whether the contribution is a good one, ask for suggestions for additional points. Alternatively, set this part for pairwork after you have completed questions 1 and 2.

Answers

Model answers:

	✔/✘	Reasons	Possible additional information
Extract 1	✔	speaks clearly expresses points well answers the question uses good fixed phrases	Banking system is often characterized by economic system Developing countries can be resistant to electronic banking
Extract 2	✘	does not speak clearly makes an attempt but does not fully answer the question gets distracted with reserve requirements poor use of visuals	
Extract 3	✔	speaks clearly explains the point clearly uses good fixed phrases has prepared well	developing countries tend to be cash-based economies
Extract 4	✘	speaks clearly, but doesn't fully answer the question points are too general and not developed too much phatic speech	

Transcript 🎧 2.7

Extract 1

I think that the banking system in developing countries is characterized by their economic system. For example, a system of private enterprise banking characterizes capitalist countries, a nationalized banking system characterizes socialist countries. In Eastern Europe, for example, the newly privatized banks had problems relating to the overhanging debt from what were previously state-owned or nationalized institutions. They also had overly complicated organization structures, lack of accountability, and poor training of staff and management. Bank networks were more labour intensive ... for example, more tellers but few or no ATMs. Electronic or Internet banking in developing countries is not extensive. Cash on delivery is still the preferred payment method for goods, and, for online orders, cash deposits into the bank account of the vendor. This not only reflects a resistance by the population to electronic payment methods, but also a lack of facilities in the banking system, such as automated clearing houses ...

Extract 2

... I think one big difference between banking in developing countries and banking in high-income economies is the cost of banking in emerging economies ... it may be very high, for a variety of reasons. The government may be unstable, the country may have a reputation for nationalizing foreign firms, or there may be the threat of a government coup d'etat, also ... high interest rate ceilings, high reserve requirements are necessary to attract customers ... So let's look at the chart and ... oh sorry, that's the wrong chart, just a minute ... right, so here is a chart showing some different reserve requirements for different countries ... you can see, I think, this difference ... do you have any questions about this chart?

Extract 3

Many developing countries have common problems relating to their banking structure. For example, high operating costs (related to interest-rate ceilings), high inflation, and little competition. Higher reserve requirements than those in high-income countries have also contributed to higher operating costs. There may be low pay scales, political interference in the management and regulatory systems of the financial sectors, with associated problems such as improper lending practices. The economies of many developing countries are cash-based because of the benefits cash offers for tax evasion, anonymity, and security. For example, where credit cards are used in these societies, every transaction may require 'explicit consent' (that is, a signature) from the card holder.

Extract 4

All business, including banking, in a foreign country always involves risk ... which is attributed to many issues. Take political stability or instability, for example ... in some countries, governments can change overnight ... next day it's a whole new ball game. I think we all agree that interest-rate ceilings and high reserve requirements tend to raise bank operating costs. Also economic factors like ... you know, the country's GDP and GNP. Inflation rates vary widely among developing countries ... in some countries it's sky high due to the economy growing too quickly. There are also the risks of operating within a developing country, for example security risk, operational risk, et cetera. Also, from the point of view of the host countries, failure of a foreign bank on their soil ... as you can imagine ... could have serious repercussions for their own banking industry.

Exercise D

Set for pairwork or group work. Tell students to analyse the data presented in Graph 1 and identify the trends relating to foreign-owned banks in each region. Then ask students to explain the trends for one region to their partner or group, specifying the reasons for the changes from their general knowledge.

Answers

Possible answers:

1/2 The graph shows commercial banks by type of ownership (private, foreign, state), measured as a percentage of total bank credit. The table reports on selected regions of the world, at three time periods: 1994, 1999 and 2004. Each region starts from different positions, with China, India and Central Europe dominated by state-owned banks. This is not surprising, as at this time these countries largely followed a socialist economic model. In 2004 this structure had not changed significantly in China or India. In Central Europe, however, the collapse of the Soviet Union, and the emergence of free market democratic states in Central Europe, led to a significant restructuring of their banking industries. As can be seen in the graph, the state-owned commercial banks' share of credit decreased significantly, from 45% to 10%, while the foreign-owned commercial banks' share increased significantly (from 21% to 77%). This was the result of the privatization of state-owned banks, and changes in regulations, that enabled and encouraged direct foreign investment.

In Latin America, due to restructuring after a financial crisis, the number and size of foreign banks increased from 6% (of total bank investment) in 1994, to 42% in 2004. This growth was at the expense of private domestic commercial banks, which decreased (mainly due to consolidations) from 79% in 1994 to 47% in 2004.

The category 'Other Asia', which includes Indonesia, Korea, Malaysia and Thailand, also experienced restructuring and consolidation in its domestic banking sectors. Collectively, the domestic banks' share of credit fell from 73% in 1994 to 56% in 2004. Interestingly, this is the only region where state-controlled commercial banks have increased their share of credit (from 16% in 1994 to 30% in 2004). A possible explanation for this is that restrictive regulations and perceived country risk have discouraged foreign bank participation.

Exercise E

Students should work in the same groups as their research groups from Lesson 3, Exercise F. They will need to have with them the research they have done individually on the group's chosen topic.

Decide how you want students to present their information, e.g.,

- short talk with/without Powerpoint, OHT, or other visual medium
- to the whole class or to another group

Make sure that students understand what the options are for the presentation types.

1 Tell students to use the Cornell note-taking system then redo their notes using the first of the 5Rs, i.e., record and reduce.

2 Ask each group to discuss the information that they have found and agree on the best definition and developing country examples they have researched.

3 In deciding how best to include this information, students need to decide where it is most relevant. Encourage students to use the record, reduce, recite, reflect technique to prepare for their seminar.

4 In preparing the seminar, students will need to decide who is going to speak when and say what. Encourage them to practise presenting to each other before talking to the whole class.

5 Allow each group a maximum of five minutes for the presentation. Then allow some time for questions. If more than one group have done the same topic, encourage disagreement and critical analysis. Remind the groups when discussing to use all the *good* techniques and phrases they have learnt.

Exercise F

Set for pairwork. Ask students what the information in Table 2 relates to. Then get them to analyse the data, and identify the most significant information for each region. Ask students to explain the key information to their partner.

Accept all reasonable answers.

Answers

Possible answers:

1 The table shows the host and source regions for bank FDI in the period 2000 to 2004.

2 Sub-Saharan Africa receives bank FDI from all the regions.

3 Europe and Central Asia is the biggest recipient of bank FDI from high-income economies.

Sub-Saharan Africa receives the largest bank FDI (14.12%) from within its own region, compared to the other host regions.

South Asia receives 19.51% of bank FDI from Sub-Saharan Africa, which represents the most significant investment from a developing region source to a developing region host.

East Asia & Pacific, Latin America & Caribbean, and Middle East & Northern Africa don't receive any bank FDI from other developing region sources except their own region.

Closure

Give students a vocabulary quiz using fixed phrases from this unit (see *Vocabulary bank*). This can be done individually to start with. Read out the first word in each fixed phrase. Students then add a second word to make a fixed phrase, preferably from this unit. Set for pairwork checking, with the pairs making new phrases. This could be done as a timed exercise.

Feed back with the whole class. Accept all reasonable answers.

This unit contains a lot of technical and semi-technical vocabulary. Students will need lots of practice with the vocabulary.

1 Work through the *Vocabulary bank* and *Skills bank* if you have not already done so, or as revision of previous study. Use the *Vocabulary bank* to check that the group can remember the meaning, spelling and pronunciation of the vocabulary in this lesson.

2 Use the *Activity bank* (Teacher's Book additional resources section, Resource 9A).

A Set the crossword for individual work (including homework) or pairwork.

Answers

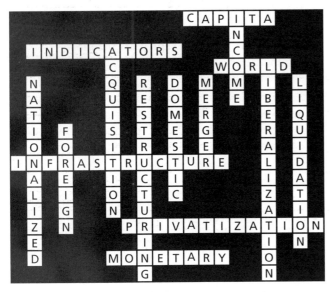

B Ask students to look at the list of nouns in the box: are plural forms of the nouns possible? Tell students to use an English-English dictionary or online definitions to help them find out the answers to the following questions.

1 Which forms are countable and which uncountable?

2 Do the countable and uncountable forms have different meanings?

Answers

Noun	Countable or uncountable	Notes
acquisition	C	see note for *merger*
development	C/U	usually U, as in the phrase *economic development*
economy	both	*The economy* usually refers to that part of a country's affairs that focuses on the financial situation.
income	C/U	
indicator	C	
industry	C/U	
infrastructure	C/U	
merger	C	often used in plural in the phrase *mergers and acquisitions*
ownership	U	
trade	C/U	usually U, as in the phrases *bilateral trade* or *trade agreement*

3 Put students in groups of three. Ask them to answer the questions below and prepare a short presentation for the class. They will need to use a number of resources including the research they have done during the lessons in this unit, their Cornell notes, and relevant information from Internet resources. When each group gives its presentation, the class will take Cornell-style notes. You may like to revise note-taking symbols and abbreviations (see extra activity 4 below) before commencing this exercise with the students.

The period 1997 to 2007 saw a substantial increase in foreign direct investment by the international banks in many developing countries.

1 *What are the main explanations for this?*

2 *What are the advantages and disadvantages of these investments for the host developing country?*

3 *Explain why foreign direct investment in their banking industries remained low in the rapidly developing countries of India and China.*

Answers

Possible answers:

Some developing countries experienced serious financial losses during the 1990s. For example, East Asia during 1997 to 1998, Russia in 1998, Brazil and Turkey during 1998 to 1999, and Argentina in

2001. As a result of the crisis, some of these countries were forced to restructure their banking systems. A combination of methods including privatization, banking consolidation and deregulation encouraged foreign direct investment in many of these developing economies.

Studies suggest productive, allocative and dynamic efficiency tend to be lower in banking systems dominated by state-owned banks, while privatization and an increased role for foreign banks help to improve at least some aspects of efficiency. Foreign banks introduce best-in-class systems and procedures. They train local staff, who over time circulate through local banks with their new skills.

Foreign banks often introduce new banking products to the local market, which helps bank customers and increases competition.

Some negative perceptions are that foreign banks earn high profits and do not comply with the political direction of the host-country government. In some developing countries, state banks are required to offer products dictated by the government – for example, low-interest loans to certain sectors of society in support of a socialist welfare policy. This restricts the ability of the state-owned banks to compete with private banks.

China and India escaped the financial crisis that affected many developing countries during the 1990s and early 2000 years. Both these countries continue to have regulations restricting foreign investment in their banking industries. The political systems in both China and India have, in the past, been based on a socialist market, with an emphasis on centralized state control of the banking industry. This situation is slowly changing with the privatization of some state banks.

4 Revise note-taking symbols – see the list at the back of the Course Book. Check back to Unit 5 if necessary. Give the meanings and ask students to write down the symbol (or do it the other way round). Then ask students to think about and discuss which symbols they actually use. Are there any other ones they have come across that they think are useful?

Alternatively, write the meanings on a set of cards. Put students in groups of about six with two teams in each group. Give each group a pile of cards. A student from each team picks a card and, without showing the members of his/her team, draws the appropriate symbol. The members of his/her team must say what the symbol stands for. If the student writes the correct symbol and the team gets the meaning right, the team gets a point. If the student writes the wrong symbol and/or the team gets it wrong, the team loses a point. The teams take it in turns to pick a card.

5 Do the same as the previous activity with banking abbreviations (including those from this unit) which will be useful for your students. For example, if they are studying in a UK or European-based context:

Banking abbreviation	Meaning
FDI	foreign direct investment
AIM	alternative investment market
OECD	Organisation for Economic Co-operation and Development
LDC	less developed country
HIPC	highly indebted poor country
IMF	International Monetary Fund
MDB	multilateral development bank
MFIs	multilateral financial institution
IBRD	International Bank for Reconstruction and Development
EIB	European Investment Bank
Co	company
plc	public limited company
NGO	non-governmental organization
CEO	chief executive officer
SME	small and medium-sized enterprise
MIGA	Multilateral Investment Guarantee Agency
GDP	gross domestic product
NIC	newly industrialized country

Some useful glossaries can be found at:

www.lse.co.uk/FinanceGlossary.asp

www.economist.com/countries/

www.ibgbusiness.com/glossary_of_terms.htm

www.world-english.org/

www.investorwords.com/4446/

www.moneyextra.com/dictionary/

wps.prenhall.com/wps/media/objects/213/218150/glossary.html

10 BANKING AND ETHICS

Unit 10 focuses on the development of ethical issues in banking, in particular the growth of socially responsible investments (SRIs). The first reading text looks at the reasons behind this growth and also discusses the impact of the Equator Principles on banking. Lessons 3 and 4 consider the issues involved in seeking bank finance for socially responsible business projects.

Skills focus

Reading

- recognizing the writer's stance and level of confidence or tentativeness
- inferring implicit ideas

Writing

- writing situation–problem–solution–evaluation essays
- using direct quotations
- compiling a bibliography/reference list

Vocabulary focus

- 'neutral' and 'marked' words
- fixed phrases from banking
- fixed phrases from academic English

Key vocabulary

capital	lending criteria	socially responsible investment (SRI)
charity credit cards	lending practices	slump (n and v)
core business	loan (n and v)	short-term
Equator Principles	long-term	transaction fee
ethics	medium-term	transparency
finance (n and v)	monitor	working capital
financial instruments	operating costs	
funds	project finance	
investor	regulatory	

10.1 Vocabulary

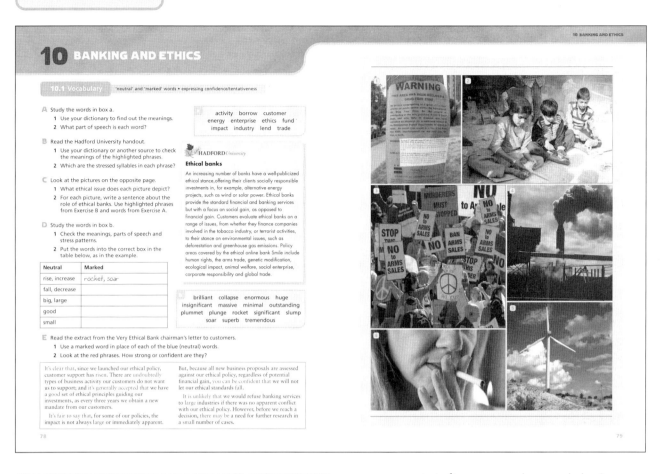

General note

Read the *Vocabulary bank* at the end of the Course Book unit. Decide when, if at all, to refer your students to it. The best time is probably at the very end of the lesson or the beginning of the next lesson, as a summary/revision.

Lesson aims

- understand when words are 'neutral' and when they are 'marked' (see *Vocabulary bank*)
- understand and use phrases expressing confidence/tentativeness (see *Vocabulary bank*)

Further practice in:

- fixed phrases/compound nouns from the discipline
- fixed phrases from academic English
- stress within words and phrases
- synonyms

Introduction

1 Revise banking words and phrases from the previous unit such as:

acquisitions – when a company buys an asset, e.g., another company, a building, etc.

economic indicators – various statistics (e.g., unemployment rate) indicating short-term and long-term economic performance

financial liberalization – making laws or systems relating to money less strict

gross domestic product – the total value of goods and services produced by a country in a year

industrialized country – country (political unit) having a lot of industry and factories

mergers – when two or more companies join together

liquidation – closing a company and selling its assets, often because it is unable to pay its debts

per capita income – the amount of income for each individual person

restructuring – organizing a company in a new way to make it operate more efficiently

Give definitions and ask students for the words/phrases.

2 Revise the following phrases used in academic writing. Ask students what sort of information will follow these phrases.

On the other hand, …

In conclusion, …

To put it another way, …

As Smith (2002) pointed out, …

Research has shown that …

Part of the difficulty is …

To start with, …

This can be defined as …

As a result, …

Finally, …

Given what has been shown above, …

Exercise A

Set for individual work and pairwork checking. Feed back with the whole class.

Answers

Model answers:

Word	Part of speech	Meaning/synonym
activity	n (C or U)	work
borrow	v (T)	use or take on a temporary basis something belonging to someone else lend (= antonym)
customer	n (C)	client
energy	n (U)	power
enterprise	n (C or U)	business organization
ethics	n (C)	values or morals
fund	n (C); v (T)	finance, provide money for
impact	v (I or T); n (U)	influence
industry	n (C or U)	business or business sector
lend	v (T)	loan
trade	n (C); v (I)	business; do business

Language note

There is no suggestion that banks which do not advertise themselves as 'ethical' are actually 'unethical'. It is more that social responsibility plays a role in decision making in an 'ethical' business whereas it may not in other businesses. An unethical business actually behaves in a way which is directly against the moral code of the society it operates in and this is not the case with a bank which, e.g., lends to tobacco companies, since smoking is legal.

Exercise B

1 Set for individual work and pairwork checking. Other sources besides dictionaries could be business textbooks, other reference books, or the Internet.

2 Show students how they can draw the stress pattern for the whole word as well as just locating the stressed syllable. If they use the system of big and

small circles shown below, they can see the pattern for the whole phrase quite easily.

Answers

Model answers:

1

ethical stance	moral attitude
socially responsible	beneficial to society
social gain	benefit to society
environmental issues	matters concerning damage to our surroundings/the natural world
policy areas	issues on which an organization takes a specific view
corporate responsibility	a company's duty to act ethically

2

'ethical stance	Ooo O
'socially responsible	Ooo oOoo
'social gain	Oo O
environ'mental issues	oooOo Oo
'policy areas	Ooo Ooo
'corporate responsibility	Ooo oooOoo

Exercise C

Set for pairwork or class discussion. Monitor and check vocabulary as necessary. Encourage students to speculate about what might be happening. Students should use the highlighted phrases and other words that are useful from the text in Exercise B; they can also use words from Exercise A.

Feed back with the whole class. Accept any reasonable answers.

Answers

Possible answers:

1 illegal drugs trade: Ethical banks will not *fund* projects connected to the drugs trade, as they only support **socially responsible** investments.

2 child labour: Ethical banks will not *lend* money to businesses which use goods produced by child labour.

3 arms dealing: Because of their **ethical stance**, ethical banks do not fund *enterprises* such as the arms *trade* which do not focus on **social gain**.

4 release of CO_2 into the atmosphere: **Environmental issues** such as factory emissions are important **policy areas** to ethical banks.

5 renewable energy: A business may ask to *borrow* money from an ethical bank, for activities such as wind power, whose *impact* on the environment is positive.

6 tobacco industry: Ethical banks will not support the tobacco *industry* because it does not take

corporate responsibility for the damage caused to people's health and the environment.

Exercise D

Introduce the idea of 'neutral' and 'marked' vocabulary (see *Language note* below and *Vocabulary bank*). Set for individual work and pairwork checking.

Feed back, discussing any differences of opinion about whether the words are marked, and in what sense they are marked. (Some students may argue that *minimal*, *significant* and *insignificant* are not marked, for example. Others may argue that they are marked, because they suggest not just that something is big/small, but that it is important/unimportant. Compare *There is a small problem with the program* and *There is an insignificant problem with the program*.)

Answers

Model answers:

Neutral	Marked
rise, increase	'rocket, soar (v)
fall, decrease	co'llapse (v and n), 'plummet (v), plunge (v and n), slump (v and n)
big, large	e'normous, huge, 'massive, sig'nificant, tre'mendous* (adj)
good	'brilliant, out'standing, su'perb, tre'mendous* (adj)
small	insig'nificant, 'minimal (adj)

**tremendous* can mean both very large and very good, so students may place this word in either category

Language note

One way of looking at vocabulary is to think about 'neutral' and 'marked' items. Many words in English are neutral, i.e., they are very common and they do not imply any particular view on the part of the writer or speaker. However, there are often apparent synonyms which are 'marked' for stance or opinion. Neutral words typically might be verbs or adjectives but other parts of speech are possible (e.g., nouns). The words are usually thought of as basic vocabulary (the adjectives often have opposites, e.g., *big/small*; *light/dark*). Marked words tend to be less frequent and are therefore learnt later.

The marked words in Exercise D are not totally synonymous. Their appropriate use and interpretation will be dependent on the context and also on collocation constraints. For example, one can say that a building is 'massive' but not (in the same sense) 'significant'.

Exercise E

1 Set for individual work and pairwork checking. Make sure that students understand any words they are not sure of. Feed back with the whole class by asking individual students to read out a sentence. Make sure that the pronunciation and stress patterns of the marked words are correct.

2 Put the table from the Answers section on the board. Make sure that students understand *tentative*. Elicit answers from the whole class and complete the table. Point out that these phrases are usually found in conversation or in informal writing such as this. Academic writing also requires writers to show degrees of confidence and tentativeness. The mechanisms for this will be covered in the next lesson.

Answers

Model answers:

1 It's clear that since we launched our ethical policy, customer support has (*risen*) soared/rocketed. There are undoubtedly types of business activity our customers do not want us to support; and it's generally accepted that we have a (*good*) tremendous/superb set of ethical principles guiding our investments, as every three years we obtain a new mandate from our customers.

It's fair to say that, for some of our policies, the impact is not always (*large*) enormous/significant/massive or immediately apparent. But because all new business proposals are assessed against our ethical policy, regardless of potential financial gain, you can be confident that we will not let our ethical standards (*fall*) plummet/collapse.

It is unlikely that we would refuse banking services to (*large*) massive/significant/huge industries if there was no apparent conflict with our ethical policy. However, before we reach a decision, there may be a need for further research in a (*small*) minimal/insignificant number of cases.

2

	Very confident	Fairly confident	Tentative (= not confident)
It's clear that	✔		
undoubtedly	✔		
It's generally accepted that		✔	
It's fair to say that		✔	
you can be confident that	✔		
It's unlikely that		✔	
there may be			✔

Closure

1 For further practice of neutral and marked vocabulary, ask students to write down some basic words, e.g., four verbs, four nouns and four adjectives. Put a list of these on the board and ask students if they are neutral or marked. See if you can find any opposites. Ask students to find some synonyms for neutral words – they can use a dictionary. A synonyms dictionary or Microsoft Word thesaurus can be useful here as well.

2 Ask pairs or groups to define, as accurately as they can, three of the fixed business phrases from the *Vocabulary bank*. Give them a few minutes to think of their definitions, then feed back and discuss as a class.

10.2 Reading

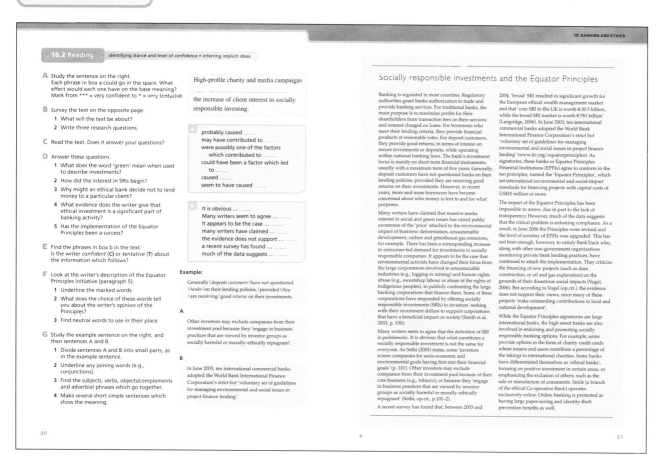

General note

Read the *Skills bank* at the end of the Course Book unit. Decide when, if at all, to refer students to it. The best time is probably at the very end of the lesson or the beginning of the next lesson, as a summary/revision.

Lesson aims

- identify the writer's stance on information from the use of marked words
- identify the writer's level of confidence in the research or information
- infer implicit ideas

Further practice in:

- finding the main information in a sentence

Introduction

Introduce the idea of degree of confidence in information, which is usually shown in academic writing. More often than not, writers will avoid categorical statements such as 'X was the cause of Y' and will demonstrate the extent to which they are sure

about something through various different linguistic devices, such as modals and hedging words and phrases.

Use this table to help explain the idea:

100% *** definitely true The writer is very confident	X caused Y
75% ** probably true. The writer is a little tentative	X probably/is likely to have caused Y
50% * possibly true The writer is very tentative	X may/might/could have/possibly caused Y

Exercise A

Make sure students understand the idea of 'socially responsible investing' (i.e., when making investment decisions, banks take into account the full impact of their investment on communities and the environment, by balancing the needs of their investors against their need to make a profit). Ask students what they think the effects of this might be on banking operations.

Set the exercise for pairwork. Feed back with the whole class, pointing out the aspects of the language that contribute to the degree of confidence.

169

Answers

Model answers:

Word/phrase	Rating	Words which show less than 100% confidence
probably caused	**	probably
may have contributed to	*	may contributed (i.e., there were other reasons)
were possibly one of the factors which contributed to	*	possibly one of the factors (i.e., there were several factors) contributed
could have been a factor which led to	*	could a factor (i.e., there were other factors)
caused	***	–
seem to have caused	**	seem

Exercise B

Explain to the students that surveying the text means skim-reading to get an approximate idea of the text contents. They should:

- look at the title
- look at the first few lines and the final few lines of the text
- look at the first sentence of each paragraph.

Note that this is in order to get a very approximate idea of the contents of the text. This will enable students to formulate questions about the text for which they might try to find answers. Students should be discouraged from reading deeply at this point, as they will be able to do this later.

Set for individual work and pairwork discussion. Each pair should agree three questions. Feed back with the whole class. Write some research questions on the board.

Exercise C

Set for individual work followed by pairwork discussion. Feed back with the whole class. Ask whether the questions you have put on the board have been answered in the text.

Exercise D

These questions require students to 'infer' information – that is, understand what is not directly stated.

Set for individual work and pairwork checking. Feed back with the whole class, making sure that students understand the answers. Accept all reasonable answers.

Answers

Possible answers:

1 Investments in businesses that are perceived to be environmentally positive and supportive of sustainable development.

2 Initial interest was driven by the media not by banks or investors.

3 Investment decisions might be made on the basis of an organization's business practices or the core industry it is in.

4 Core SRI in the UK totalled €30.5 billion; broad SRI adds up to €782 billion.

5 Opinions vary. Many NGOs are not satisfied with compliance and the Principles had to be revised. However, evidence suggests that projects do bring positive social benefits.

Exercise E

Set for individual work and pairwork checking. Feed back with the whole class. Point out that these phrases are very important in academic writing and will help to determine whether something is a fact or an opinion – an important aspect of reading comprehension. They are also used by writers in developing their arguments for or against a particular point of view.

Answers

Model answers:

It is obvious that what constitutes a socially responsible investment is not the same for everyone.	C
Many writers seem to agree that the definition of SRI is problematic.	T
It appears to be the case that environmental activists have changed their focus from the large corporations …	T
Many writers have claimed that massive media interest in social and green issues has raised public awareness of the 'price' attached to the environmental impact of business …	T
… *the evidence does not support* their views, since many of these projects …	C
A recent survey has found that, between 2003 and 2004, 'broad' SRI resulted in significant growth for the European ethical wealth management market	C
… *much of the data suggests* that the critical problem is enforcing compliance.	T

Exercise F

Set for pairwork. Feed back with whole class. Discuss any differences in students' answers, and whether marked equivalents are hard to find for some of the words.

Answers

Possible answers:

1 The impact of the Equator Principles has been <u>impossible</u> to assess, due in part to the lack of transparency. However, much of the data suggests that the <u>critical</u> problem is enforcing compliance. As a result, in June 2006 the Principles were revised and the level of scrutiny of EPFIs was <u>upgraded</u>. This has not been enough, however, to satisfy BankTrack who, along with other non-government organizations monitoring private bank lending practices, have continued to <u>attack</u> the implementation. They <u>criticize</u> the financing of new projects (such as dam construction, or oil and gas exploration) on the grounds of their <u>disastrous</u> social impacts (Vogel, 2006). But according to Vogel (op.cit.), the evidence does not support their views since many of these projects 'make <u>outstanding</u> contributions to local and national development'.

2 The writer's choice of words suggests that the Equator Principles are the subject of strong opinions and disagreement.

3

Marked word	Neutral alternative
impossible	difficult
critical	main
was upgraded	was improved
attack	disagree with
criticize	say they don't like
disastrous	negative
outstanding	positive

Exercise G

Draw the table from the Answers section on the next page on the board. Ask students to look at the example sentence and say which box each part of the sentence should go in. Complete the table for the example sentence as shown. Point out how the noun phrases can be made up of more than one word. In each case, elicit which words are the core of the noun phrases (shown in bold in the table). Do the same with the verb phrases. Ask students to suggest how the sentence can be rewritten in several short, very simple sentences in which noun phrases and verb phrases are reduced to their core meaning as far as possible. Demonstrate with these examples if necessary:

Banks have policies.

Customers receive returns.

Customers have not questioned banks on policies if returns are good.

This is generally true.

Point out how in the actual sentences the noun phrases have been expanded so that there is:

customers – deposit customers

policies – lending policies

returns – good returns on their investments

Set questions 1–4 (relating to sentences A and B) for individual work and pairwork checking. Feed back with the whole class.

Answers

Model answers:

1/2 A Other investors | may exclude | companies | from their investment pool | <u>because</u> | they | 'engage in | business practices | <u>that</u> | are viewed | by investor groups | as socially harmful <u>or</u> morally-ethically repugnant'.

 B In June 2003, | ten international commercial banks | adopted | the World Bank International Finance Corporation's | strict, <u>but</u> 'voluntary | set of guidelines | for managing | environmental <u>and</u> social issues | in project finance lending.'

	Subject noun phrases	Verb phrases	Object/complement noun phrases	Adverbial phrases	Notes
Example	deposit customers	have not questioned	banks	on their lending policies	*in written English an adverbial phrase introduced by prepositions can often be followed by verbs*
	they	are receiving	good **returns** on their investments	provided;	
A	Other **investors**	may exclude	companies	from their investment pool	
	they	engage in	business **practices**	because	
	(that)	are viewed		as socially **harmful** or morally-ethically **repugnant**	
B	ten international commercial **banks**	adopted	the **World Bank** International Finance Corporation's set of **guidelines** for managing environmenta land social **issues** in project finance lending	In June 2003;	

4 Possible sentences:

A Investors have an investment pool.
Companies engage in business practices.
These practices are viewed as harmful or repugnant.
Some investors may exclude such companies from their investment pool.

B The World Bank set guidelines for financing.
The guidelines are for managing social issues.
In 2003 ten banks adopted the guidelines.

Language note

1 Subjects and objects will always be nouns, with or without modifying adjectives. Complements can be nouns, adjectives or adverbs.

2 There are several types of conjunction in English.
Coordinating conjunctions such as *and*, *or*, *but* link elements of equal grammatical status.
Correlative conjunctions have two items: *either … or …*; *both … and ….*
Subordinating conjunctions relate clauses to each other using single words (e.g., *that* with verbs of saying, thinking, etc., *after, as, before, if, although, while*) or phrases (e.g., *as soon as, in order to, provided that …*).
See a good grammar reference book for full explanations.

3 *Adverbial phrases* add information about the actions or processes described by the verb phrase.

Closure

Here is some promotional language from the website of an ethical bank that sells 'green' banking products. Ask students to identify any marked vocabulary items in each sentence and to suggest more neutral words. Point out to students that the words do not need to be synonyms, but should be appropriate for conveying a particular message. Feed back, comparing answers and discussing any differences of opinion.

Brilliant solutions to make your house a dream ecological home!

Innovative investments in environmentally enhancing projects!

Exceptional-value finance for energy-effective housing!

Buy our exclusive charity credit cards in a robust yet alluring design!

Do you need some inspiration? We have some great investments in socially important projects!

Halt exploitation of workers in 'sweatshop' environments by not supporting businesses that actively participate in violating human rights!

Possible changes:

(*Brilliant solutions*) <u>Good</u> <u>ideas</u> to make your house a (*dream*) <u>model</u> ecological home!

(*Innovative*) <u>New</u> /<u>good</u> investments in environmentally (*enhancing*) <u>sound/trustworthy</u> projects!

(*Exceptional-value finance*) <u>Affordable/inexpensive</u> loans for energy (*effective*) <u>efficient</u> housing!

Buy our (*exclusive*) special charity credit cards in a
(*robust yet alluring*) strong but attractive design!

Do you need some (*inspiration*) ideas? We have some
(*great*) good investments in socially (*important*)
responsible projects!

(*Halt*) Stop exploitation of workers in ('*sweatshop*')
low-wage environments by not supporting businesses
that (*actively participate*) engage in (*violating*) ignoring
human rights!

10.3 Extending skills

10.3 Extending skills — recognizing essay types • problem–solution–evaluation essays

A Read the four essay questions on the right. What types of essay are they?

B Look at text A on the opposite page. Copy and complete Table 1 below.

C Look at text B on the opposite page. Copy and complete Table 2 below.

D Read the title of Essay 4 again.
1 Make a plan for this essay.
2 Write a topic sentence for each paragraph in the body of the essay.
3 Write a concluding paragraph.

1 Outline the problems and solutions in obtaining bank finance for a business involved in alternative energy.

2 Explain, from a bank's viewpoint, the dilemma it faces in providing socially responsible investments for customers.

3 Consider a bank that provides finance for sustainable development projects. What questions might the bank ask a business applying for project finance?

4 A company is planning to develop a waste recycling business. It wants to obtain finance from a bank supporting socially responsible investments. Explain the business plan and discuss the risks, benefits and finance needs of the project.

Table 1

Situation	
Problems	
Solutions	

Table 2

Solution	
Argument in favour	
Argument against	

10.4 Extending skills — writing complex sentences • quotations • references

A Expand these simple sentences. Add extra information. Use the ideas in Lesson 3.
1 The proposal is for waste recycling.
2 The practice of dumping waste in a landfill will create a long-term environmental risk.
3 A risk to the project is competition from other entrants to the market.
4 The business plan is sound.
5 This is a long-term business plan.

Table 1: *Referencing books*

Author(s)	Publisher	Date	Place

Table 2: *Referencing journals*

Name of journal	Volume	Pages

B Look at text C on the opposite page. Copy and complete Tables 1–3.

C Look at text D on the opposite page.
1 Complete a further row of Table 1.
2 How could you write this as a reference?

Table 3: *Referencing websites*

Retrieval date	URL

D What do the abbreviations in the blue box mean?

&	©	cf.	edn.	ed(s).	et al.
ibid.	n.d.	op. cit.	p.	pp.	vol.

E Look again at the text in Lesson 2 and text B on the opposite page.
1 Find all the direct quotations and their source references.
2 What words are used to introduce each direct quote? Why does the writer choose each word?
3 What punctuation is used to introduce each direct quote?

F Write out a reference list for your essay in Lesson 3, Exercise D.

82

Case Study 1

In 2000, John Goodman decided to start a small business specializing in sustainable energy, namely developing and manufacturing solar panels for home owners. John prepared a business plan to show that, while initially expensive to install, over time his solar power panels would be energy- and cost-efficient, provided they were correctly installed.

He applied to his bank for a ten-year loan for fixed capital costs, and a three-year loan for working capital. His high street bank refused him a loan on the grounds that his business idea was 'too exotic', and argued that, as the market was a niche not mainstream market, it was too small to provide even reasonable returns. It also argued that governments were more interested in nuclear and biofuels as an alternative, as solar power was not yet proven to be

cost effective. Furthermore, like most traditional banks, its focus was mainly on short-term financial instruments.

Following his bank's refusal to loan him the finance, John searched the Internet for banks offering funding for sustainable energy projects. After selecting three possible banks as sources of finance for his project, he re-read their lending criteria and refined his technology and business plans before submitting his application to a retail bank selling itself as an 'ethical bank'. On its Internet site, the 'ethical bank' stated that it refused to lend or invest in companies with poor environmental records. This time John was successful in his loan application. And unlike traditional banks, the 'ethical bank' was prepared to grant John both a ten-year loan and a three-year loan.

(Waller, 2005)

In the past, a bank's investment customers relied on the bank to provide good returns and did not question the bank's lending policies. Increasingly today, investors are seeking socially responsible investments such as those offered by banks promoting themselves as 'ethical banks'. As Sparkes (2002) states, an 'ethical bank' refuses, for example, 'to lend or invest in companies that have poor environmental records...' (p. 73) Investors in 'ethical, socially responsible and environmental funds include in their investment criteria judgments based on a moral assessment of what a business does ...' (Hancock, 2005, p. 41). However, as Hancock (op.cit.) also points out, 'it would not be socially responsible or, indeed, ethical to throw investors' money into businesses with little hope of success, however well meaning they may be.' (p. 45) There is a dilemma for the bank in balancing its customers' requests for socially responsible investments with its legitimate commercial needs.

Reference list

International Finance Corporation (n.d.). *Equator principles.* Retrieved July 7, 2007, from www.ific.org/equatorprinciples

Langridge, K. (2006). 'Green' or ethical financial services set to become more mainstream. *Banking Business Review: Online.* Retrieved September 20, 2007, from http://www.banking-business-review.com/article_feature.asp?guid=7 D72B1BF-3380-4192-BAA8-7CC878489B66

Sethi, S.P. (2005). Investing in socially responsible companies is a must for public pension funds – because there is no better alternative. *Journal of Business Ethics, 36,* 99–129.

Smith, R.C. and Walter, I. (2003). *Global banking.* (2nd Ed.). New York: Oxford University Press.

Vogel, D. (2006). *The market for virtue: the potential and limits of corporate social responsibility.* Washington D.C.: The Brookings Institution Press.

Case Studies in Sustainable Energy Projects

Brian Waller

Wentworth & Bourne

First published in 2000
by Wentworth & Bourne Ltd.
11 Vine Lane, London EC4P 5EJ
© 2000 Brian Waller
Reprinted 2007

All rights reserved. No part of this publication may be reproduced, stored in a retrieval system, or transmitted in any form or by any means, electronic, mechanical, photocopying, recording or otherwise without the prior written permission of the Publishers.

British Library Cataloguing in Publication Data
A catalogue record for this book is available from the British Library

Typeset by Glenda Graphics, Barnstaple, Devon, UK
Printed and bound by PW Enterprises, Bucks, Cornwall, UK
ISBN 0-321-09487-3

83

Lesson aims

- understand situation–problem–solution–evaluation structure in essays
- understand the use of information in this type of essay structure to:
  describe
  give cause and effect
  compare
  evaluate
  argue for

Further practice in:
- identifying required essay types
- producing an outline
- writing key sentences – which can be expanded in the next lesson into longer sentences

Introduction

Revise the different types of essay that were examined in Unit 8. Say or write on the board some key words or phrases from essay titles such as the following:

State …

Outline …

Describe …

Compare …

Evaluate …

Discuss …

Why …?

How …?

To what extent …?

How far …?

Ask students to say
- what type of essay is required
- what type of organizational structure should be used

Point out that the type of essay required may change, depending on the words following the instructional verbs, for example: *Outline the process for …* indicates descriptive writing, whereas *Outline the advantages and disadvantages …* indicates comparison.

174

Possible answers:

Descriptive	State ... Outline ... Describe ...
Comparison	Compare ... Evaluate ... Discuss ...
Analytical	Why ...? How ...?
Argument	To what extent ...? How far ...?

If students find this difficult, refer them to the *Skills bank* for Unit 8.

Ask students to add more instructional verbs.

Exercise A

Set for individual work and pairwork checking. Feed back with the whole class.

Point out that in real life, essays given by lecturers often involve several types of writing in one essay. This is the case with essay 4.

Tell students that in fact a possible structure for essay 4 would be the following, which is commonly found in many types of writing (including newspapers and academic writing).

Possible structure of essay 4:

Situation: description of the project, giving reasons and background information
Problem(s): the problems which this project intends to address
Solution(s): the likely benefits and possible risks
Evaluation of solution(s): how the solutions address the risks; identification of finance needs + justification

Tell students they will plan (and possibly write) this essay.

Answers

Model answers:

1 comparison
2 analytical
3 descriptive
4 descriptive, comparison/analysis, description/argument

Exercise B

Set for individual work and pairwork checking. It may be useful to tell students to make a table in their notebooks as in the Answers section.

Feed back with the whole class.

Answers

Model answers:

Situation	John Goodman needed finance to start a business manufacturing solar panels for home owners.
Problems	His bank would not give him a loan on the grounds that: his market was too small; it was not a mainstream market; his product had not yet proven to be cost-effective; the ten-year loan was too long-term.
Solutions	• do an Internet search for banks supporting alternative energy initiatives • read carefully their lending criteria • refine technology and business plans before submitting an application

Exercise C

Set for individual work and pairwork checking. Feed back with the whole class.

Answers

Model answers:

Solution	'Ethical banks' provide socially responsible investments for customers.
Argument in favour	They support businesses whose ventures have positive social and environmental outcomes.
Argument against	Customers may have commercial expectations which are not met by socially responsible investments.

Exercise D

1 Set for pairwork discussion. Remind students to refer to the texts they have discussed in this lesson for ideas and information. Remind students about the basic structure of an essay (introduction – main body – conclusion).

If you wish, you can give students the first two columns of the table in the Answers section, with the third column empty for them to complete. The table is reproduced in the additional resources section (Resource 10B) for this purpose.

For each paragraph give students the first idea in the examples. Elicit additional ideas. Check understanding of non-banking concepts, e.g., recycling business.

Feed back with the whole class. Build the plan on the board, using the ideas in the Answers section to help. Accept all reasonable suggestions.

2 Ask students to write some topic sentences for the four body paragraphs, using the information in the plan. Remind students that topic sentences need to be very general. Set for individual work.

Feed back with the whole class, writing some of examples on the board.

3 Set for pairwork, then discussion with the whole class. Or if you prefer, set for individual homework. The ideas should be those of the students. Remind them to introduce their ideas with suitable phrases.

Note: Students will need their essay plans again in Lesson 4.

Answers

1 Possible essay plan:

		Examples of ideas
Introduction introduce the topic area give the outline of the essay		business ➔ applying for bank's SRI funding ➔ business plan required *In this essay, I will discuss a business proposal by ...(situation)* *I will illustrate/describe current problems ... (examples + consequences)* *I will consider ... (solutions+ risks)* *Finally I will evaluate solutions and risks, and identify funding requirements.*
Body	**Para 1**: situation: description and background	• project ➔ plastics, glass + paper recycling • location ➔ outskirts of main city in small tropical island nation • justification ➔ current practice = dumping all waste in landfill • long-term environmental risk ➔ land (toxic contamination)
	Para 2: problems (specific examples)	• no current facility • community health risks • increasing environmental problem • affects land, i.e., a finite resource • affects tourism, i.e., main industry • too remote to interest large investors
	Para 3: solutions (benefits) and risks	benefits • reduces toxic waste + fumes generated by landfill • reduces growth in landfill • provides economic benefit by recycling waste • creates employment • enhances the skills of the employees • creates other businesses through the development of alternative uses for the recycled waste material risks • competition from other entrants to the market ➔ no other current competitors – too remote; better business alternatives elsewhere • delays in shipment/setting up plant ➔ built into business plan • insufficient supply of waste material • rise in collection and processing costs
	Para 4: evaluation of solutions	business plan is sound • expertise + experience to operate a recycling business • approval from local city government obtained • plant + location approved • no adverse environmental/social consequences identified therefore, funding needs are: • ten-year-term loan ➔ to finance the construction of the recycling plant ➔ estimated cost $10 million • three-year working capital loan ➔ to finance the initial start-up and day-to-day operating costs of the business • business plan indicates estimated amount required ➔ $2 million
Conclusion		business plan = long-term profitable business + positive ecological and social outcomes *In my view/As I see it, the best option is ... because ...* *Firstly ...Secondly ... Thirdly ...*

2 Possible topic sentences:

Para 1	The project proposal is to create a waste recycling facility.
Para 2	The lack of a waste recycling facility is currently creating a mumber of problems for the island.
Para 3	There are a number of possible benefits and some risks associated with the proposed project.
Para 4	The business plan is sound and sets out a realistic funding proposal.

3 Students' own concluding paragraphs.

Language note

Although 'situation–problem–solution–evaluation of solution' is often said to be an organizing principle in writing, in practice it is sometimes difficult to distinguish between the situation and the problem: they may sometimes seem to be the same thing. The important thing is to be clear about the main *focus* of the essay – that is, the answer to the question 'What am I writing about?' – and to structure the essay around this.

Closure

Set up a role-play where business representatives try to persuade a panel of bankers to invest in their project (by means of a business plan and discussion). The bankers work for banks with a socially responsible investment policy, and have adopted the Equator Principles. The business representatives are requesting finance for business projects that focus first and foremost on desirable social and environmental outcomes. The bankers try to find out whether the business representatives have really got a good idea, and whether they have done the necessary preparation and planning to demonstrate that the project has the intended social and ecological benefits as well as being financially sound.

Put students in groups of four. Within each group, students work in pairs. Pair A (business representatives) should think of an idea for an environmentally sustainable business. Pair B (bankers from banks who have adopted the Equator Principles) should think of all the risks and benefits on which they will assess the business plan. Students can use the notes in Resource 10C (in the Teacher's Book additional resources section) to help them prepare.

The business representatives should prepare a short business plan for their idea, which should include why it is a good idea, how they plan to put it into operation, how much money they will need and where they plan to get it. They should also decide how much to ask the bankers for, and for what purpose – bearing in mind that their focus is not on maximizing profits but on creating a socially and environmentally beneficial business.

The bankers should prepare their list of identified risks plus a list of the criteria that have to be met in their socially responsible investment policy.

When both pairs are ready, they should take it in turns to be the business representatives and the bankers. The business representatives should try to persuade the bankers to invest in their business for a reasonable return on their investment plus positive social and environmental effects. The bankers need to be sure that the idea is a good one and that it meets their socially responsible investment criteria.

10.4 Extending skills

10.3 Extending skills · recognizing essay types • problem–solution–evaluation essays

A Read the four essay questions on the right. What types of essay are they?

B Look at text A on the opposite page. Copy and complete Table 1 below.

C Look at text B on the opposite page. Copy and complete Table 2 below.

D Read the title of Essay 4 again.
1 Make a plan for this essay.
2 Write a topic sentence for each paragraph in the body of the essay.
3 Write a concluding paragraph.

① Outline the problems and solutions in obtaining bank finance for a business involved in alternative energy.

② Explain, from a bank's viewpoint, the dilemma it faces in providing socially responsible investments for customers.

③ Consider a bank that provides finance for sustainable development projects. What questions might the bank ask a business applying for project finance?

④ A company is planning to develop a waste recycling business. It wants to obtain finance from a bank supporting socially responsible investments. Explain the business plan and discuss the risks, benefits and finance needs of the project.

Table 1

Situation	
Problems	
Solutions	

Table 2

Solution	
Argument in favour	
Argument against	

10.4 Extending skills · writing complex sentences • quotations • references

A Expand these simple sentences. Add extra information. Use the ideas in Lesson 3.
1 The proposal is for waste recycling.
2 The practice of dumping waste in a landfill will create a long-term environmental risk.
3 A risk to the project is competition from other entrants to the market.
4 The business plan is sound.
5 This is a long-term business plan.

Table 1: Referencing books

Author(s)	Publisher	Date	Place

Table 2: Referencing journals

Name of journal	Volume	Pages

B Look at text C on the opposite page. Copy and complete Tables 1–3.

C Look at text D on the opposite page.
1 Complete a further row of Table 1.
2 How could you write this as a reference?

D What do the abbreviations in the blue box mean?

Table 3: Referencing websites

Retrieval date	URL

& © cf. edn. ed(s). et al.
ibid. n.d. op. cit. p. pp. vol.

E Look again at the text in Lesson 2 and text B on the opposite page.
1 Find all the direct quotations and their source references.
2 What words are used to introduce each direct quote? Why does the writer choose each word?
3 What punctuation is used to introduce each direct quote?

F Write out a reference list for your essay in Lesson 3, Exercise D.

82

Case Study 1

In 2000, John Goodman decided to start a small business specializing in sustainable energy, namely developing and manufacturing solar panels for home owners. John prepared a business plan to show that, while initially expensive to install, over time his solar power panels would be energy- and cost-efficient, provided they were correctly installed.

He applied to his bank for a ten-year loan for fixed capital costs, and a three-year loan for working capital. His high street bank refused him a loan on the grounds that his business idea was 'too exotic', and argued that, as the market was a niche not mainstream market, it was too small to provide even reasonable returns. It also argued that governments were more interested in nuclear and biofuels as an alternative, as solar power was not yet proven to be cost effective. Furthermore, like most traditional banks, its focus was mainly on short-term financial instruments.

Following his bank's refusal to loan him the finance, John searched the Internet for banks offering funding for sustainable energy projects. After selecting three possible banks as sources of finance for his project, he re-read their lending criteria and refined his application to a retail bank selling itself as an 'ethical bank'. On its Internet site, the 'ethical bank' stated that it refused to lend or invest in companies with poor environmental records. This time John was successful in his loan application. And unlike traditional banks, the 'ethical bank' was prepared to grant John both a ten-year loan and a three-year loan.

(Waller, 2005)

In the past, a bank's investment customers relied on the bank to provide good returns and did not question the bank's lending policies. Increasingly today, investors are seeking socially responsible investments such as those offered by banks promoting themselves as 'ethical banks'. As Sparkes (2002) states, an 'ethical bank' refuses, for example, 'to lend or invest in companies that have poor environmental records…' (p. 73) Investors in 'ethical, socially responsible and environmental funds include in their investment criteria judgments based on a moral assessment of what a business does …' (Hancock, 2005, p. 41). However, as Hancock (op.cit.) also points out, 'it would not be socially responsible or, indeed, ethical to throw investors' money into businesses with little hope of success, however well meaning they may be.' (p. 45) There is a dilemma for the bank in balancing its customers' requests for socially responsible investments with its legitimate commercial needs.

Reference list

International Finance Corporation (n.d.). *Equator principles*. Retrieved July 7, 2007, from www.ifc.org/equatorprinciples

Langridge, K. (2006). 'Green' or ethical financial services set to become more mainstream. *Banking Business Review: Online*. Retrieved September 20, 2007, from http://www.banking-business-review.com/article_feature.asp?guid=7D7281BF-3380-4192-BAA8-7CC878489B66

Sethi, S.P. (2005). Investing in socially responsible companies is a must for public pension funds - because there is no better alternative. *Journal of Business Ethics, 56,* 99–129.

Smith, R.C. and Walter, I. (2003). *Global banking.* (2nd Ed.). New York: Oxford University Press.

Vogel, D. (2006). *The market for virtue: the potential and limits of corporate social responsibility.* Washington D.C.: The Brookings Institution Press.

Case Studies in Sustainable Energy Projects

Brian Waller

Wentworth & Bourne

First published in 2008
by Wentworth & Bourne Ltd.
11 Vine Lane, London EC4P 1EI
© 2008 Brian Waller
Registered 2007

All rights reserved. No part of this publication may be reproduced, stored in a retrieval system, or transmitted in any form or by any means, electronic, mechanical, photocopying, recording or otherwise without the prior written permission of the Publishers.

British Library Cataloguing-in-Publication Data
A catalogue record for this book is available from the British Library

Typeset by Glenda Craghorn, Barnstaple, Devon, UK
Printed and bound by PW Enterprises, Bude, Cornwall, UK
ISBN 8-321-49487-3

83

General note

This lesson focuses on writing references for a bibliography according to the APA (American Psychological Society) system. Before the lesson, it would be useful to familiarize yourself with this system. See the *Skills bank*, and for more detailed information, websites such as http://owl.english.purdue.edu/owl/resource/560/10/ or http://www.westwords.com/guffey/apa.html (at the time of writing).

Lesson aims

- use quotations with appropriate punctuation and abbreviations such as ibid.
- write a bibliography (APA system)

Further practice in:

- the reverse activity to Lesson 2, i.e., putting extra information into simple sentences in an appropriate way

Introduction

Introduce the idea of using sources in writing. Look back at the text in Lesson 2 and ask students to find all the places where a reference to a source is mentioned. Ask them to find a quotation and a paraphrase. What are the main differences?

Exercise A

Remind students of the essay plan in Lesson 3. If you wish, you can reproduce the following table for them. They should try to get all the information in each numbered point into one sentence.

<table>
<tr><td colspan="2">

From Para 1:
1. project ➜ plastics, glass + paper recycling
   location ➜ outskirts of main city in small tropical island nation
2. justification ➜ current practice = dumping all waste in landfill
   long-term environmental risk ➜ land (toxic contamination)

</td></tr>
</table>

From Para 1:
1. project ➜ plastics, glass + paper recycling
   location ➜ outskirts of main city in small tropical island nation
2. justification ➜ current practice = dumping all waste in landfill
   long-term environmental risk ➜ land (toxic contamination)

From Para 3:
risks
3. competition from other entrants to the market ➜ no other current competitors – too remote; better business alternatives elsewhere

From Para 4:
4. business plan is sound
   • expertise + experience to operate a recycling business
   • approval from local city government obtained
   • plant + location approved
   • no adverse environmental/social consequences identified

From Conclusion:
5. business plan = long-term profitable business + positive ecological and social outcomes

Do the first sentence with the whole class as an example on the board. Students should feel free to add words as appropriate to make a coherent sentence; they can also paraphrase. Set the remaining sentences for individual work.

Answers

Possible answers:

1 The proposal is to set up a plastics, glass and paper recycling business, located on the outskirts of the main city of a small tropical island nation.

2 The current practice, where all waste is disposed of in a landfill, is likely to lead to long-term environmental problems, especially through toxic contamination of the land.

3 Although competition is a possible risk to the project, at this stage the remoteness of the location and the existence of better business alternatives elsewhere have deterred competitors from entering the market.

4 There are a number of factors which indicate that the business plan is built on a sound foundation: firstly, the business has the expertise and experience to confidently build and operate a recycling business; secondly, the project (and the location) have met with approval from the local city government; and thirdly, no adverse environmental or social consequences have been identified.

5 This business plan looks to create a business which will be profitable over the long term, while at the same time generating positive ecological and social outcomes.

Exercise B

Tell students that this is a list of references from the text in Lesson 2. Note that it is called a reference list because it lists all the references actually given (it is not a list of all the references the author might have consulted but not referred to – that is a bibliography).

Set for individual work and pairwork checking. Tell students they will need to pay close attention to the detail of the layout which is in the APA style (the American Psychological Association). See the *Skills bank* for relevant websites which give further details. In particular, students should note and will need to practise:

● putting the names of writers and multiple writers in the correct alphabetical order according to family name, with the right spacing and punctuation

● writing all numbers correctly, including dates and page references

● using punctuation including the role and placing of full stops and commas.

● laying out the references in the correct style with the correct positions (e.g., use of indents and tabs)

● using standard APA style features such as italic and brackets

Answers

Table 1:

Author(s)	Publisher	Date of publication	Place of publication
Smith, R.C., & Walter, I.	Oxford University Press	2003	New York
Vogel, D.	The Brookings Institution Press	2006	Washington

Table 2:

Name of journal	Volume	Pages
Journal of Business Ethics	56	99–129

Table 3:

Retrieval date	URL
July 7, 2007	www.ifc.org/equatorprinciples
Retrieved September 20, 2007	http://www.banking-business review.com/article_feature. asp?guid=7D7281BF-338041-92-BAA8-7CC878489B66

Language and subject note

In the case of journals, there is an increasing tendency to refer to the volume number only in reference lists, omitting the issue number. Thus, for example, *English for Specific Purposes, 16 (1),* 47–60 might become *English for Specific Purposes, 16, 47–60.*

Exercise C

Set for individual work and pairwork checking.

Answers

1

Author(s)	Publisher	Date of publication	Place of publication
Waller, B.	Wentworth & Bourne Ltd.	2005	London

2 Waller, B. (2005). *Case studies in sustainable energy projects*. London: Wentworth & Bourne.

Language and subject note

In the APA system, titles of books (but not articles or journal titles) are in italics, sentence case – that is, initial capital letter only, unless the title contains a proper noun. If the title contains a colon, the first word after the colon is also capitalized.

Journal titles are in italics and 'headline' or 'title' style – that is, all key words are capitalized but not conjunctions and prepositions. For example: *Journal of Business Ethics*.

Journal articles are sentence case, no italics.

Exercise D

Most of these were covered in Unit 5, so ask students to check back if they are not sure; they can also check online at the APA site and/or the other sites given in the *Skills bank*.

Set for individual work and pairwork checking.

Answers

Model answers:

&	and
©	copyright
cf.	compare
edn.	edition
ed(s).	editor(s)
et al.	and other authors
ibid.	same place in a work already referred to
n.d.	no date (used in a reference list if there is no date – as is often the case with web articles)
op. cit.	the work already referred to
p.	page
pp.	pages
vol.	volume

Exercise E

Remind students (if you have not done so already) of the two main ways in which students can use sources (i.e., references to other writers' work) in their writing:

- by giving the exact words used by another writer
- by paraphrasing another writer's ideas, i.e., rewriting the ideas using their own, different words but retaining the meaning

The first method is referred to as quotation or direct quotation. Direct quotations are in quotation marks, usually single: '... '.

The second method is referred to as paraphrase, summary or indirect quotation. Note that for copyright reasons around 90% of the paraphrase should be new words.

Set for individual work. Tell students to look for all the direct quotations. They should identify the introducing phrases used, plus the punctuation, and also locate the source in the reference list on page 83 of the Course Book.

Feed back with the whole class for the first two answers. Make sure that students understand why the different introducing verbs were chosen. Students in groups then complete the rest of the exercise. Monitor, then build up the answers on the board with the whole class.

Answers

Model answers:

Lesson 2:

Quote	Introducing phrase + reason for choice	Punctuation around the quote	Source	Comment
'seeking with their investment dollars to support corporations that have a beneficial impact on society'	No introductory verb. Reason: the quote is embedded within the syntax of the main sentence.	'xxx'	page 100 of: Smith, R.C., and Walter, I. (2003). *Global banking.*(2nd Ed.) New York: Oxford University Press.	The quote is a clause at the end of a sentence. It begins with a lower case letter. It is followed by (Smith et al., 2003, p. 100) and then a full stop.
'investors screen companies for socio-economic and environmental goals having first met their financial goals'.	As Sethi (2005) states, some … Reason: this is Sethi's opinion.	'xxx'	page 101 of Sethi, S.P. (2005). Investing in socially responsible companies is a must for public pension funds – because there is no better alternative. *Journal of Business Ethics*, 56, 99–129.	The quote is a clause in the sentence. There are some words missing which were in the original sentence – so the quote does not begin with a capital letter.
'engage in business practices that are viewed by investor groups as socially harmful or morally– ethically repugnant'	No introductory verb. Reason: the quote is embedded within the syntax of the main sentence	'xxx'	the same as above	The quote is a clause at the end of a sentence. It begins with a lower case letter. It is followed by (Sethi, op. cit., p. 101–2) and then a full stop.
'voluntary set of guidelines for managing environmental and social issues in project finance lending'	No introductory verb Reason: the quote is embedded within the syntax of the main sentence	'xxx'	International Finance Corporation (n.d.). *Equator principles.* Retrieved July 7, 2007, from www.ifc. org/equatorprinciples	The quote is a clause in the sentence. There are some words missing which were in the original sentence – so the quote does not begin with a capital letter.

Lessons 3/4:

Quote	Introducing phrase + reason for choice	Punctuation around the quote	Source	Comment
'to lend or invest in companies that have poor environmental records…'	As Sparkes (2003) states Reason: the writer is giving a definition	'xxx'	page 73 of Sparkes, R. (2002). *Socially responsible investment: a global revolution.* Chichester: John Wiley & Sons.	The quote is a clause in the sentence. There are some words missing which were in the original sentence – so the quote does not begin with a capital letter.
'ethical, socially responsible and environmental funds include in their investment criteria judgments based on a moral assessment of what a business does…'	No introductory verb. Reason: the quote is embedded within the syntax of the main sentence	'xxx'	page 45 of Hancock, J. (2005). *Investing in corporate social responsibility: a guide to best practice, business planning and the UK's leading companies.* London: Kogan Page.	The quote is a clause in the sentence. There are some words missing which were in the original sentence – so the quote does not begin with a capital letter
'It would not be socially responsible or, indeed, ethical to throw investors' money into businesses with little hope of success, however well meaning they may be.'	However, as Hancock (op. cit.,) also points out, … Reason: this is the writer's opinion	'Xxx.'	the same as above	The quote is a full sentence. It begins with a capital letter and ends with a full stop inside the quotation mark. It is preceded by a comma since it follows 'As Hancock points out …'

Exercise F

Set for individual work, possibly for homework. Students should refer back to their essay plan for Lesson 3 (Exercise D) and decide which of the references from the list on page 83 they would use (they can add other sources they are familiar with if they wish). They should then write out the full reference list. This may seem a mechanical exercise, as they have now either examined or written out all the references in the Course Book. However, it is good practice, as reference lists are notoriously difficult to get right.

Language and subject note

An ampersand is used with multiple authors, preceded by a comma.
The full stop at the end of the reference is omitted in the case of URLs.
Dates are (for example) April 7 not April 7th.

Closure

Refer students to the *Skills bank* for a summary of writing references. Study how the following are used:

- names (order)
- punctuation (capital letters, full stops, commas, colons)
- layout (indentation, spacing)
- style features (italics, brackets)

For further practice, use Resource 10D from the additional resources section. Ask students to check the references on a library database or on the Internet (discuss which sources are likely to be the most accurate and give them all the information they need – often the best way to check bibliographical details is to use a university library catalogue, as information found on the Internet is frequently inaccurate or incomplete). They should also make any necessary changes to ensure the references fit the APA models used in this unit. If possible, they should use the online website references (see *Skills bank*) to help them. Remind students that they will also need to put the references in the right alphabetical order.

Correct versions are:

Hardenbrook, A. (2007). The Equator Principles: the private financial sector's attempt at environmental responsibility. *Vanderbilt Journal of Transnational Law, 40,* 197–232.

Heffernan, S. (2005). *Modern banking.* Chichester: John Wiley & Sons.

Shim, Jae K. & Costas, M. (2001). *Encyclopedic dictionary of international finance and banking.* Boca Raton: St. Lucie Press.

Smith, R.C., and Walter, I. (2003). *Global banking* (2nd Ed.). New York: Oxford University Press.

Sparkes, R. (2002). *Socially responsible investment: a global revolution.* Chichester: John Wiley & Sons.

Vogel, D. (2006). *The market for virtue: the potential and limits of corporate social responsibility.* Washington D.C.: The Brookings Institution Press.

Extra activities

1 Work through the *Skills bank* and *Vocabulary bank* if you have not already done so, or as revision of previous study.

2 Use the *Activity bank* (Teacher's Book additional resources section, Resource 10A).

A As in the previous unit, students will need lots of practice with the technical and semi-technical terms relating to socially responsible investments. Set for individual work (including homework) or pairwork. Tell students to focus on the main meanings of the words in banking.

Answers

Word expression	Part of speech	Noun – countable or uncountable?	Verb – transitive or intransitive?
account*	n	C	
borrow	v		T
client	n	C	
ethics	n	(pl)	
lend	v		T
monitor	v		T
overheads	n	(pl)	
project	n	C	
transparency	n	U	

* there is also a verb: *account for*

B Set for individual work (including homework) or pairwork. Accept all reasonable answers. Students should be able to explain the meaning.

Answers

Possible answers:

bank	loan, account
business	start-up, plan
capital	investment
financial	instruments, liberalization
investment	proposal, opportunity
lending	criteria
operating	costs
personal	loan
transaction	fee
working	capital

3 Ask students to choose one of the other essays in Lesson 3 and make a plan. They can also write topic sentences for each paragraph in the essay.

11 INFLUENCES ON BANKING STANDARDS

This unit looks at the range of external influences which can negatively affect banking standards – including globalization, new technology, political regulation, the economic cycle and ethical issues. The first lecture looks in detail at the way changes in technology have created the potential for Internet and ID fraud. It also looks at the way financial targets can sometimes compromise banking standards. The second lecture examines the failure of proper regulation and how this can lead to fraud within a banking organization.

Skills focus

🎧 Listening
- recognizing the speaker's stance
- writing up notes in full

Speaking
- building an argument in a seminar
- agreeing/disagreeing

Vocabulary focus

- words/phrases used to link ideas (*moreover*, *as a result*, etc.)
- stress patterns in noun phrases and compounds
- fixed phrases from academic English
- words/phrases related to technological issues

Key vocabulary

See also the list of fixed phrases from academic English in the *Vocabulary bank* (Course Book page 92).

account holders	diversification	log management	regulation
biometric	due diligence	money laundering	scamming
bounced cheque	encryption software	ombudsman	security
client	ethics policy	overdrawn	serial numbers
code of conduct	fraud	password	smart card
compliance	fraudulent	protection	spyware
computer hacking	ID theft	penalty rate	sub-prime mortgage
conflict of interest	jurisdiction	pharming	technology
data protection	keylogger	phishing	Trojan horse
default (n and v)	laser printer	proxy server	two-factor ID
deregulation	legislation	reconciliation	verification

11.1 Vocabulary

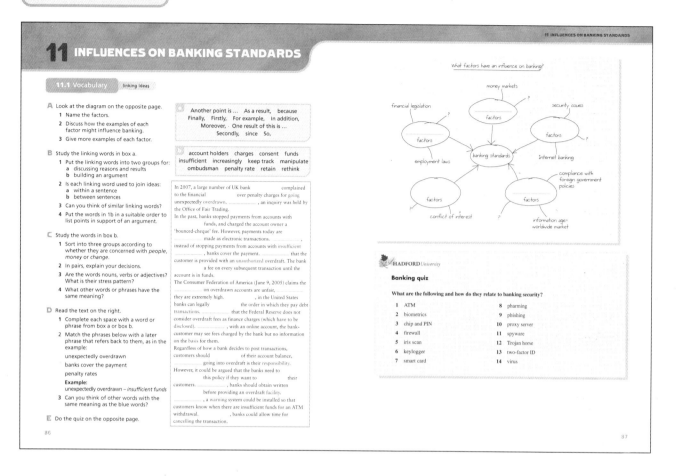

General note

Read the *Vocabulary bank* at the end of the Course Book unit. Decide when, if at all, to refer your students to it. The best time is probably at the very end of the lesson or the beginning of the next lesson, as a summary/revision

Lesson aims

- use rhetorical markers: to add points in an argument; to signal cause and effect (between- and within-sentence linking)
- further understand lexical cohesion: the use of superordinates/synonyms to refer back to something already mentioned; building lexical chains

Further practice in

- synonyms, antonyms and word sets from banking

Introduction

1 Revise some vocabulary from previous units. Give students some key words, below. Ask them to think of terms connected with them (for example, some key phrases from banking). Ask them to make sentences that illustrate their banking meanings:

ethical policy, investment opportunities, policy conflict, corporate responsibility, socially responsible investments, lending criteria, lack of transparency, investment criteria

2 Introduce the topic: before asking students to open their books, ask them what the term 'banking standards' means in general. Accept any reasonable suggestions. What kind of things do banks need to pay attention to outside their own organizations? Tell the students that they first met some of these concepts in Unit 7 and Unit 8, but here they are going to consider these topics in more detail.

Exercise A

Ask students to open their books and look at the diagram on page 87.

Check the meaning of the words in the diagram. If necessary give some examples.

1 Set for pairwork. Feed back with the class.

2/3 With the whole class, discuss the technological factors. What can they remember about technology in Unit 4? Ask students to explain how computers affect banking, e.g., new services, new products. Discuss with the class the positive and negative aspects of Internet banking: for example, customers no longer constrained to banking hours but have access to their accounts virtually anywhere at any time. On the other hand, there are security issues, reductions in staff, etc.

Next discuss with the class the effects of globalization. Ask the class to suggest how globalization might affect banking standards. Remind them of issues discussed in Unit 8 pertaining to offshore banking, e.g., reduction of government controls. Accept any reasonable suggestions.

Set the remaining factors for pairwork discussion. Ask a few pairs to feed back to the class. Accept any reasonable answers.

Answers

Possible answers:

1 See diagram below.

2 Answers depend on the students.

3 Some more examples of factors are:

Technological factors

    credit + smart cards
    staff need new skills
    new business model

Globalization factors

    different business norms and cultures
    reduction of government controls
    increased competition
    growth of new economies

development of new/changing financial instruments
global organizations such as the World Bank and the United Nations
international conventions and agreements such as Basel I and Basel II

Political factors

    deregulation
    privatization
    control by governments

Economic factors

    economic/business cycle
    taxes
    changes in financial legislation, e.g., monetary controls

Add some of these to the diagram, as appropriate and as students suggest them. Make a large poster-sized copy of the diagram, on an OHT or other visual medium, to which you can add more examples as the unit progresses.

Exercise B

1 Set for individual work and pairwork checking. Feed back with the whole class, building the table in the Answers section.

2 Explain what is meant by 'within' and 'between' sentences: 'within-sentence linkers' join clauses in a sentence; 'between-sentence linkers' connect two sentences. Demonstrate with the following:

Within-sentence linker:

The bank charged bounced-cheque fees <u>because</u> the customer had insufficient funds to meet the payment.

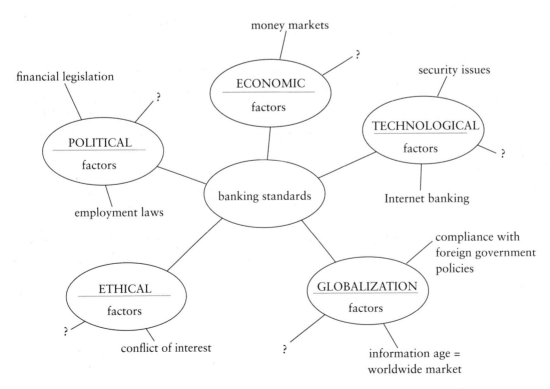

Make sure that students can see that within-sentence linkers precede dependent clauses.

Between-sentence linker:

The customer had insufficient funds to meet the payment. <u>As a result</u>, the bank charged bounced-cheque fees.

Point out that between-sentence linkers usually have a comma before the rest of the sentence.

Ask students to say which words in box a are 'between' and which are 'within'.

3 Ask for suggestions for synonyms and add to the table.

4 First make sure that students understand the basic principle of an argument which is:

Statement

+

one or more support(s) for statement (= more facts, reasons, results, examples, evidence, etc.)

Constructing a complex argument will usually entail a statement plus several supports.

With the whole class, elicit suggestions for how to use the linkers when constructing an argument. Build the table below on the board.

Answers

Possible answers:

1/2/3

Linking words	Use for	Within or between sentence linker	Other similar words/phrases
Another point is …	building an argument	between	And another thing,
As a result,	reasons and results	between	Consequently,
because	reasons and results	within	as
Finally,	building an argument	between	Lastly,
Firstly,	building an argument	between	To begin with/To start with; For one thing,
For example,	building an argument	between	For instance,
In addition,	building an argument	between	Also,
Moreover,	building an argument	between	Furthermore,
One result of this is …	reasons and results	between	One consequence of this is … Because of this,
Secondly,	building an argument	between	Next, Then,
since	reasons and results	within	as
So,	reasons and results	between	Therefore, Thus, Hence,

Language note

1 Note that within-sentence linkers may be placed at the beginning of the sentence with a comma after the first clause, as in:

<u>Because</u> the customer had insufficient funds to meet the payments, the bank charged bounced-cheque fees.

2 Although the between-sentence linkers are described above as joining two sentences, they can of course link two independent clauses joined by coordinating linkers *and* or *but*, as in:

The customer had insufficient funds to meet the payment and, <u>as a result</u>, the bank charged bounced-cheque fees.

4 A typical argument is constructed like this:

Firstly,	making the first major support point
For example,	supporting the point with a specific example
In addition,	adding another related point in support
Secondly,	making the second major support point
Another point is …	adding another related point in support
Moreover,	adding more information to the point above
Finally,	making the last point

Exercise C

1 Set for individual work. Note that students must decide to put each word into one of the three categories, even if it is not immediately clear how it could be relevant. If they are not sure which category to use, they should try to think of a phrase containing the word and imagine how it could be relevant to one of the categories.

2 Put students in pairs to compare their answers and to justify their choices. Feed back with the whole class, discussing the words for which students feel the category is not obvious. If no decision can be reached, say you will come back to the words a little later.

3/4 Set for pairwork. Feed back with the whole class if you wish.

Answers

Possible answers:

Words/phrases	Suggested categories	Part of speech	Other words/phrases
a'ccount 'holders	people	n, pl	bank customers
'charge	money	v (T)	require (payment)
con'sent	people	n (U)	agreement, permission
funds	money	n, pl	money needed
insuf'ficient	money	adj	inadequate
in'creasingly	change	adverb	more and more
keep 'track	change	v (I, T)	monitor
ma'nipulate	change	v (T)	influence
'ombudsman	people	n (C)	organization that deals with complaints
'penalty rate	money	n (C)	fine
re'tain	change	v (T)	keep
'rethink	change	v (T)	alter, change

Exercise D

Students should first read through the text to get an idea of the topic.

1 Set for individual work and pairwork checking. Feed back with the whole class.

2 Set for individual work and pairwork checking. Feed back with the class.

It is common to use synonymous words and phrases to refer back to something already mentioned. Point out that these words are not general synonyms but are dependent on the context.

3 Set for individual work and pairwork checking. Feed back with the whole class.

Point out that having done these exercises, students should now be able to say whether the words in box b can be put into a 'change', 'money' or a 'people' group. The point here is that the context

will make clear what the meaning of a word should be. This is important when it comes to making a guess at the meaning of a word which one is not sure of initially.

Tell the students that a particular topic will have groups of words which are connected to or associated with it – known as 'lexical chains'. These lexical chains show us the themes that run through the text and which help 'glue' the ideas together to make a coherent piece of text. It is a good idea, therefore, to learn vocabulary according to topic areas.

Answers

Model answers:

1 In 2007, a large number of UK bank account holders complained to the financial ombudsman over penalty charges for going unexpectedly overdrawn. As a result, an inquiry was held by the Office of Fair Trading.

In the past, banks stopped payments from accounts with <u>insufficient</u> funds and charged the account owner a 'bounced-cheque' fee. However, payments today are <u>increasingly</u> made as electronic transactions. <u>So</u>, instead of stopping payments from accounts with insufficient <u>funds</u>, banks cover the payment. <u>One result of this is</u> that the customer is provided with an unauthorized overdraft. The bank <u>charges</u> a fee on every subsequent transaction until the account is in funds.

The Consumer Federation of America (June 9, 2005) claims the <u>penalty rates</u> on overdrawn accounts are unfair, <u>since</u> they are extremely high. <u>Moreover</u>, in the United States banks can legally <u>manipulate</u> the order in which they pay debt transactions. <u>Another point is</u> that the Federal Reserve does not consider overdraft fees as finance charges (which have to be disclosed). <u>For example</u>, with an online account, the bank customer may see fees charged by the bank but no information on the basis for them.

Regardless of how a bank decides to post transactions, customers should <u>keep track</u> of their account balance, <u>because</u> going into overdraft is their responsibility. However, it could be argued that the banks need to <u>rethink</u> this policy if they want to <u>retain</u> their customers. <u>Firstly</u>, banks should obtain written <u>consent</u> before providing an overdraft facility. <u>Secondly</u>, a warning system could be installed so that customers know when there are insufficient funds for an ATM withdrawal. <u>In addition</u>, banks could allow time for cancelling the transaction.

2

unexpectedly overdrawn	insufficient funds
penalty rates	overdraft fees
banks cover the payment	customer is provided with an unauthorized overdraft

3

going … overdrawn	exceeding credit balance
insufficient	inadequate
unauthorized	without permission
transactions	payments
disclosed	revealed
basis	reason
responsibility	duty
facility	service
warning	alerting
cancelling	stopping

Exercise E

Set for individual work then pairwork checking. Feed back with the whole class.

Finally ask students to define what is meant by the term *fraudulent behaviour*. Accept all reasonable suggestions. Ask students in pairs to come up with examples of bank employee behaviour which might be considered fraudulent.

Language note

There is no precise legal definition of fraud. Many examples of 'fraud' can be offences under the Theft Acts of 1969 and 1978. When it comes to occupational fraud, the term covers acts such as: embezzlement; false accounting; bribery and corruption; and making fraudulent statements for personal gain (e.g., falsely claiming overtime or travel expenses).

Source:
http://fraudadvisorypanel.org/newsite/PDFs/advice/Model%20Fraud%20Policy%20Statements%20Feb05.pdf

Answers

Model answers:

1 automated teller machine, used to dispense cash via debit cards. If a card and its PIN are stolen, cash can be withdrawn from a customer's account.

2 a scientific technique for identifying an individual from his or her unique physical attributes

3 the use of a computer chip embedded in a credit or debit card, together with a Personal Identification Number, to verify the cardholder's identity

4 a means of controlling computer access to or from external networks

5 a technique which analyses the unique appearance of a person's eye, in order to verify identity

6 spyware which records every keystroke to allow information to be transmitted to an unknown third party

7 a card (generally the same size as a credit card) which can process electronic information

8 infusing false information into a server so that users are directed to a fraudulent site

9 sending an email that falsely claims to be from a legitimate source, to obtain private information for use in identity theft

10 web server which intercepts all requests to the real server

11 software that gathers information (e.g., email addresses, passwords, credit card numbers) by monitoring user activity on the Internet

12 product unwittingly installed on a computer when the user installs something else

13 the use of two checks in order to verify someone's identity

14 a program that can replicate itself and attack a computer without the knowledge of the user

Closure

Give students vocabulary revision of phrases from this lesson. Say the first word and ask students to complete the phrase – for example, you say *penalty* (students say *rate*).

account holders

insufficient funds

overdrawn account

written consent

unauthorized overdraft

bounced cheque

electronic transaction

ATM withdrawal machine

proxy server

11.2 Listening

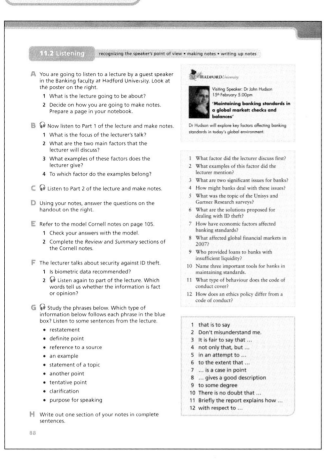

banking operations they have compromised bank security.

Ask students to say whether they think this is true or not. Elicit phrases they can use before the sentence to show how certain they are about their opinion.

Dictate or write on the board the following phrases. Ask students to say what the effect of each phrase is when put before the sentence on the board. In each case, does it make the writer sound confident or tentative?

> *The research shows that ...*
>
> *A survey found that ...*
>
> *The evidence does not support the idea that ...*
>
> *It appears to be the case that ...*
>
> *The evidence suggests that ...*
>
> *The evidence shows that ...*
>
> *It is clear that ...*
>
> *It is possible that ...*

2 Revise the Cornell note-taking system. Elicit the R words. Ask students to describe how to divide up the page (refer to Unit 9). Revise the other ways to take notes (see Units 1 and 3).

3 Revise note-taking symbols and abbreviations (see units 5 and 9, and Unit 9 extra activity 4).

General note

Read the *Skills bank*. Decide when, if at all, to refer students to it. The best time, as before, is probably at the very end of the lesson or the beginning of the next lesson, as a summary/revision.

Lesson aims

- recognize and understand phrases that identify the speaker's point of view
- convert notes into full sentences and paragraphs

  Further practice in:
- making notes (the use of headings systems and abbreviations)
- referring to sources
- general academic words and phrases

Introduction

1 Review phrases indicating a speaker's view of the truth value of a statement. Write a sentence like the following on the board (i.e., a 'fact' about which there may be differences of opinion):

While technological advances have revolutionized

Exercise A

Refer the students to the Hadford University lecture announcement. Tell them to look at the title and the summary of the talk.

Check that they know the meaning of 'checks and balances' (factors which may have a limiting or controlling effect on banking practice).

Set the exercises for pairwork discussion. Feed back with the whole class.

Answers

Possible answers:

1 Accept any reasonable suggestions.

2 The lecturer is clearly going to list causes and effects. This suggests that possibly a flowchart or spidergram might be a suitable form of notes (as in Unit 1), as well as the Cornell system (which is used here) or the more conventional numbered points system.

🎧 Exercise B

Play Part 1 once through *without* allowing students time to focus on the questions.

Put students in pairs to answer the questions by referring to their notes. Feed back with the whole class, building a set of notes on the board if you wish. If necessary, refer students back to the spidergam in Lesson 1 to remind them of the five factors relating to banking standards. Note that 4 is a general knowledge question – which students should be able to answer from their background knowledge.

Add the examples to your spidergram from Lesson 1 if you have not already done so.

Ask students which method they are going to use to make notes, having now listened to the introduction. They should now make any adjustments necessary to the page they have prepared in their notebooks.

Answers

Model answers:

1 the problems banks face in maintaining banking standards; the policies and procedures required to address these problems

2 technological and globalization

3 how to enforce compliance in different jurisdictions; dealing with a country whose business practices are dubious

4 globalization

Transcript 🎧 2.8

Part 1

Good morning. Today I'm going to focus on banking standards. That is to say, I shall be looking at some of the factors which may affect, or compromise, the way banks operate in their day-to-day banking, including some of the fraudulent behaviour banks have to deal with. Don't misunderstand me, I don't want to imply that banks, or their employees, commonly engage in fraudulent behaviour, but as we all know, banking scandals and crises are not uncommon.

To some degree, all banks today need to be aware of how their actions, anywhere in the world, affect and are perceived by their customers. It is fair to say that as a result of technological advances banking operations are more complex. Not only that, but globalization means banks need to be aware of the government policies of the country or countries with whom they operate. For example, how does a bank enforce compliance on a subsidiary in another jurisdiction? Should a bank handle funds from a country with dubious business practices when the origin of the funds is unclear? These questions and many more demonstrate the

complexity of situations banks face. So, in an attempt to keep this discussion of banking standards and responsibilities reasonably simple, I'm going to summarize a few of the more interesting problems banks may be exposed to, and will conclude briefly with the policies and procedures required for maintaining standards in the industry.

🎧 Exercise C

Before playing Part 2 of the recording, write the words *pharming*, *phishing* and *sub-prime mortgage* on the board. Review the meaning, pronunciation and spelling.

Play the whole of the rest of lecture through once without stopping. Students should make notes as they listen.

Answers

See Notes section of the table in Answers to Exercise E.

Transcript 🎧 2.9

Part 2

To start with, let's look at technological factors. Banking is an information-based industry involved in the collection and use of a wide variety of its clients' personal information, including bank account numbers and bank balances. Moreover, banks hold information on their clients' creditworthiness and banking history – for example, whether they have been issued with credit, debit or smart cards.

While information technology has revolutionized banking operations (increasing efficiency and providing new products and services, such as Internet banking), it has compromised bank security.

Computer hacking has become widespread and increasingly more sophisticated to the extent that Internet fraud, through phishing, pharming, and spyware, is now a major area of concern for banks. The process known as 'spear phishing' is a case in point. The bank customer may receive a personalized e-mail purporting to come from the bank, which tricks the account holder into divulging their online banking password and other personal and financial information. In other scams, such as Trojan horse or keylogger, spyware is planted onto personal computers to steal personal identity numbers and financial account credentials. In the case of pharming, the computer user is directed to fraudulent websites via proxy servers, even though the URL seen on the browser appears to be correct. (For those of you unfamiliar with these terms, webopedia.com gives a good description.)

It's quite clear that privacy and data protection continue to be significant issues for financial institutions. Because of the risks of fraud, many customers choose to only *view* their accounts online and refrain from carrying out online banking transactions. This is a problem for the banks, however, who want to encourage greater use of Internet banking. This means ultimately that the onus is on the banks to provide protection against Internet fraud. Client education programmes can, to some degree, raise customers' awareness of new forms of fraud, and of the need to notify their bank, as soon as they receive suspect e-mails. However, what banks really need is staff with the technical expertise to ensure that Internet access to their services is safe.

There is no doubt that fraud is a global concern. In 2005 Unisys conducted a survey into the increasing prevalence of online identity theft. At that time, 17% of US and 11% of UK consumers reported being a victim. In 2006 a Gartner Research survey found a 50% increase in ID theft victims compared to 2003. All the evidence shows that, as the acceptance of financial products such as credit cards grows, the risk of ID fraud also increases. What seems obvious is that banks (and their customers) have a responsibility for remaining vigilant and up to date with online security measures in order to protect themselves from Internet hackers. Some people claim that biometric data, such as iris scans and fingerprints, could provide the answer. However, it could be argued that this will not solve the problem, as the usefulness of biometrics depends on the quality (and therefore the cost) of the machine and the technology used.

Other people favour 'two-factor identification'. In addition to a password, confirmation by cell phone is required. Two-factor identification puts another step in the way of criminals. Meanwhile, the US Department of Justice is updating and improving current federal laws so that identity thieves are appropriately penalized for using malicious spyware and keyloggers; and so that threats to steal or corrupt data on a victim's computer become illegal.

So far, we have been discussing behaviour external to the banks. However, problems can also arise *within* banks.

Economic factors, such as the current trend of diversification within banking, have encouraged banks into non-traditional activities, like bancassurance and other fee-related business and

can lead to possible conflicts of interest. Within the banking industry, as Heffernan (2004, p.21) points out, 'conflict-of-interest issues continue to surface. Banks are accused of fraud for inflating prices on stock firms and initial public offerings (IPOs).'

Problems may also occur on an international scale. In this information age, new technology has extended the global 'reach' of many businesses. Consequently, events in one country impinge on others. For example, in 2007 a 'sub-prime' mortgage crisis, originating in the United States, affected global financial markets. American mortgage agents had received financial incentives to sell mortgages. As a result, vast numbers of mortgage loans were sold to low-income families with no assessment of their credit risk. The American banks sold these loans on to large investment banks who packaged these debts into bonds, sold largely to foreign investors. The originating banks were not overly concerned about the borrower's ability to repay because they were intending to sell the loans. Rising defaults by sub-prime American mortgage borrowers resulted in banks becoming nervous about getting their money back and being unwilling to lend to one another. In the US, Europe, Japan and England, central banks, as lenders of the last resort, provided short-term funds to banks with insufficient liquidity. It's quite clear that ethical questions need to be addressed regarding the originating banks' relaxation of standards and responsibility. Why were sub-prime loans granted to risky borrowers (many based on fraudulent loan applications) who subsequently defaulted?

Banks also need to continually reaffirm their standards in relation to how they manage their operations. It's quite clear that if the standards applied by banks fall, customer confidence is eroded. In March 2006, economic factors led to an investigation into work-related stress at the Bank of New Zealand. Briefly, the resulting report explains how lack of staff and the constant pressure to meet unrealistic sales targets by cross selling and selling to family and friends, were the main causes of staff stress. Setting sales targets or introducing 'pay for performance' may also compromise employees' compliance with stated banking standards.

There are three important tools that enable a bank to establish and maintain its standards: firstly, a code of conduct; secondly, clearly set out departmental operating procedures; and finally, a clearly communicated ethics policy.

A code of conduct provides all bank employees, from the executive team to the entry-level employees, with specific information about what is and is not acceptable business behaviour, with respect to receiving unsolicited gifts and benefits, waiver of fees, prior disclosure of possible conflicts of interest, and so on.

Departmental operating procedures provide the internal controls that ensure consistency and quality of bank performance by specifying step-by-step instructions on the procedures carried out by each department. For example, the operating procedures in a bank's loans department would specify the procedures to be followed by the bank loans officer in processing a loan.

Ethical behaviour is described by the International Dictionary of Banking and Finance (2000, p.137) as 'an action that conforms to the moral constraints of an industry or society ... Professional ethics restrict a number of undesirable practices that are not strictly illegal.' An ethics policy should express the bank's underlying values. The World Bank Code of Professional Ethics, in a publication entitled *Living Our Values* (1999) 'is intended to serve as a guide for staff and managers to use in day-to-day interactions and decision making'. The focus of an ethics policy is relationships within and outside the bank. This includes person-to-person relationships, workplace relationships, and the bank's relationship with the wider community. Many financial institutions have an ethics policy but few conduct 'ethics training', that is, training in dealing with unpredictable situations. Ethics education is not about teaching morality. It is about risk and risk management. It should also cover staff queries and matters arising from the code of conduct. The rules that inform banking practice are not static. The challenge for banks is to balance the business demands of profit-making with the need for good working relationships, both within the bank and with the wider community.

Now, I'm going to stop at this point. Does anybody have any questions?

Exercise D

Put students in pairs to answer the questions by referring to their notes. Feed back with the class to see how much they have been able to get from the lecture. If they can't answer something, do not supply the answer.

Answers

Model answers:

1 technological factors
2 Internet banking; Internet fraud: phishing, pharming and spyware
3 privacy and data protection
4 client education programmes; recruiting staff with the appropriate technological expertise
5 identity theft
6 biometrics, two-factor ID, legal measures
7 conflict-of-interest problems
8 US sub-prime mortgage crisis
9 central banks, as lender of last resort
10 a code of conduct; clearly set out departmental operating procedures; a clear ethics policy
11 specific information for all staff on appropriate behaviour, e.g., accepting unsolicited gifts
12 An ethics policy focuses on relationships both within the bank and with the wider community. It is about risk and risk management.

Note

Source references for lecture:

Bennett, H. (2006). *Stress risk assessment*. BNZ Finsec Members Summary Report

Clarke, J. (2000). *International dictionary of banking and finance*. London: Routledge

Heffernan, S. (2005). *Modern banking*. Chichester: John Wiley & Sons

World Bank. (1999). *Living our values*. Retrieved Oct 1, 2007 from http://go.worldbank.org/YV72RDGSW0

Exercise E

1 Set for individual work.

2 Set for individual work and pairwork checking.
  Feed back with the whole class.

Answers

Possible answer:

Review	Notes

Influence of technological factors …?	1 <u>Technological factors</u>
	a) information technology
	➜ revolutionized banking operations:
	   • efficiency
	   • new services, e.g., Internet banking
	➜ compromised bank security:
	   • Internet fraud (phishing, pharming, spyware)

Major concerns for banks …?	b) key issues: data protection and privacy ➜ client education ➜ staff with technical expertise

ID theft: research results …?
 	
Solutions …?
	c) ID theft
	   • Unisys research ➜ (2005) 17% US, 11% UK consumers = victims
	   • Gartner research ➜ ID theft (2003–6) ⬆ 50%
	Proposed solutions:
	   • biometrics – quality/ cost?
	   • 2-factor ID i.e., password + mobile phone confirmation
	   • US Dept. Justice ➜ appropriate penalties; computer fraud illegal

Other factors…?
 	
Other factors which affect banking …?
	2 <u>Other factors</u>
	   • economic ➜ conflicts of interest
	   • globalization: events in one country influence world markets, e.g., 2007 US sub-prime mortgage defaults ➜ central banks (US, Europe, Japan, England) = lenders of last resort to banks with insufficient liquidity
	   • bad practice: BNZ (2006) ➜ unrealistic sales targets ➜ employee stress ➜ ? non-compliance with banking standards

3 tools for maintaining standards …	<u>How to maintain banking standards?</u>
	   • code of conduct ➜ specific info on acceptable business behaviour
	   • departmental procedures ➜ specific step-by-step instructions
	   • ethics policy ➜ expresses bank's underlying values
	   See World Bank Code of Ethics
	     ◦ unpredictable situations in day-to-day operations
	     ◦ relationships ➜ person to person, workplace, bank's relationship with outside community

Summary: Technological factors have revolutionized banking operations, but compromised security. Internet fraud is increasing, requiring banks to find ways of making Internet banking secure. Globalization and other factors also put pressure on banking standards. Three important tools to maintain standards: code of conduct, clear operating procedures, and ethics policy.

🎧 Exercise F

1 Discuss question 1 with the whole class. Ask them if they can remember any phrases which signal whether the comments are true or just opinion.

2 Play the extract. Ask students to tell you to stop the recording when they hear key phrases. Write the phrases on the board.

Remind the students that it is important to recognize when someone is giving only their opinion, which others might well disagree with.

Answers

Model answers:

1 The lecturer expresses reservations about the effectiveness of biometrics, because of the quality of the technology that may be used.

2

There is no doubt that (fraud is a global concern).	This phrase is used by the speaker when giving a strong opinion.
All the evidence shows that (... risk of ID fraud also increases).	This phrase is used to support strongly the speaker's opinion.
What seems obvious is that (banks ... have a responsibility for remaining vigilant ...)	This is clearly the lecturer's opinion, but there is an assumption that it is shared by the listeners.
Some people claim that (biometric data ... could provide the answer).	This phrase can be used to give both a speaker's own opinion as well as an opposing view.
However, it could be argued that (this will not solve the problem).	This phrase is used to introduce a counter argument.

Transcript 🎧 2.10

There is no doubt that fraud is a global concern. In 2005 Unisys conducted a survey into the increasing prevalence of online identity theft. At that time, 17% of US and 11% of UK consumers reported being a victim. In 2006 a Gartner Research survey found a 50% increase in ID theft victims compared with 2003. All the evidence shows that, as the acceptance of financial products such as credit cards grows, the risk of ID fraud also increases. What seems obvious is that banks (and their customers) have a responsibility for remaining vigilant and up to date with online security measures in order to protect themselves from Internet hackers. Some people claim that biometric data, such as iris scans and fingerprints, could provide the answer. However, it could be argued that this will not solve the problem, as the usefulness of biometrics depends on the quality (and therefore the cost) of the machine and the technology used. Other people favour 'two-factor identification'. In addition to a password, confirmation by mobile phone is required. Two-factor identification puts another step in the way of criminals.

🎧 Exercise G

Allow students time to read the phrases and the types of information, making sure that they understand any difficult words. Remind students that 'type' of information tells you what the speaker intends to do with the words. The words themselves are something different.

Ask students to try to match the phrases and types of information as far as they can. Note that it is not always possible to say what the function of a phrase is outside its context, so they may not be able to match all the phrases and information types before hearing the sentences. Note that some types of information are needed more than once.

When the students have done as much as they can, play the sentences one at a time allowing time for them to identify the type of information which follows. Check answers after each sentence, making sure that students understand the information that actually follows the phrase. If possible students should also give the actual words.

Answers

Model answers:

Fixed phrase	Type of information which follows the phrase
that is to say	restatement
Don't misunderstand me.	clarification
To some degree,	tentative point
It is fair to say that …	tentative point
not only that, but …	another point
in an attempt to …	purpose for speaking
to the extent that …	clarification
with respect to …	statement of a topic
… is a case in point	an example
… gives a good description	reference to a source
Briefly, the report explains how …	reference to a source
There is no doubt that …	definite point

Transcript 🎧 2.11

Extract 1

Good morning. Today I'm going to focus on banking standards. That is to say, I shall be looking at some of the factors which may affect, or compromise, the way banks operate in their day-to-day banking, including some of the fraudulent behaviour banks have to deal with.

Extract 2

Don't misunderstand me, I don't want to imply that banks, or their employees, commonly engage in fraudulent behaviour, but as we all know, banking scandals and crises are not uncommon.

Extract 3

It is fair to say that as a result of technological advancements banking operations are more complex.

Extract 4

Not only that, but globalization means banks need to be aware of the government policies of the country or countries with whom they operate.

Extract 5

So, in an attempt to keep this discussion of banking standards and responsibilities reasonably simple, I'm going to summarize a few of the more interesting problems banks may be exposed to …

Extract 6

Computer hacking has become widespread and increasingly more sophisticated to the extent that Internet fraud, through phishing, pharming, and spyware, is now a major area of concern for banks.

Extract 7

The process known as 'spear phishing' is a case in point.

Extract 8

For those of you unfamiliar with these terms, webopedia.com gives a good description.

Extract 9

Client education programmes can, to some degree, raise customers' awareness of new forms of fraud, and of the need to notify their bank, as soon as they receive suspect e-mails.

Extract 10

There is no doubt that fraud is a global concern.

Extract 11

Briefly, the resulting report explains how lack of staff and the constant pressure to meet unrealistic sales targets, by cross selling and selling to family and friends, were the main causes of staff stress.

Extract 12

A code of conduct provides all bank employees, from the executive team to the entry-level employees, with specific information about what is and is not acceptable business behaviour, with respect to receiving unsolicited gifts and benefits, waiver of fees, prior disclosure of possible conflicts of interest, and so on.

Exercise H

Use this section from the Cornell notes to demonstrate what to do:

Notes

1 Technological factors:

  a) information technology

- revolutionized banking operations: efficiency
new services, e.g., Internet banking
- compromised bank security:
Internet fraud (phishing, pharming, spyware)

b) key issues: data protection and privacy

- client education
- staff with technical expertise

Elicit from students suggestions on how to write up the notes in complete sentences. Write the suggestions on the board.

Ask students to say what they need to add in to the notes to make a good piece of writing, e.g.,

Grammar: relative pronouns, articles and determiners, prepositions, auxiliary verbs, linking words, 'there was/were' clauses (in italics below).

Vocabulary: some vocabulary may need to be added, particularly where symbols are used in the notes, or where extra words are needed to make sense of the information or give a good sense of flow in the writing (in bold below).

Note that this, of course, works the other way: when making notes, these elements can be excluded from the notes.

Possible rewrite of the Notes:

Information technology *has* revolutionized banking operations, *for example*, *by* **increasing** efficiency, *and* **providing** new services, *such as* Internet banking. *It has also* compromised bank security, *especially in the* **area** of Internet fraud (*with the* **growth** *of* **scams**, *such as* phishing, pharming *and* spyware).

Two key issues *for* **banks continue** *to be* data protection and privacy. *These can be* **dealt with** *by* educating clients *about the* **dangers**, *and by* **hiring** staff with *the* technical expertise *to* **maintain security**.

Set another section for individual writing in class or for homework. Either ask students to refer to their own notes, or to the Cornell notes on page 105 in the Course Book.

Closure

1 Tell students to review and make a list of the main topics and arguments presented in this lesson. Then ask them to summarize the viewpoints, using some of the language they have practised.

2 They could also give a two- or three-sentence summary of anything that they themselves have read, e.g., *I read a useful article on X by Y. It said that* …

3 Ask students to do some research and to make a list of useful or interesting books/articles/websites on the topics in this lesson. They should draw up a list, including correct referencing, and share their sources with other students.

11.3 Extending skills

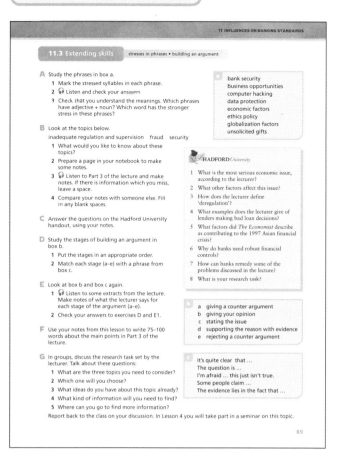

Lesson aims

- recognize stress patterns in noun phrases
- understand how to develop an argument:

  stating the issue

  giving a counter argument

  rejecting a counter argument

  giving opinions

  supporting opinions
- understand more general academic words and phrases mainly used in speaking

Further practice in:

- expressing degrees of confidence/ tentativeness
- reporting back

Introduction

1 Revise the lecture in Lesson 2. Ask students to use the model Cornell notes. They should cover up the notes section and use the review and summary sections (which they completed in Lesson 2) to help recall the contents of the lecture. They could work in pairs to do this.

2 Revise phrases which express degrees of confidence in 'facts'. Dictate these phrases. Do they show that the speaker is certain or doubtful or tentative?

> *There is no question that* (= certain)
>
> *We have to accept the evidence* (= certain)
>
> *Some people claim that* (= doubtful)
>
> *What seems obvious is that* (= certain)
>
> *As everyone is aware* (= certain)
>
> *To some degree* (= tentative)
>
> *This means ultimately that* (= certain)
>
> *It's quite clear that* (= certain)
>
> *We could argue that* (= tentative)

🎧 Exercise A

1/2 Set for individual work and pairwork checking. This is an exercise in perceiving rhythm. At this point there is no need to distinguish between different levels of stress. Students can underline all the stressed syllables. They will also need to count all the syllables.

Feed back with the whole class, checking pronunciation of the phrases and meanings.

3 Discuss this with the class first. Demonstrate with ,bank 'security showing how if you say 'bank ,security, it appears that a contrast is being made with another type of security. Tell students that the usual pattern for a noun + noun phrase is for the heavier stress to go on the second noun. Eco'nomic ,factors is, however, different: it is a compound made from an adjective + noun, and the heavier stress goes on the first noun.

Set students to pick out the other phrases made from an adjective + noun. Elicit the stress patterns and give students time to practise the phrases.

Note that 'ethics ,policy and globali'zation ,factors are exceptions. In these noun + noun compounds, the first word is used to differentiate from other factors or policies.

Answers

Model answers:

1/2 ,bank se'curity

,business oppor'tunities

com,puter 'hacking

,data pro'tection

eco'nomic ,factors

'ethics ,policy

globali'zation ,factors

'unsolicited ,gifts

3 unsolicited gifts, economic factors; the heavier stress falls on the first word.

Transcript 🎧 2.12

,bank se'curity

,business oppor'tunities

com,puter 'hacking

,data pro'tection

eco'nomic ,factors

'ethics ,policy

globali'zation ,factors

'unsolicited ,gifts

🎧 Exercise B

1 Look at the topics. Discuss with the class what they know already about these topics and find out what opinions they may have. Put students in pairs and ask each pair to write down one question to which they would like an answer in the lecture.

2 Set for individual work.

3 Play Part 3 straight through; students make notes.

4 Put students in pairs to compare their notes and fill in any gaps they may have.

Transcript 🎧 2.13

Part 3

Turning now to the effect of economic factors on banking standards … Of course, a major concern is the development of new and changing financial instruments. This is partly a result of technological and globalization factors, and partly a result of deregulation of the banking industry. Deregulation means a reduction of government controls, therefore we have to accept that banks must determine their *own* risk profile. But the question is: are banks capable of regulating themselves?

Some people claim that the current system has sufficient checks and balances. I'm afraid, however, that examples of lenders from around the world taking very little responsibility for their lending decisions suggest that this just isn't true. For example, those involved in the finance chain of the US sub-prime mortgages, from mortgage broker to investment bank, focused too much on the business opportunities. They didn't consider the consequences of mortgagees defaulting on their loans.

There are other examples from different parts of the world. On December 9, 2003, the *Jakarta Post* published a report on fraud, involving US$200 million, in export loans to a number of local companies by the state-owned BNI , Indonesia's second largest bank. The bank had failed to conduct proper credit appraisals before providing export loans to several local businessmen who used, as collateral, letters of credit guaranteed by banks in foreign countries, including Kenya. They claimed to be exporting commodities to Africa but I'm afraid that just wasn't true.

In another example, an article in *The Economist*, June 30, 2007, on the causes of the Asian financial crisis of 1997 identified feeble regulation and supervision, alarming mismatches between assets and liabilities, wasteful investment, inadequate bank regulation, and corruption as contributing factors. An audit by PricewaterhouseCoopers into Bank Bali at the time, uncovered 'numerous' indications of fraud. Key government officials (including the finance minister, and the central bank governor) were implicated. Bribery, in the form of unsolicited gifts and kickbacks to senior bank officials who approved loans, was commonplace at the time.

It's quite clear that all financial institutions, and banks in particular, need robust financial controls – especially when a significant amount of business activity is located in another jurisdiction. Some of the responsibility, for example, for the fraudulent use of Barings Bank's money by rogue trader, Nick Leeson, lies in the fact that the bank's London-based executives did not have controls in place to monitor the activities in their Singapore office. If banks don't take responsibility for what is happening and do something about it, governments will step in. The evidence for this lies in the fact that the Sarbanes-Oxley Act was rushed into US law in 2002, after the large bankruptcies of Enron (in which nine US banks were implicated) and WorldCom.

Unless they want to be subject to tighter government regulation, banks need to develop initiatives which appeal to their consumers' need for security, yet don't compromise the banks' profit-making objective. It is argued that banks have a moral responsibility to ensure that their clients' personal details and financial affairs are secure and that active controls are in place to provide total data protection from, for example, computer hacking. Continual advances in technology, particularly computer technology, mean this is an ongoing concern. Banks need to invest in highly skilled personnel whose job is to keep themselves up to date with the latest technology and threats to bank security. Many of these bank IT employees are relatively young technical people, yet the nature of their work will provide them with access to the personal and financial data of bank clients. It is therefore important that a comprehensive ethics policy and high banking standards are in place to guide these employees in the disclosure of this client data.

Now, I'm going to set you a task which will involve investigating some of the points I've raised. I want you to do some research into one of the following three topics which affect banking standards, namely, inadequate regulation and supervision; fraud and security problems; and deregulation. For your chosen topic, I would like you to identify causes and consequences. Secondly, I'd like you to suggest some solutions – in other words, what banking needs to think about to improve its standards. So, to repeat, your task is to identify the causes and consequences, and to suggest solutions.

Exercise C

Set for individual work and pairwork checking. Feed back with the class on question 6 to make sure that it is clear.

Answers

Model answers:

1 the development of new and changing financial instruments

2 technological, globalization, political (deregulation)

3 a reduction of government controls

4 sub-prime mortgages, US; BNI bank's export loans, Indonesia; fraud and bribery at Bank Bali

5 feeble regulation and supervision; mismatch between assets and liabilities; wasteful investment; inadequate bank regulations; corruption

6 to prevent fraudulent activity, especially in operations located in foreign jurisdictions

7 implement robust financial controls; improve security, particularly Internet security; provide total security of all data; invest in IT personnel knowledgeable in the latest technology and bank security threats; establish a comprehensive ethics policy and high banking standards to guide employees

8 to choose one topic from: inadequate regulation and supervision; fraud and security problems; and deregulation; then to identify causes and consequences, and suggest what banking needs to think about to improve its standards

Exercise D

1 Set for pairwork discussion. Explain that a 'counter argument' means an opinion which you do not agree with or think is wrong. 'Issue' means a question about which there is some debate.

2 Set for individual work and pairwork checking.

Do not feed back with the class at this point but move on to Exercise E.

🎧 Exercise E

1 Play the extract. Tell students to stop you when they hear each phrase from box c. Make sure students can say exactly what the words are in each case. Ask them also to paraphrase the words so that it is clear that they understand the meanings.

2 If necessary play the extract again for students to check that they have the phrases and types of statement correct.

Answers

Exercises D and E model answers:

See table below.

Type of statement	Phrase	Lecturer's words
c stating the issue	The question is …	*The question is:* are banks capable of regulating themselves?
a giving a counter argument	Some people claim …	*Some people claim* that the current system has sufficient checks and balances.
e rejecting a counter argument	I'm afraid … this just isn't true.	*I'm afraid*, however, that examples of lenders from around the world taking very little responsibility for their lending decisions suggest that *this just isn't true*.
b giving your opinion	It's quite clear that …	*It's quite clear that* all financial institutions, and banks in particular, need robust financial controls.
d supporting the reason with evidence	The evidence lies in the fact that…	*The evidence lies in the fact that* the Sarbanes-Oxley Act was rushed into US law in 2002 …

Transcript 🎧 2.14

But the question is: are banks capable of regulating themselves? Some people claim that the current system has sufficient checks and balances. I'm afraid, however, that examples of lenders from around the world taking very little responsibility for their lending decisions suggest that this just isn't true.

It's quite clear that all financial institutions, and banks in particular, need robust financial controls. The evidence lies in the fact that the Sarbanes-Oxley Act was rushed into US law in 2002, after the large bankruptcies of Enron (in which nine US banks were implicated) and WorldCom.

Exercise F

Set for individual work – possibly homework – or else a pair/small group writing task. If the latter, get students to put their writing on an OHT or other visual medium, so that the whole class can look and comment on what has been written. You can correct language errors on the OHT.

Exercise G

Set students to work in groups of three or four. Make sure they understand that they should choose to focus on one of the three topics: inadequate regulation and supervision; fraud and security problems; deregulation. Allow each group to choose their topic. Make sure that each topic is covered by at least one, preferably two groups. Ask one person from each group to present the results of the group's discussion.

Tell the class that they should carry out research into their group's topic. You will also need to arrange the date for the feedback and discussion of the information – this is the focus of Exercise G in Lesson 4.

Closure

Arguments, counter arguments and giving opinions

Before you ask students to look at the statements below, tell them they should think about the methods seen above to present an argument and/or a counter argument, and to give an opinion. Then ask them to think about whether they agree with the statements below. They should prepare a brief summary of their viewpoints on the topics; they should also try and use some of the phrases used in this lesson:

1 A major concern is the development of new and changing financial instruments.
2 The current system is one in which lenders take very little responsibility for their lending decisions.
3 All banks need robust financial controls.
4 Governments will step in if banks don't take responsibility for what happens in their industry.

11.4 Extending skills

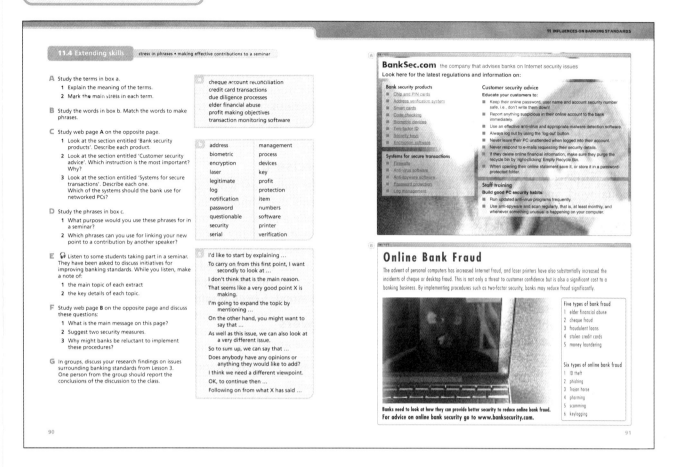

11.4 Extending skills stress in phrases • making effective contributions to a seminar

A Study the terms in box a.
1 Explain the meaning of the terms.
2 Mark the main stress in each term.

B Study the words in box b. Match the words to make phrases.

C Study web page **A** on the opposite page.
1 Look at the section entitled 'Bank security products'. Describe each product.
2 Look at the section entitled 'Customer security advice'. Which instruction is the most important? Why?
3 Look at the section entitled 'Systems for secure transactions'. Describe each one.
Which of the systems should the bank use for networked PCs?

D Study the phrases in box c.
1 What purpose would you use these phrases for in a seminar?
2 Which phrases can you use for linking your new point to a contribution by another speaker?

E Listen to some students taking part in a seminar. They have been asked to discuss initiatives for improving banking standards. While you listen, make a note of:
1 the main topic of each extract
2 the key details of each topic.

F Study web page **B** on the opposite page and discuss these questions:
1 What is the main message on this page?
2 Suggest two security measures.
3 Why might banks be reluctant to implement these procedures?

G In groups, discuss your research findings on issues surrounding banking standards from Lesson 3. One person from the group should report the conclusions of the discussion to the class.

Box a:
cheque account reconciliation
credit card transactions
due diligence processes
elder financial abuse
profit making objectives
transaction monitoring software

Box b:
address	management
biometric	process
encryption	devices
laser	key
legitimate	profit
log	protection
notification	item
password	numbers
questionable	software
security	printer
serial	verification

Box c:
I'd like to start by explaining …
To carry on from this first point, I want secondly to look at …
I don't think that is the main reason.
That seems like a very good point X is making.
I'm going to expand the topic by mentioning …
On the other hand, you might want to say that …
As well as this issue, we can also look at a very different issue.
So to sum up, we can say that …
Does anybody have any opinions or anything they would like to add?
I think we need a different viewpoint.
OK, to continue then …
Following on from what X has said …

BankSec.com the company that advises banks on Internet security issues
Look here for the latest regulations and information on:

Bank security products
■ Chip and PIN cards
■ Address verification system
■ Smart cards
■ Code checking
■ Biometric devices
■ Two-factor ID
■ Security keys
■ Encryption software

Systems for secure transactions
■ Firewalls
■ Anti-virus software
■ Anti-spyware software
■ Password protection
■ Log management

Customer security advice
Educate your customers to:
■ Keep their online password, user name and account security number safe, i.e., don't write them down!
■ Report anything suspicious in their online account to the bank immediately.
■ Use an effective anti-virus and appropriate malware detection software.
■ Always log out by using the 'log out' button.
■ Never leave their PC unattended when logged into their account.
■ Never respond to e-mails requesting their security details.
■ When you delete online financial information, make sure they purge the recycle bin by 'right-clicking' Empty Recycle Bin.
■ When opening their online statement save it, or store it in a password-protected folder.

Staff training
Build good PC security habits:
■ Run updated anti-virus programs frequently.
■ Use anti-spyware and scan regularly, that is, at least monthly, and whenever something unusual is happening on your computer.

Online Bank Fraud

The advent of personal computers has increased Internet fraud, and laser printers have also substantially increased the incidents of cheque or desktop fraud. This is not only a threat to customer confidence but is also a significant cost to a banking business. By implementing procedures such as two-factor security, banks may reduce fraud significantly.

Five types of bank fraud
1 elder financial abuse
2 cheque fraud
3 fraudulent loans
4 stolen credit cards
5 money laundering

Six types of online bank fraud
1 ID theft
2 phishing
3 Trojan horse
4 pharming
5 scamming
6 keylogging

Banks need to look at how they can provide better security to reduce online bank fraud.
For advice on online bank security go to www.banksecurity.com.

90

91

Lesson aims

- recognize stress in compound phrases
- link your contribution to previous contributions when speaking in a seminar
- understand vocabulary in the area of environmental issues

Further practice in:
- taking part in seminars:
  introducing, maintaining and concluding a contribution
  agreeing/disagreeing with other speakers

Introduction

1 Remind students that they are going to be presenting their research findings later in this lesson. Check that they can remember the main points from Lesson 3 lecture extracts; key phrases from the lecture could be used as prompts, e.g.,

Some lenders take very little responsibility for their lending decisions (i.e., should they be made more accountable?)

The question is: are banks capable of regulating themselves? (How are banks going to manage these problems?)

Many bank IT employees are relatively young. (Do they have the necessary experience, maturity and ethics given their responsibilities?)

2 The following activity is a good way to check that students are familiar with the terminology and vocabulary from Lesson 3. Ask students to write down five to ten words or expressions from the previous lesson relating to bank security. Then use two or three students as 'secretaries'. Ask the class to dictate the words so that the secretaries can write the vocabulary on the board. Use this as a brainstorming session.

	Main topic	Key details
Extract 1	cheque fraud	impact of new technologies, e.g., laser printer methods for preventing cheque fraud, e.g., policy on stop payments, timely account reconciliations, updated staff training
Extract 2	'know your customer' controls	transaction monitoring software due diligence for unusual activity
Extract 3	ethics and integrity	clear leadership from senior management clearly communicated ethics policy ethics training for all staff
Extract 4	elder financial abuse	unexplained transactions and suspicious activity in elderly people's accounts staff training to recognize and report signs of such abuse

🎧 Exercise E

Before the students listen, tell them to read the instructions. Check that students understand the topic for the seminar discussion. Ask them what they might expect to hear.

Play each extract one at a time and ask students to identify the main topic and also the key points for each topic.

Feed back with the whole class.

Answers

Model answers:

See table above.

Transcript 🎧 2.15

Extract 1

MAJED: The lecturer we listened to last week introduced a number of interesting issues. In my part of the seminar, I would like to build on what he said about the impact of new technologies and talk specifically about cheque fraud. The advent of personal computers and PC-driven laser printers that can replicate documents with high resolutions has contributed significantly to a rise in cheque fraud. It's obvious that there's a lot the bank can do to prevent cheque fraud. For example, they should have a very clear policy on the duration and placement of stop payments. Performing cheque account reconciliations quickly may lead to early detection of fraudulent or questionable items. The reconciliation policies must include information on how to handle duplicate serial numbers, and on checking for numbers that are too short, too long, or in an unusual range, colour or size. The policy needs to clearly specify the notification process, if a suspect item is found, and the time in which it is to be dealt with. Time may be critical in achieving a satisfactory outcome. For the banks, the benefits of continuously updating the training of their cheque reconciliation staff, as well as having sufficient trained staff to deal with the volume of cheque fraud, will far outweigh the costs.

Extract 2

EVIE: That seems like a very good point Majed is making. What I'd like to discuss is one important initiative for dealing with the opening of new accounts and the monitoring of existing ones. To hopefully avoid fraud losses and prevent money laundering, and to counter terrorism financing, bank staff should receive training in 'know your customer' (KYC) procedures. A key aspect of KYC controls is monitoring a customer's transactions against their recorded profile and the history of their accounts. For this task, banks increasingly use specialized transaction monitoring software, particularly names-analysis software and trend-monitoring software. If unusual activity is identified, then due diligence processes, using all sources of information on the subject, including the Internet, are utilized to determine whether a transaction or activity is suspicious and should be reported to the authorities. Does anybody have any opinions or anything they would like to add?

Extract 3

JACK: Right. Thank you, Evie. I'm going to expand the topic by mentioning ethics and integrity. Because bank employees are exposed to significant sums of money, some are tempted into fraudulent behaviour. The research indicates, however, that it is the perceived examples from the bank's chief executives – that is, overt or covert messages regarding their work standards and ethics – that have the most influence on bank staff behaviour. Clearly then, the ethics policy must be communicated from the top of the organization downwards. Managers and departmental heads responsible for implementing the policies could attend ethical leadership courses. However, sometimes the message may be confusing. Let me try and make this clearer with an example. For instance, in February 2007 the *Wall Street Journal* reported that Bank of America was offering credit cards to illegal immigrants. While the bank argued that it was doing nothing illegal, critics said that they should not be helping people who violated the country's immigration laws, and that the bank was only concerned about getting the business of an untapped market of 10 to 20 million illegal immigrants. The question is: while the bank may have acted within the law, are its actions ethical? So to sum up, I would like to point out that it takes years to build a reputation and minutes to ruin it. Ethics is not a luxury but a necessity.

Extract 4

LEILA: Well, I'm going to explain about detecting elder financial abuse, in the context of banking. I feel that this needs addressing as the population ages. Basically, it's financial abuse committed against people 65 years old and over. In the US, states have passed legislation requiring bank employees to report suspected cases of elder financial abuse. Some of the features of this phenomenon include: sudden changes in an elder person's bank accounts, or practices; uncharacteristic or unexplained withdrawals of large sums of money by an elder or someone representing them; large credit card transactions or cheques written to unusual recipients. Other examples may include large transfers of funds to a family member or acquaintance without reasonable explanation, new signatories to an elder person's account, or newly formed joint accounts with another person. Staff should also look for elderly people who appear nervous when accompanied by another person, or appear to be bullied, or give incoherent explanations for a withdrawal. Elderly people who appear confused about increases in credit card transactions, or about bank fees that have been incurred are possibly victims. Suspicion should be raised about signatures that look to be forged on financial transactions and applications for new items, for example, credit cards. It is in the bank's interest to take a proactive role by training their employees to recognize and report this. It also gives a positive message to the growing number of elderly customers. In my view, banks have a capacity to provide services to the community while making a legitimate profit.

Exercise F

1/2 Set for pairwork. Tell students to study the Online Bank Fraud web page (B). Feed back with the whole class. Make sure students understand the terminology in the web page.

3 Set for small group discussion. Feed back with the whole class. Accept all reasonable responses.

Answers

Possible answers:

1 Banks need to provide better security against online fraud.

2 Two-factor authentification, 'know your customer' procedures, password protection, encryption software, quick identification of financial irregularities.

3 They can be expensive for banks to implement and inconvenient for customers (e.g., carrying tokens). They require staff to have appropriate skills and frequent training to update those skills.

Exercise G

In their groups students should now present their research findings on the topic they chose from Lesson 3: inadequate regulation and supervision; fraud and security problems; deregulation. Remind them that the task was to:

● identify causes and consequences
● suggest some solutions, i.e., how banking might improve its standards

Encourage students to use the seminar language practised in this unit and earlier units. In addition, students can, of course, make use of the information in Lesson 4.

As a group students should try to come to an overall conclusion. This conclusion should be presented to the rest of the class, together with supporting evidence from students' own research.

Closure

1 Ask students to do an Internet search for products and systems to add to the BankSec web page. Students should report back to the class explaining their findings.

2 Ask students to listen again to the seminar presentations in Exercise E and discuss these questions:

Did the presenters meet the seminar objectives? If not, why not?

Which presentation was the best? Why?

Answers

Possible answers:

issue and cause	consequences	solutions
inadequate regulation and supervision *cause*: failure to implement or comply with appropriate policies and procedures	● poor lending practices ● weak corporate governance ● lack of transparency for depositors ● weak risk assessment ● complicated new product structures	● central bank supervisory role ● compliance ● higher transparency of bank policies and practices
fraud and security problems *cause*: the rapid increase in information technology, and the ability of highly skilled hackers to penetrate bank systems	● customer data not secure ● threat to customer confidence ● wide range of different technical security 'solutions' ● growing knowledge gap between older executives and young employees with technology expertise ● customers with inadequate knowledge of IT security	● improving the current technology ● increasing industry-specific security hardware and software ● adopting worldwide standards and procedures for risk management ● ensuring worldwide availability of standardized products and services ● ensuring speedy customer-data delivery services ● independent auditing overview of all technology changes
deregulation *cause*: political decision to reduce government controls	● increasing competition ● focus on global expansion ● new financial instruments ● diversification in service providers, e.g., supermarkets providing credit cards ● investment in more technology to increase competitive edge	● sustainable investments ● strong central bank with responsibility for oversight and standard setting ● bank directors held responsible for adequate internal controls ● oversight committee to perform risk assessment of all significant investment and products

Extra activities

1 Work through the *Vocabulary bank* and *Skills bank* if you have not already done so, or as revision of previous study.

2 Use the *Activity bank* (Teacher's Book additional resources section, Resource 11A).

A Set for individual work (including homework) or pairwork. Check students understand meanings.

Answers

client	education
laser	printer
log	management
money	laundering
online	security
proxy	server
serial	numbers
Trojan	horse

B Set the wordsearch for individual work (including homework) or pairwork.

Answers

Possibe two-word phrases are:

account reconciliation

biometric data

bounced cheque

computer hacking

due diligence

encryption software

financial ombudsman

ID theft

smart card

sub-prime mortgage

3 Use Resource 11B, in Teacher's Book additional resources section, to provide students with further practice of some of the concepts they have studied in this unit.

Set for individual work or pairwork. Feed back with whole class.

Answers

computer hacking	10	modifying a program, often in an unauthorized manner, by changing the code itself
conflict of interest	13	a situation where an opportunity for private benefit clashes with a person's (or organization's) public responsibilities
data compromise	9	when unauthorized user gains access to private information
fraudulent site	7	false location on the world wide web
keylogger	5	surveillance software which records every keystroke to allow information to be transmitted to an unknown third party
pharming	2	infusing false information into a server so that users are directed to a fraudulent site
phishing	1	sending an e-mail that falsely claims to be from a legitimate source, to obtain private information for use in identity theft
proxy server	6	web server that intercepts all requests to the real server
scamming	8	stealing information from a computer
spyware	3	software that gathers information (e.g., e-mail addresses, passwords, credit card numbers) by monitoring user activity on the Internet
sub-prime mortgage	12	loan made to someone with poor credit record, which attracts very high interest rates
Trojan horse	4	product unwittingly installed when the user installs something else
unsolicited gifts	11	presents which the recipient has not requested and may not be for legitimate business reasons

12 BANKING GOVERNANCE

This unit provides an opportunity for revision of many of the concepts and vocabulary items used in the book. It explores the issues of banking governance and looks at some of the measures that banks need to put in place in order to meet compliance standards. The reading text in Lesson 2 looks at a case study of a bank which failed to enforce its compliance procedures.

Skills focus

Reading
- understanding how ideas in a text are linked

Writing
- deciding whether to use direct quotation or paraphrase
- incorporating quotations
- writing research reports
- writing effective introductions/conclusions

Vocabulary focus

- verbs used to introduce ideas from other sources (*X contends/suggests/asserts that ...*)
- linking words/phrases conveying contrast (*whereas*), result (*consequently*), reasons (*due to*), etc.
- words for quantities (*a significant minority*)

Key vocabulary

accountability	governance	procedure
compliance	implicit	proliferation
control	integrity	provision
dysfunction	norms	regulatory
explicit	observance	supervisory
fiduciary	proactive	transparency

12.1 Vocabulary

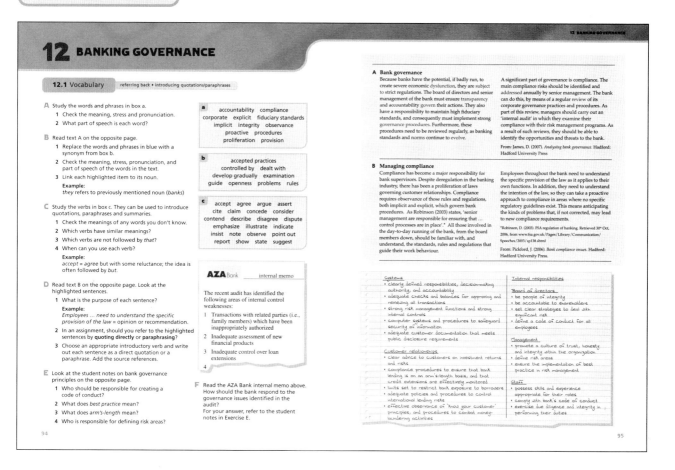

Read the *Vocabulary bank* at the end of the Course Book unit. Decide when, if at all, to refer your students to it. The best time is probably at the very end of the lesson or the beginning of the next lesson, as a summary/revision.

Lesson aims

- understand deictic reference – pronouns and determiners
- refer to sources: the choice of introductory verb and stance of writer towards reference
- choose whether to quote or paraphrase

Further practice in:

- words and phrases from banking

Introduction

1   Revise the following words and phrases from the two previous units. Ask students to say which grammar class the words belong to and to provide definitions of them.

    overheads (n, pl) (US, overhead)

    consent (n, U)

    evaluate (v, T)

    ombudsman (n, C)

    inadequate (adj)

    equity (n, C/U)

    subsequent (adj)

    finance (n, C/U); (v, T)

    loan (n, C); (v, T)

    impact (v, T)

    ethics (n, C)

2   Introduce the topic of the unit: write the words *governance* and *controls* on the board. Ask students what they signify for banking. *What factors do banks need to take into consideration in their daily activities? What processes do they need to go through when they are thinking about new products and cross-border banking?*

Have a class discussion on the non-commercial factors bank directors and management need to consider in operating a successful bank. Accept any reasonable suggestions. Do not elaborate, but tell students that this will be the topic of this unit.

Exercise A

1/2 Ask students to mark the most strongly stressed syllable in compounds.

Feed back with the whole class, checking meanings.

Answers

Model answers:

Word (part of speech)	Meaning
accounta'bility (n, U)	responsibility
com'pliance (n, U)	agreement, obedience
'corporate (adj)	relating to a big company
ex'plicit (adj)	clear, exact
fi'duciary standards (n, pl)	trustworthiness with other people's money
im'plicit (adj)	suggested
in'tegrity (n, U)	moral principles
ob'servance (n, U)	obedience
pro'active (adj)	taking action without being asked
pro'cedures (n, C/U)	set of agreed actions
prolifer'ation (n, U)	large increase, growth
pro'vision (n, C)	requirement

Exercise B

Introduce the idea of textual cohesion, created by referring back to words or ideas already mentioned with pronouns such as *it* and *this* (pronouns and determiners). Say that this is an important way in which the sentences in a text are 'held together'. In reading and understanding it is important to know what is being referred to by such words.

You can build up the answers to question 3 by copying Resource 12B in the additional resources section onto an OHT or other visual medium.

1/2 Set for individual work and pairwork checking. Feed back with the whole class.

3 Set for individual work. Ask students to list the referring words and try to decide why each is used. Feed back, building the table shown opposite, top.

Answers

Model answers:

1/2

Word (part of speech)	Synonym
dys'function (n, U)	problems
'subject to (adj)	controlled by
tran'sparency (n, U)	openness
'govern (v, T)	guide
'governance procedures (n, pl)	rules
norms (n, pl)	accepted practices
e'volve (v, T)	develop gradually
a'ddressed (v, T)	dealt with
re'view (n, C)	examination

3

Bank governance

Because banks have the potential, if badly run, to create severe economic dysfunction, they are subject to strict regulations. The Board of Directors and senior management of the bank must ensure transparency and accountability govern their actions. They also have a responsibility to maintain high fiduciary standards, and consequently must implement strong governance procedures. Furthermore, these procedures need to be reviewed regularly, as banking standards and norms continue to evolve.

A significant part of governance is compliance. The main compliance risks should be identified and addressed annually by senior management. The bank can do this, by means of a regular review of its corporate governance practices and procedures. As part of this review, managers should carry out an internal audit in which they examine their compliance with their risk management programs. As a result of such reviews, they should be able to identify the opportunities and threats to the bank.

Language note

This is a complex area of written language. The reference words here are commonly found and arguably students should be able to use them in their writing. There are, of course, various other ways to refer back to a word or idea, such as when comparing: *the former … the latter …*; *some … others …* . For more information, see a good grammar reference book.

Exercise C

1–3 Set for individual work or pairwork. Feed back. Discuss any differences of opinion in question 2 and allow alternative groupings, with reasonable justifications. Establish that not all the verbs have equivalents.

The verb *cite* is very similar to the verb *quote* in meaning. Both verbs introduce the ideas of others. But *quote* is normally followed by the actual

Word	Refers to	Comments
the + noun	a previously mentioned noun	one of several ways in which choice of article is governed
they	a noun	• generally refers to the nearest suitable noun previously mentioned or the subject of the previous sentence • other pronouns used in text for reference: *he, she, it*
its, their	a previously mentioned noun, indicating possession	other possessive pronouns used in text for reference: *his, her, hers, theirs,* etc.
this	an idea in a phrase or a sentence	• often found at the beginning of a sentence or a paragraph; a common mistake is to use 'it' for this purpose • also used with prepositions (e.g., *for this*)
this/these + noun	a previously mentioned noun/noun phrase	also used with prepositions (e.g., *by this method*).
such + noun	a previously mentioned noun	Meaning is: 'Xs like this'. Note that when referring to a singular noun, *such a X* is used (e.g., *in such a situation*).

words, whereas *cite* can also be followed by a paraphrase, e.g.,

Brown quotes Smith as saying, 'The reason for this problem is ...'

Brown cites Smith as agreeing with this idea.

4 Discuss this with the whole class, building the table in the Answers section. Point out to students that the choice of introductory verb for a direct or indirect quote or a paraphrase or summary will reveal what they think about the sources. This is an important way in which, when writing essays, students can show a degree of criticality about their sources. Critically evaluating other writers' work is an important part of academic assignments, dissertations and theses.

Answers

Possible answers:

2 accept, agree, concede
argue, assert, claim, contend, insist
consider, note, observe, point out, state
disagree, dispute
illustrate, indicate, show

3/4 See table below.

Verb	Followed by	Used when the writer ...
accept	*that*	reluctantly thinks this idea from someone else is true
agree	*that*	thinks this idea from someone else is true
argue	*that*	is giving an opinion that others may not agree with
assert	*that*	is giving an opinion that others may not agree with
cite	+ noun	is referring to someone else's ideas
claim	*that*	is giving an opinion that others may not agree with
concede	*that*	reluctantly thinks this idea from someone else is true
consider	*that*	is giving his/her opinion
contend	*that*	is giving an opinion that others may not agree with
describe	*how;* + noun	is giving a description
disagree	*that; with* + noun	thinks an idea is wrong
dispute	+ noun	thinks an idea is wrong
emphasize	*that*	is giving his/her opinion strongly
illustrate	*how;* + noun	is explaining, possibly with an example
indicate	*that*	is explaining, possibly with an example
insist	*that*	is giving an opinion that others may not agree with
note	*that*	is giving his/her opinion
observe	*that*	is giving his/her opinion
point out	*that*	is giving his/her opinion
report	*that*	is giving research findings
show	*that*	is explaining, possibly with an example
state	*that*	is giving his/her opinion
suggest	*that;* + gerund	is giving his/her opinion tentatively; *or* is giving his/her recommendation

Exercise D

Discuss with the students when it is better to paraphrase and when to quote directly. Refer to the *Skills bank* if necessary.

1/2 Set for individual work and pairwork checking. Feed back with the whole class.

3 Set for individual work. Remind students that if they want to quote another source but to omit some words, they can use three dots (…) to show some words are missing.

Answers

Possible answers:
See table below.

Original sentence	The writer is …	Direct quote or paraphrase?	Suggested sentence
a Compliance has become a major responsibility for bank supervisors.	giving an opinion	quote directly	Pickford (2006) points out that compliance has become a major responsibility for bank supervisors.
b Compliance requires observance of those rules and regulations, both implicit and explicit, which govern bank procedures.	is giving an opinion that others may not agree with	paraphrase	Pickford (2006) argues that, in banking compliance, implicit and explicit rules must be followed.
c As Robinson (2003) states, 'senior management are responsible for ensuring that … control processes are in place'*.	quoting from another writer; the other writer is making a strong statement.	quote the other writer directly	Pickford (2006) cites Robinson, who insists that 'senior management are responsible for ensuring … control processes are in place'. (Robinson, 2003).
d Employees throughout the bank need to understand the specific provision of the law as it applies to their own functions.	giving an opinion or recommendation	paraphrase with a direct quotation	Pickford (2006) suggests that employees should understand how the law 'applies to their own functions'.
e This means anticipating the kinds of problems that, if not corrected, may lead to new compliance requirements.	is giving an opinion that others may not agree with	quote directly	As Pickford (2006) contends, 'This means anticipating the kinds of problems that, if not corrected, may lead to new compliance requirements.' (p.24)

Exercise E

Set for pairwork discussion. Feed back with the whole class if necessary. Accept any reasonable suggestions.

Answers

Possible answers:

1 The board of directors, because it is the governing body representing the shareholders/owners of the bank.

2 The model way of accomplishing a task.

3 A contract in which all parties are not connected in any way.

4 Management is responsible for defining risk areas.

Exercise F

Set for pairwork discussion. Monitor to make sure students are referring to the student notes. Feed back with the whole class building the table in the Answers section. Accept any reasonable suggestions.

Answers

Possible answers:
See table below.

Closure

Ask students to write a paragraph describing an environment where staff would feel comfortable communicating concerns over fraudulent activity. They need to consider the management culture and the management response to such concerns.

Answers

Accept any reasonable answers.

Possible answer:

The bank culture should include positive reinforcement of the personal values of trust and integrity. These values should be supported in the bank's code of conduct and be well communicated to all employees. Employees must believe that there will not be any negative effects on their career from communicating their concerns over fraudulent activity. Such communications should be acknowledged positively and publicly within the bank. Management must investigate any such communications and inform employees of the outcome.

Governance problem	Recommendation
Transactions with related parties (i.e., family members) which have been inappropriately authorized	Have a comprehensive code of conduct and ensure all staff receive training and understand it. Have bank policies and procedures that ensure all transactions are appropriately authorized and approved.
Inadequate assessment of new financial products	Ensure the bank has appropriately trained and experienced staff to assess all new product risk, and to price products accordingly. Ensure product risk fits within the risk strategies set by the board of directors.
Inadequate control over loan extensions	Ensure that comprehensive procedures are prepared for granting loan extensions, and that appropriate authorization levels are set. Ensure rigorous internal checks are carried out on an ongoing basis.

12.2 Reading

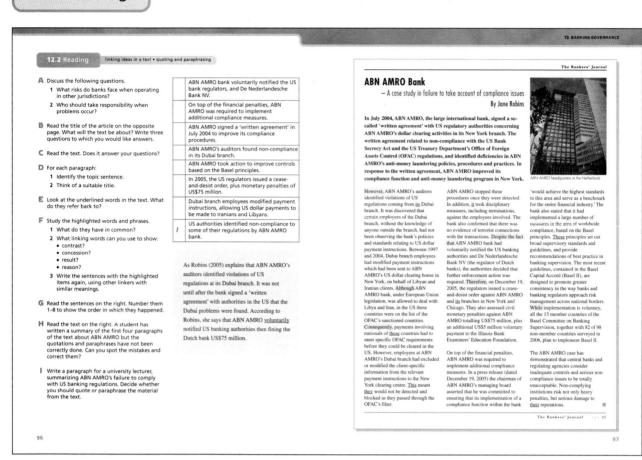

General note

Read the *Vocabulary bank* and *Skills bank* at the end of the Course Book unit. Decide when, if at all, to refer students to them. The best time is probably at the very end of the lesson or the beginning of the next lesson, as a summary/revision.

Lesson aims

- understand rhetorical markers in writing (*but* and *so* categories)
- use direct quotations from other writers:
  - common mistakes
  - missing words
  - fitting to the grammar of the sentence
  - adding emphasis to a quote
  - continuing to quote from the same source

Further practice in:

- indirect quotations/paraphrases/summaries
- summarizing with a series of topic sentences
- rhetorical markers (adding points)
- deictic reference and relative pronouns

Introduction

Revise the main governance principles from Lesson 1 and ask: *Who should take responsibility for what?*

To prepare students for the lesson's theme, ask them to think of a situation they have read about where there has been a governance problem for a bank. Identify the problem, and discuss who should be responsible, and why.

Exercise A

Set for pairwork or class discussion. Accept any reasonable suggestions.

Answers

Possible answers:

1 Banks may face some of the following risks when operating in other countries: differences between cultures, varying structural models and public policies, different laws and regulations, different compliance rules.

2 The board of directors is ultimately responsible. Refer to the bank governance principles in Lesson 1.

Exercise B

Remind students about surveying a text (skim-reading to get an approximate idea of the text contents by looking at the title, looking at the beginning few lines and the final few lines of the text, and by looking at the first sentence of each paragraph).

Set for individual work and pairwork discussion. Each pair should agree three questions. Feed back with the whole class. Write some questions on the board.

Exercise C

Set for individual work followed by pairwork discussion. Feed back with the whole class. Ask whether the questions you have put on the board have been answered in the text.

Exercise D

1/2 Set for individual work and pairwork discussion. The topic sentences should suggest a suitable title.

Answers

Possible answers:

	Topic sentence/phrase	Para title
Para 1	In 2004, ABN AMRO signed a 'written agreement' with US regulatory authorities concerning its dollar clearing activities in New York.	ABN AMRO's compliance problems with US regulatory authorities
Para 2	ABN AMRO's auditors identified violations of US regulations coming from its Dubai branch.	Dubai branch violates US regulations
Para 3	ABN AMRO stopped these procedures once they were detected.	the consequences of the violations
Para 4	On top of the financial penalties, ABN AMRO was required to implement additional compliance measures.	compliance measures and Basel principles
Para 5	The ABN AMRO case has demonstrated that regulating agencies consider serious non-compliance issues to be totally unacceptable.	the risks of non-compliance

Exercise E

Set for individual work and pairwork checking.

Answers

Model answers:

Word	Refers to
its	ABN AMRO
these	Libya and Iran
this	employees at ABN AMRO's Dubai branch had excluded or modified ... information
they	payment instructions
it	ABN AMRO
its	ABN AMRO
these	the Basel principles
their	non-complying banks

Exercise F

1 Refer students to the highlighted words. Elicit that they are all linking words or phrases.

2 With the whole class, elicit from the students some linking words that can be used for:

   contrast and concession (i.e., words which have a *but* meaning)

   result and reason (i.e., words which have a *so* or *for* meaning)

   Build the table in the Answers section (on the following page) on the board, reminding students of the difference between *between-* and *within-* sentence linkers (refer to Unit 11 *Vocabulary bank*).

3 Set for individual work. Encourage students to rewrite the sentences using a different type of linking word from the original (i.e., swapping between- and within-sentence linkers).

Answers

Possible answers:

2

	Within-sentence linkers	Between-sentence linkers
Contrast (*but*) used when comparing	... but ..., (but also) ... whereas ... ... while ...	However, ... In/By contrast, ... On the other hand, ... Compared with ...
Concession (*but*) used to concede/accept a point which simultaneously contrasts with the main point of a sentence or paragraph	... although ... ... despite/in spite of the fact that ... ... while..., (although)	Although ... At the same time ... Nevertheless, ... Despite the fact that... In spite of (*this*/noun), ... Yet, ...
Result (*so*)	..., so ... ... so that ... ... with the result that ...	So, ... As a result, ... Consequently, ... Therefore, ...
Reason (*for*)	... because ... ... since ... ... as ... ... due to/owing to the fact that ...	Because of (*this*/noun), ... Owing to (*this*/noun), ... Due to (*this*/noun), ...

3 *Nevertheless/Despite this*, ABN AMRO's auditors identified violations of US regulations coming from its Dubai branch.

ABN AMRO bank, under European Union legislation, was allowed to deal with Libya and Iran. *However*, in the US these countries were on the list of the OFAC's sanctioned countries.

As a result/So, payments involving nationals of these countries had to meet specific OFAC requirements before they could be cleared in the US.

Although ABN AMRO bank had voluntarily notified the US banking authorities and De Nederlandesche Bank NV (the regulator of Dutch banks), the authorities decided that further enforcement action was required.

OR

ABN AMRO bank had voluntarily notified the US banking authorities and De Nederlandesche Bank NV (the regulator of Dutch banks). *Despite this*, the authorities decided that further enforcement action was required.

Consequently/As a result, on December 19, 2005, the regulators issued a cease-and-desist order against ABN AMRO and its branches in New York and Chicago.

Although implementation is voluntary, all the 13 member countries of the Basel Committee on Banking Supervision, together with 82 of 98 non-member countries surveyed in 2006, plan to implement Basel II.

Language note

The first of these sentences is the beginning of a paragraph and the linker links to the previous paragraph. Therefore, a between-sentence linking word must be used.

Exercise G

Set for individual work and pairwork checking. This activity could also be done using Resource 12C in the additional resources section. Photocopy and cut up the sentences and hand them out in a jumbled order. Tell students to put them in the correct order.

Answers

Model answers:

5	ABN AMRO bank voluntarily notified the US bank regulators, and De Nederlandesche Bank NV.
7	On top of the financial penalties, ABN AMRO was required to implement additional compliance measures.
2	ABN AMRO signed a 'written agreement' in July 2004 to improve its compliance procedures.
4	ABN AMRO's auditors found non-compliance in its Dubai branch.
8	ABN AMRO took action to improve controls based on the Basel principles.
6	In 2005, the US regulators issued a cease-and-desist order, plus monetary penalties of US$75 million.
3	Dubai branch employees modified payment instructions, allowing US dollar payments to be made to Iranians and Libyans.
1	US authorities identified non-compliance to some of their regulations by ABN AMRO bank.

Exercise H

Set for individual work and pairwork checking. Feed back with the whole class.

Answers

Model answers:

Corrected version	Comments
As Robins (2005) explains,	Note the grammar here: either *As Robins (2005) explains* or *Robins (2005) explains that* but not both. This is a common mistake.
'ABN AMRO's auditors identified violations of US regulations [at] its Dubai branch'.	1. The words which are the same as the original need quotation marks. 2. Because the word *at* is different from the original, it is put in square brackets. It is important that a quote is exactly the same as the original. Any changes need to be clearly shown.
It was not until after they signed a 'written agreement' with authorities in the US that the Dubai problems were found.	Note that much of the text here has been paraphrased – which is the better option for information.
Robins (ibid.) further points out that	1. When continuing to refer to a source you can use 'further' or 'also' or other similar words; 'says' is not a good choice of introductory verb since it is too informal. You do not need 'according to' as well as a verb of saying. 2. When referring to the same place in the same source, use 'ibid.' instead of the full source reference. If it is the same publication (but not the same place in the text), use 'op. cit.'
ABN AMRO '*voluntarily* notified the US banking authorities' [italics added] who then fined the Dutch bank US $75 million.	1. The words which are the same as the original need quotation marks. 2. If you want to emphasize a part of a quote, use italics and then put '[italics added]' after the quote. 3. It is important to make a quotation fit the grammar of a sentence. Failing to do this properly is a common mistake.

Exercise I

Set for individual work, possibly for homework. Alternatively, set for pair or small group work. Students can write the paragraph on an OHT or other visual medium, which you can display and use to give feedback to the whole class.

Closure

Ask students to discuss these questions.

1 What aspects of ABN AMRO's customer relationship policies and procedures were compromised as a result of their experience with the US bank regulators? What improvements can be made?

2 Imagine you work in ABN AMRO's head office. You are in the team responsible for developing the bank's systems and reporting procedures when operating in other jurisdictions. What will you recommend?

Accept any reasonable suggestions.

Note:

The information relating to the cease-and-desist order and the fines imposed on ABN AMRO is a matter of public record and is available on the following websites.

www.dnb.nl

www.federalreserve.org

www.abnamro.com

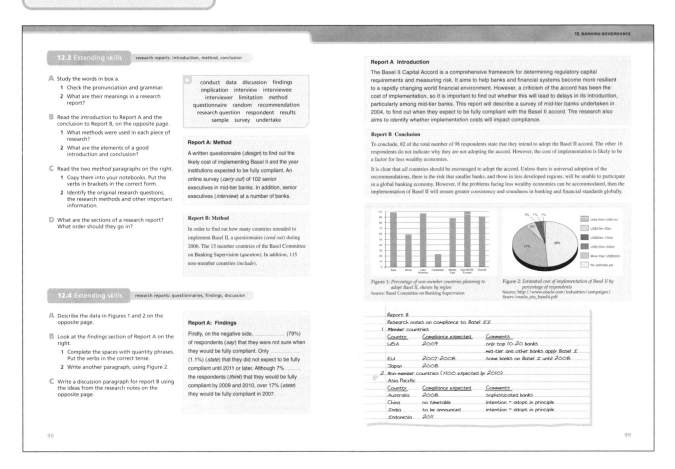

Lesson aims

- structure a research report:
  - introduction
  - method
  - conclusion

Further practice in:

- essay structure
- research methods

Introduction

In preparation for looking at the structure of a research report, revise the sections for an *essay*: introduction, body, conclusion.

Ask students what should go in each section. Elicit ideas for introductions and conclusions. Do not correct at this point.

Remind students about the methods for doing research (see Unit 5). Ask students what kinds of research would be appropriate if you want to find out what customers think of a bank's products or services. (Primary sources are best: survey, questionnaire, interview, quantitative and qualitative methods.)

Ask students what kinds of research would be appropriate if you want to find out what products and services a particular bank offers. (Secondary sources are the easiest: e.g., Internet research, company reports, business magazines.)

Tell students that the next two lessons will focus on writing up research in reports. Ask for suggestions for suitable sections of a research report. Do not correct at this point.

Language note

In the models presented here, the report is executed at a very simple level. For instance, in a real academic research report, there will be a literature review section before the methods section, and the research questions will be linked with this review. There are also different models for reports. For example, a business report (as opposed to an academic research report) may put conclusions and recommendations near the beginning and the findings as the final section.

Exercise A

Set for individual work and pairwork checking. Feed
back with the whole class.

Answers

Model answers:

Word	Notes on pronunciation and grammar	Meaning in a research report
con'duct	v (noun is pronounced: 'conduct)	do (some research, a survey, an experiment)
'data	pl n	information; can be numerical (quantitative) or verbal (qualitative)
dis'cussion	n (U/C)	The title of the section in a research report which discusses the findings. Sometimes the discussion is included in the findings/results section.
'findings	pl n	The title of the section in a research report which details what has been found out; each finding should be linked with a research question. The title 'results' can also be used for this section.
impli'cation	n (C)	possible effect or result of the findings
'interview	n (C), v	noun: when someone is asked questions in a survey verb: to ask someone questions in a survey
interview'ee	n (C)	the person being questioned
'interviewer	n (C)	the person asking the questions
limi'tation	n (C)	a problem with the research methods; an aspect which the research could not address
'method	n (C)	Title of the section in a research report which explains how the research was carried out. In the plural it refers to the research methods used.
question'naire	n (C)	a written set of questions
'random	adj	in no fixed order; with no organizing principle
recommen'dation	n (C)	suggestion for action as a result of the findings of the research
re'search ,question	n (C)	what the researcher wants to find out
res'pondent	n (C)	a person taking part in a questionnaire survey
re'sults	pl n	same as 'findings'; used more or less interchangeably
'sample	n (C), v	the group of people taking part in the research
'survey	n (C), v	a type of research in which the researcher sets out to describe a situation or set of ideas or behaviours, by reading a variety of documents or asking people questions
under'take	v	do (some research, a survey)

Exercise B

Explain to the students that these are examples of a typical introduction and conclusion. Set for pairwork discussion. Feed back with the whole class. Bring the class's attention to the tenses that are used here (present perfect, present simple, future) as well as the use of the passive.

Answers

Model answers:

1 Report A: Probably a written survey and interviews.

Report B: Probably a written questionnaire.

2

Good introduction	Example sentence(s)
Introduce the topic.	The Basel II Capital Accord is a comprehensive framework for determining regulatory capital requirements and measuring risk.
Give some background information.	It aims to help banks and financial systems become more resilient to a rapidly changing world financial environment.
Say why the topic is important.	However, a criticism of the accord has been the cost of implementation, so it is important to find out whether this will lead to delays in its introduction, particularly among mid-tier banks.
Say what you will do in the report. Give a general statement of the purpose of the research.	This report will describe a survey of mid-tier banks undertaken in 2004, to find out when they expect to be fully compliant with the Basel II accord. The research also aims to identify whether implementation costs will impact compliance.

Good conclusion	Example sentence(s)
Give a general summary/restatement of findings.	To conclude, 82 of the total number of 98 respondents state that they intend to adopt the Basel II accord. The other 16 respondents do not indicate why they are not adopting the accord. However, the cost of implementation is likely to be a factor for less wealthy economies.
Say what your recommendations are.	It is clear that all countries should be encouraged to adopt the accord.
Set out the implications of not taking action.	Unless there is universal adoption of the recommendations, there is the risk that smaller banks, and those in less developed regions, will be unable to participate in a global banking economy.
Comment on future possibilities if action is taken.	However, if the problems facing less wealthy economies can be accommodated, then the implementation of Basel II will ensure greater consistency and soundness in banking and financial standards globally.

Exercise C

Explain to students that these paragraphs are examples of the method section of a research report.

1 Set for individual work. Ask students to copy the text into their notebooks and put the verbs into the correct form. Feed back with the whole class, drawing students' attention to the use of the past tense when reporting methods of research, as well as the use of the passive.

2 Set for individual work and pairwork checking. Tell students that they should transform the research questions into real, direct questions. Feed back with the whole group; point out that the information given in the method section should include these types of details.

Answers

Possible answers:

	Research questions	Research method	Other important information
Method (A) A written questionnaire (*design*) <u>was designed</u> to find out the likely cost of implementing Basel II and the year institutions expected to be fully compliant. An online survey (*carry out*) <u>was carried out</u> of 102 senior executives in mid-tier banks. In addition, senior executives (*interview*) <u>were interviewed</u> at a number of banks.	1. How much does your institution expect to spend on setting up systems, processes and procedures to be compliant with Basel II?	online survey	102 senior executives surveyed
	2. When does your institution expect to be fully compliant with Basel II?	interview	
Method (B) In order to find out how many countries intended to implement Basel II, a questionnaire (*send out*) <u>was sent out</u> during 2006. The 13 member countries of the Basel Committee on Banking Supervision (*question*) <u>were questioned</u>. In addition, 115 non-member countries (*include*) <u>were included</u>.	How many banks in your country plan to adopt the recommendations of the Basel II accord?	written questionnaire containing closed questions	done in 2006 13 member countries and 115 non-member countries of the Basel Committee on Banking Supervision were questioned

Exercise D

Use this to confirm that students understand the organization of a general research report. Elicit the answers from the whole class. You may need to tell students as a prompt that there are five sections. Elicit the names of the sections and their order in a research report.

Answers

Model answers:

Section	Order in a research report
introduction	1
method	2
findings/results	3
discussion	4
conclusion	5

Language note

Different disciplines and reports for varying purposes may have different section names or organization. The model suggested here is a rather general one, and is a pattern commonly adopted in an academic context, though there are variations depending on the level of the writing (whether, for example, it is a master's or PhD dissertation). If students are going to write about 500 words only, you may wish to include *discussion* with *findings/results* or with the *conclusion*.

Closure

1 Refer students to the *Skills bank* to consolidate their understanding of the sections of a research report and their contents.

2 Ask students to choose a bank into which they would like to carry out some customer research. They should think about aspects such as products and services, reliability, customer requirements, etc. For example, students may like to choose an ethical bank (see Unit 10), an international bank (see unit 7), an Internet bank (see unit 11), or an offshore bank (see Unit 8). *What topics would they ask customers about in a questionnaire?*

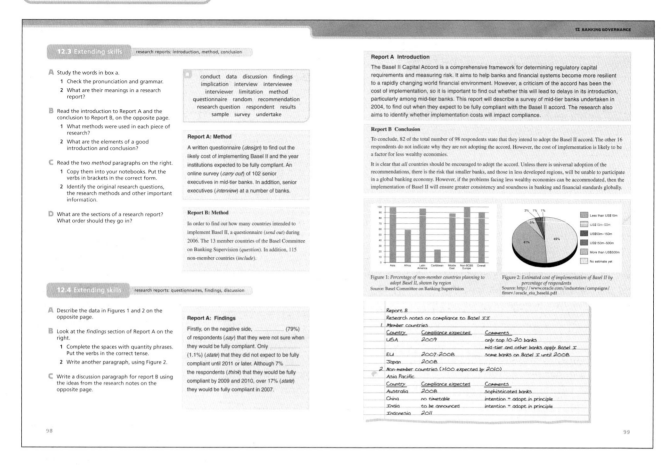

Lesson aims

- write part of a research report: findings and discussion
- analyse and use research data and information

Further practice in:

- using rhetorical markers for adding/listing points
- talking about numbers and quantities

Introduction

Write up the table below on the board. Give some example phrases and ask students to say approximately what percentage they represent, e.g., *a large majority = 80% approximately.*

A/An	overwhelming large significant slight small insignificant tiny	majority	(of + noun)
		minority	
		number	
Over	than	half a quarter a third	
More			
Less		x%	

Note that *of* is needed if the category for the numbers is given: *A slight minority of respondents said that …* but *A slight minority said that …*

Ask students: what is the difference between *many* and *most*?

Exercise A

Set students to work in pairs to talk about the key elements of the numbers shown in the charts. If you wish, ask students to write some sentences. Feed back with the whole class, writing some example sentences on the board. Note: tell students that they do not have to comment on every section of the graph, generally just those that show the majority, the average, and the minority. Ask the class what these results show about the Basel II accord. (Answer: most banks and financial institutions support it.)

Answers

Possible answers:

Figure 1

The graph shows that the overwhelming majority (98%) of non-member countries in Asia intend to adopt the Basel II accord. Also, the overwhelming majority of countries in non-BCBS Europe (97%) and

Latin America (96%) plan to adopt the accord. However, a minority (25%) of Caribbean countries plan to adopt it.

Figure 2

A significant minority (41%) of respondents said they expected to spend less than US$10 million to be compliant with Basel II.

A slight minority/Just under half of respondents (49%) said they were not yet able to estimate the total cost of implementing Basel II.

A tiny minority (1% and 1%) estimated they would spend between US$150m and US$500m or more than US$500m.

Exercise B

1 Set for individual work and pairwork checking. They will need to practise the expressions they used for quantity in Exercise A. Tell students that each space may be for more than one word.

Feed back with the whole class, pointing out the use of past tenses when reporting findings.

2 Set for individual work. Remind students to use linking words and to begin with a topic sentence. This paragraph continues the *findings* section of Report A.

Answers

Possible answers:

1 Findings

Firstly, on the negative side, a large majority (79%) of respondents (*say*) said that they were not sure when they would be fully compliant. Only a tiny minority (1.1%) (*state*) stated that they did not expect to be fully compliant until 2011 or later. Although 7% of the respondents (*think*) thought that they would be fully compliant by 2009 and 2010, over 17% (*state*) stated they would be fully compliant in 2007.

2 The survey also revealed some positive aspects. A significant minority (41%) of respondents said they expected to spend less than US$10 million to be compliant with Basel II. Just under half of respondents (49%) said they were not yet able to estimate the total cost of implementing Basel II. A tiny minority (1% and 1%) estimated they would spend between US$150m and US$500m or more than US$500m.

Exercise C

Ask students to look at the research notes for Report B on the right-hand page. These are the results of Internet searches to obtain an update on compliance to Basel II. Tell students that the discussion section of a report is where they can give their opinions on their findings.

They should write a paragraph using the research notes. Set for individual work.

Answers

Possible answers:

Discussion

It is clear that those countries whose banks have strong financial backing, such as the top 10 to 20 US banks, the sophisticated Australian banks, and EU and Japanese banks are best able to achieve an early implementation of the Basel II accord. It seems that Basel I will be an option for mid-tier banks. From a practical point of view, in a world of changing governments, changing financial technology and globally different financial and legal institutions, the time and expense required to achieve compliance will be more difficult for large developing countries. However, China and India have indicated an intention to achieve compliance, although neither has given a firm commitment, whereas Indonesia expects to be compliant by 2011. There is a worldwide perception that Basel II has a role to play in an era of increasing globalization and financial markets. Consequently, over 100 non-member countries are expected to reach compliance by 2010.

Closure

Ask students to work out the original questions used in the research for Reports A and B.

First, suggest some question types for questionnaires. Elicit the following:

- yes/no
- multiple choice
- open-ended

Tell students to concentrate on the *yes/no* or *multiple choice* types (*open-ended* questions will elicit qualitative information which is often hard to analyse) and to look at the data in Figures 1 and 2 and the sample *findings* paragraph. They should try to formulate the actual questions given in the customer survey questionnaire.

Set for pairwork. Feed back with the whole class, writing examples of good questions up on the board.

Possible answers:

Do you intend to adopt the Basel II accord?

How much do you expect to spend on the implementation of Basel II?

- less than US$10 m
- US$10m–US$50m
- US$50m–US$150m
- US$150m–US$500m
- more than US$500m
- don't know

1 Work through the *Vocabulary bank* and *Skills bank* if you have not already done so, or as revision of previous study.

2 Use the *Activity bank* (Teacher's Book additional resources section, Resource 12A).

   A Set the crossword for individual work (including homework) or pairwork.

   Answers

   B Set for individual work and pairwork checking.

   Answers

95%	the great majority
70%	a significant majority
53%	just over half
50%	half
48%	slightly less than half
10%	a small proportion
2%	a tiny minority

3 Ask students to practise making questionnaires for bank surveys. They should write questionnaires, carry out the research amongst a suitable group of respondents (20–40 people is fine) and then write up the report. They could choose from the following topics (or other appropriate topics):

   training: a questionnaire for bank staff

   customer relationships: a questionnaire for bank customers

Both questionnaires should have a focus on issues of governance and compliance. Refer to the bank governance principles in Lesson 1 and/or direct students to relevant websites, for example: www.bii-compliance.com/pdf/basel2/Bank_Govern ance_and_Basel2.pdf

For model questionnaires, see Resources 12D and 12E in the additional resources section.

Activity bank

A Solve the crossword.

Across

1 The interest … on the savings account is 6%.
4 To charge an account with a cost.
7 … are used less frequently nowadays. Debit card use is increasing.
8 Profit on money invested.
10 To put money into something to increase its value.
13 A person or company that is owed money.
14 An amount of money lent to a person or company.
15 Money placed in a bank to earn interest.
16 I'd like to open a current … .

Down

1 Adjective from *regulate*.
2 Rules or conditions of a loan, an investment, etc.
3 Interest rates can be variable or they can be … for a specified period of time.
5 Related to money.
6 A fall in the value of an object (e.g., a car) or a currency.
7 The Japanese yen and the euro are convertible … .
9 Money paid as income on investments.
11 Another word for *variable*.
12 A local office of a large organization, especially a bank.

B Play noughts and crosses. Use the words in context or explain what they mean.

illegal	deductible	liquidity
transferable	negotiable	monetary
insufficient	illegible	transaction

EFT	gold standard	hard currency
wholesale bank	EFTPOS	MNB
ATM	central bank	retail bank

Activity bank

A Find 20 words from this unit in the wordsearch.

- Copy the words into your notebook.
- Check the definition of any words you can't remember.

H	C	M	N	M	L	C	O	U	N	T	E	R	F	E	I	T	R
T	K	H	Z	X	P	I	Y	F	B	Y	F	R	N	B	T	H	M
B	K	Z	C	G	L	N	Q	H	I	P	Y	Q	R	X	H	K	M
L	C	H	N	Q	L	T	M	U	R	N	P	L	L	M	N	K	L
K	R	E	G	U	L	A	T	E	I	E	A	W	B	N	I	R	R
K	T	R	E	C	E	I	P	T	L	D	J	N	O	N	Q	N	F
F	K	N	P	V	K	K	N	B	L	M	I	I	C	V	T	R	T
I	N	V	E	S	T	D	A	A	K	C	T	T	T	I	M	Y	G
T	L	W	Y	J	M	I	W	Y	R	A	U	I	Y	L	A	J	M
H	L	H	K	Z	T	A	L	S	L	C	S	R	C	L	J	L	E
H	N	G	F	O	R	T	K	U	E	O	H	G	R	R	M	G	G
Y	M	G	G	D	I	V	C	D	P	C	Z	A	T	E	A	R	K
L	M	E	H	D	L	R	U	E	L	Q	U	L	R	G	N	R	M
C	N	T	E	X	I	A	D	W	R	Q	U	R	T	T	M	C	J
L	I	R	N	C	R	K	R	W	L	A	F	R	I	L	E	T	Y
W	C	J	K	F	Q	V	L	R	V	W	O	J	F	T	M	R	K
Q	F	W	N	Q	R	D	V	K	T	M	V	D	T	K	Y	X	B
Y	D	E	M	A	N	D	Y	G	I	R	O	T	Z	R	P	L	K

B Choose one word from each column to make a two-word phrase. Use each word once only.

bank	depression
deposit	assets
economic	account
financial	currency
foreign	fraud
liquid	ownership
national	panic

E-banking is an umbrella term used by the banking industry.

Electronic transfers between banks were well established by the 1970s, but it was several years before bank customers benefited from computer technology.

In the 1970s, the US Federal Reserve System operated a computerized clearing house system, or interbank electronic funds transfer (EFT) system.

The retail or bulk funds transfer system handles large-volume, low-value payments, including cheques, credit transfers, direct debits, ATM and EFTPOS transactions.

Payment via the retail telecommunications network occurs as follows.

Although e-banking has had a significant impact on banking practices, inadequate customer data integration (CDI) is a major problem for banks.

E-banking is an umbrella term used by the banking industry.

Electronic transfers between banks were well established by the 1970s, but it was several years before bank customers benefited from computer technology.

In the 1970s, the US Federal Reserve System operated a computerized clearing house system, or interbank electronic funds transfer (EFT) system.

The retail or bulk funds transfer system handles large-volume, low-value payments, including cheques, credit transfers, direct debits, ATM and EFTPOS transactions.

Payment via the retail telecommunications network occurs as follows.

Although e-banking has had a significant impact on banking practices, inadequate customer data integration (CDI) is a major problem for banks.

CAD	CAL	CAM
DVD	HTML	HTTP
ISP	LCD	PIN
ROM	URL	USB
WAN	WWW	ACH
ATM	CDI	CHAPS
CHIPS	EFT	ODFI
RDFI	RTGS	SWIFT

Activity bank

A Solve the synonyms crossword. Find words with the same meaning as the clues.

Across

3 show
4 expenses
7 finally
9 it follows that
10 drop
12 fundamentally
14 numbers
15 usually
16 yearly
17 financial
document

Down

1 staff
2 change
5 client
6 in fact
8 money
11 rise
13 get better

B Play opposites bingo.

- Choose six words from the box and write one word in each square of your bingo card.
- Your teacher will call out some words. If you have the **opposite** word on your card, cross it out.
- The first person to cross out all the words on their card is the winner.

assets   credit   deficit   distributed
domestic   fall   income   lend   low
minimum   net   positive   previous
profit   relevant   sharply   specific
variable   withdraw

Verbs	Nouns	Adverbs	Adjectives
rise		gradually	
increase		sharply	
grow		slightly	
improve		markedly	
fall		significantly	
decrease		rapidly	
drop		steeply	
decline		steadily	

A Study the two-word phrases in the box.

   1 What is the meaning of each phrase?

   2 Discuss your definition with a partner.

> administrative expenses   annual report   balance sheet   bank equity   calendar year
> doubtful debts   financial position   financial year   fixed assets   interest receivable
> net income   occupancy expenses   operating income   retained profits   total assets

B Use a two-word phrase from the box to complete each of these sentences.

   1 A _____ is a statement of assets and liabilities.

   2 _____ are tangible items that have a long-term value to the organization.

   3 The value of the shareholders' interest in the bank is described in the balance sheet as _____ .

   4 _____ is the surplus remaining after deducting all expenses from revenue.

   5 The year ended 31st March 2007 was the _____ _____ for the bank.

   6 Interest earned in the period but not yet paid by the customer is classified as _____ in the statement of financial position.

   7 _____ is the amount after adjusting operating income for non-operating items such as income from investments and write-off of investments.

   8 The board of directors commented on the proposed restructuring of the bank in the _____ .

   9 Expenses of the head office organization are often classified as _____ in the annual report.

  10 The surplus arising each year after deducting income tax and dividends from net income is referred to as _____ .

  11 _____ comprise current assets, fixed assets and investments.

  12 The period 1st January to 31st December is called a _____ .

  13 The statement of _____ was previously referred to as the balance sheet.

  14 Debts which may not be paid are referred to as _____ .

  15 Office lease costs as well as telephone and electricity are included as _____ .

Poor contributions	Student A	Student B	Student C
disagrees rudely			
doesn't explain how the point is relevant			
doesn't understand an idiom			
dominates the discussion			
gets angry when someone disagrees with them			
interrupts			
is negative			
mumbles or whispers			
says something irrelevant			
shouts			
sits quietly and says nothing			
starts a side conversation			
other:			

Good contributions	Student A	Student B	Student C
allows others to speak			
asks for clarification			
asks politely for information			
brings in another speaker			
builds on points made by other speakers			
contributes to the discussion			
explains the point clearly			
gives specific examples to help explain			
is constructive			
links correctly with previous speakers			
listens carefully to what others say			
makes clear how the point is relevant			
paraphrases to check understanding			
says when they agree with someone			
speaks clearly			
tries to use correct language			
other:			

Activity bank

A Find 20 verbs from this unit in the wordsearch.

- Copy the verbs into your notebook.
- Write the noun for each verb.

L	B	C	D	F	E	M	A	N	I	P	U	L	A	T	E	V	L
K	G	N	D	G	F	N	J	R	M	Z	Q	R	Z	L	P	Y	Q
B	M	B	A	D	L	K	F	E	G	T	N	T	X	H	L	M	W
W	V	N	G	R	O	W	T	G	A	D	O	P	T	V	Q	N	B
B	A	K	Y	L	E	A	L	T	G	Z	S	U	P	P	O	R	T
M	R	V	L	P	C	Q	C	O	R	R	E	L	A	T	E	R	J
V	I	P	A	I	R	N	U	Z	M	Y	T	E	B	J	N	V	J
R	M	N	D	P	C	E	E	I	L	M	T	T	Y	N	Q	H	E
W	J	N	C	P	P	D	D	D	R	A	A	X	T	K	R	S	C
W	I	D	D	R	I	R	N	I	L	E	W	I	V	X	I	N	L
J	K	H	E	V	E	E	E	U	C	O	R	H	N	V	N	K	K
J	F	T	O	C	T	A	M	C	R	T	D	Q	R	T	D	G	L
V	M	R	F	X	R	U	S	R	I	K	T	E	M	F	A	C	R
C	P	Q	E	T	C	E	O	E	M	A	P	K	T	T	Q	I	D
B	C	K	H	C	K	B	A	H	D	U	T	C	T	M	H	N	N
T	P	G	A	J	T	W	G	S	S	L	T	E	V	Q	J	Z	Y
Y	R	R	E	G	U	L	A	T	E	F	P	J	F	C	P	J	R
W	N	T	K	N	P	I	N	T	E	R	V	E	N	E	T	R	L

B Think of a word or words that can go in front of each of the words below to make a phrase from banking. Explain the meaning.

Example: *bank = central bank, investment bank, retail bank*, etc.

accounts	analysis	assets	bank	banking	basket	bond	capital	card	currency
cycle	draft	fund	loan	note	policy	profit	rates	reserves	services	supply

Original sentence	Student A	Student B
The mandate of most central banks is to carry out their government's fiscal and monetary policy to ensure a stable economy and currency.	The objective for most central banks is to carry out policies that result in a stable currency and economy.	The majority of state banks have to execute the agreed financial goals of parliament.
	not satisfactory: not enough changes: this is patch-writing	*acceptable paraphrase: all words changed except 'banks', which is acceptable*
Some central banks set their country's official interest rate.	By setting the official interest rate of their country, central banks hope to manage the inflation rate.	A certain number of them fix the government interest rate.
	not satisfactory: although all the words except 'inflation' (which is allowable) have been changed, the meaning is different from the original	*acceptable paraphrase: use of pronoun 'them' (i.e., central banks); 'fix' as synonym for 'set'. The only words the same as the original are 'interest rate', which is allowable*
They do this to manage inflation (a rise in the price of a 'basket' of goods), as well as deflation.	Inflation involves an increase in the price of a 'basket' of goods rather than an increase in just one product or service.	This is seen as a means of controlling inflation (increasing costs of a range of products), and deflation.
	not acceptable: although all the words have been changed, the meaning is different from the original	*acceptable paraphrase: 'inflation' and 'deflation' are the same as the original but this is acceptable*

You are going to write a short report entitled *Changes in inflation rates and GDP in the Middle East and Europe over five years*.

1 Study Figure 2 (in Lesson 4) and Figure 3 below. Make notes on the main points in each.

2 Divide the notes into sections to make suitable paragraphs.

3 Decide which ideas are suitable topic sentences for the paragraphs.

4 Make full sentences from the notes, joining ideas where possible, to make one continuous text. Try to interpret and comment on the data.

5 Write a conclusion using relevant information from this unit and your own knowledge. Comment on the action a central bank could take to rectify an unfavourable trend. Use Egypt and Germany as your examples.

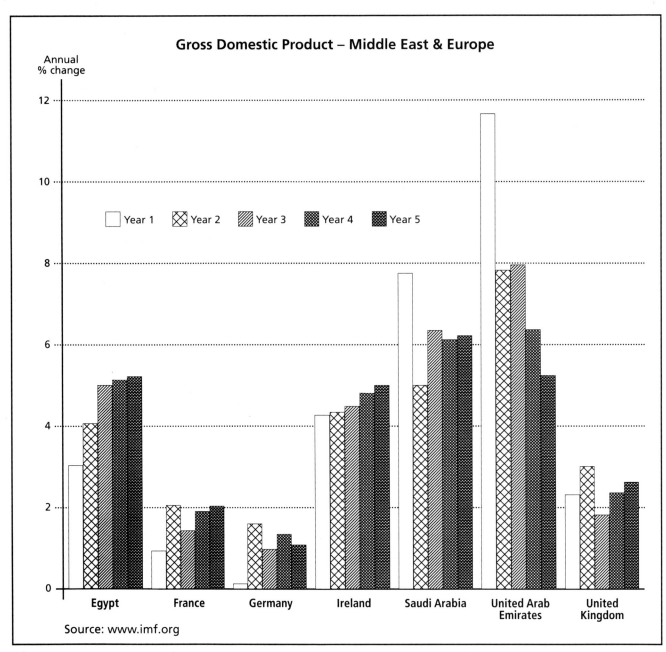

Figure 3

Changes in Inflation rates and GDP in the Middle East and Europe over five years

Figure 2 shows inflation rates for seven countries in the Middle East and Europe over a five-year period. Egypt and the UAE experienced the highest inflation rates of the sample countries during this period whereas the European countries experienced more modest inflation. Saudi Arabia is a country whose inflation rates are generally low. For example, an inflation rate of well below 1% was shown for the first three years. Saudi Arabia recorded the lowest inflation of the sample countries.

Figure 3 shows the annual percentage change in the value of a 'basket' of goods and services in the same seven countries. To calculate economic growth in a given country, a calculation is made on the annual value of the goods and services (known as gross domestic product) sold within that country in a particular year.

The UAE and Saudi Arabia recorded the highest GDP growth due to rising income from their oil revenues. Ireland was the best performing European country with GDP growth consistently over 4% per annum. Egypt had high growth but also high inflation, whereas Germany experienced an inflation rate above its GDP growth resulting in negative real growth.

If a comparison is made of GDP and inflation, Ireland represents the model developed country economy with solid GDP growth of more than 4% and a constant inflation rate of less than 2%. The United Arab Emirates is the model of a high growth economy. It has the second highest inflation rate as well as the second highest GDP. Egypt also has high growth (approximately 4%) but its inflation rates fluctuate between 11% and 4 %.

In contrast, during this period Germany is an example of an advanced country with a stagnant economy, with GDP growth averaging around 1% and inflation increasing to over 2%. The UK has a stable economy with inflation around 2% and GDP growth also around 2%.

Many central banks in developed countries have set a goal, or been mandated, to maintain inflation at below 3% per annum. Governments place a high priority on achieving and maintaining price stability. Another objective of central banks is to moderate long-term interest rates, so as to encourage investment in projects that require funding over an extended period. Central banks also control money supply as a tool for influencing growth and inflation.

The central bank of Germany should attempt to stimulate the economy by lowering interest rates and increasing money supply. The lowering of interest rates should also weaken the value of the currency and this will assist export businesses in selling more products and services.

In Egypt, in order to prevent escalating inflation, the central bank will need to increase interest rates and reduce money supply. This should slow the growth of the economy and reduce the rate of inflation.

A annual	A market	A fixed
A central	A online	A currency
A government	A share	A credit
A foreign	A economic	A bank
A investment	A personal	A promissory
A monetary	A gross	A interest
A cash	A financial	A money
B accounts	B analysis	B assets
B bank	B banking	B basket
B bond	B capital	B card
B currency	B cycle	B draft
B fund	B loan	B note
B policy	B profit	B rates
B reserves	B services	B supply

Activity bank

A Solve the crossword.

Across

5 A document to show that goods or money have been received.

7 Cash on … is only advisable when the trading partners have built up a relationship of trust.

8 A document often used in international trade. (3 words)

11 The value of one item against another, e.g., two currencies.

13 In cash with order, the goods are paid for pre-… .

14 There is a lot of documentation involved in completing a … . (3 words)

Down

1 The company exports goods worth $300 million … annum.

2 Documentary collection offers less … than a letter of credit.

3 Another word for best (e.g., financial terms).

4 Another word for goods for sale.

6 If someone is considered a credit risk, they are more likely to … on their payments.

9 A person or business that sells products to another country.

10 A person or business that brings in products from another country.

12 A request for goods.

Activity bank

Student A

B Play 'battleships'.
Answer Student B's questions about this grid.

	A	B	C	D	E	F	G	H	I	J	K	L
1	A		G	U	A	R	A	N	T	E	E	
2		G										C
3	C		R		G	O	O	D	S			O
4	O			E		I						N
5	M		P		E		T					T
6	P		R	P		M		E				R
7	O		O		A		E		M			A
8	N		D			R		N		S		C
9	E		U				T		T			T
10	N		C					S				
11	T		T									
12	S		S		S	E	C	U	R	I	T	Y

Ask Student B questions to find the following words from this unit:

- three words for money
- two verbs meaning 'to assess the risk' ending in ~ate
- four words which can be nouns or verbs, meaning: 'loss of value'; 'buying and selling'; 'an official offer to purchase'; provision of something that is needed'

Ask: *Is there a letter in 1C?*
Use this grid to mark the letters/words you find. Mark empty squares with a cross.

	A	B	C	D	E	F	G	H	I	J	K	L
1												
2												
3												
4												
5												
6												
7												
8												
9												
10												
11												
12												

Activity bank

Student B

B Play 'battleships'.
Answer Student A's questions about this grid with *No* or *Yes, it's (F)*.

	A	B	C	D	E	F	G	H	I	J	K	L
1	F				C	U	R	R	E	N	C	Y
2	I											
3	N				O	R	D	E	R			
4	A										E	T
5	N						L			T		R
6	C					L			A			A
7	E				A			L				D
8				F			U					E
9	C				C							
10	A				L		S	U	P	P	L	Y
11	S			A								
12	H		C		E	V	A	L	U	A	T	E

Ask Student A questions to find the following ten words from this unit:

- two nouns which refer to a business commitment
- three plural nouns which refer to purchases for export
- two nouns which refer to financial commitment
- two plural nouns meaning items required to complete the assembly of a product

Ask: *Is there a letter in 1C?*
Use this grid to mark the letters/words you find. Mark empty squares with a cross.

	A	B	C	D	E	F	G	H	I	J	K	L
1												
2												
3												
4												
5												
6												
7												
8												
9												
10												
11												
12												

	Fixed phrase	Followed by ...	Actual information (suggested answers)
1	An important concept (is) ...	a new idea or topic that the lecturer wants to discuss	
2	What do I mean by ... ?	an explanation of a word or phrase	
3	In financial terms, ...	a general idea put into a financial context	
4	Say ...	an imaginary example	
5	In this way ...	a concluding comment giving a result of something	
6	Looking at it another way, ...	a different way to think about the topic	
7	As you can see, ...	a comment about something visual (e.g., a diagram or lecture slide) OR a fact that has just been demonstrated	
8	The point is ...	a key statement or idea	

Student A

Payment method	cash with order (CWO)
Payment to exporter	when order is placed, prior to shipment
Title/goods available to importer	depends on contract specification, e.g., ex factory, FOB (free on board), on delivery, or on acceptance after arrival
Bank involvement	importer may require finance
Risk to importer	if exporter doesn't adhere to contract terms
Risk to exporter	very little
Not advised if/when	trading partner is a government or an established trading partner – implies lack of trust

- -

Student B

Payment method	letter of credit (L/C) • used for business transactions in which the payment of the invoice needs to be guaranteed by a third party (usually a bank), e.g., if buyer's country is economically/politically unstable • can be denominated in a stable currency, e.g., USD, euro
Payment to exporter	on submission of documents under L/C after goods arrive safely
Title/goods available to importer	when letter of credit is settled
Bank involvement	L/C is drawn by the exporter's bank on the importer's bank which promises to honour it (by confirming it) if the exporter meets the terms in it
Risk to importer	• if exporter doesn't adhere to the contract terms • possibility of fraud
Risk to exporter	• very little for a confirmed irrevocable L/C if documents comply • exporter may require FX (foreign exchange) contract to guarantee price received for the goods (if there is the potential for currency fluctuations)
Not advised if/when	• importing country is politically unstable, i.e., risk that movement of funds out will be stopped (in event of war, etc.) • profit margin is low as L/C involves added costs • goods are perishable as L/C is time-consuming

Student C   7.4

Payment method	**documentary collection** equal risk/benefit to both parties; used when parties have an established relationship and know each other well
Payment to exporter	on acceptance of bill of exchange
Title/goods available to importer	on payment or acceptance of bill of exchange by importer's bank (on behalf of the importer)
Bank involvement	exporter sends title documents (bill of exchange, bill of lading, etc.) through own bank to importer with instruction to release them to importer on acceptance/payment of bill of exchange
Risk to importer	• fraud or misunderstanding regarding goods • loss of goods
Risk to exporter	possibility of importer not accepting the bill of exchange
Not advised if/when	• importing country has weak economy or if unstable politically, e.g., it may place restrictions on foreign currency payments • it is a government order, as payment is not released until goods are certified by government agency, i.e., goods handed over (for certification) before payment

Student D   7.4

Payment method	**cash on delivery (COD)** exporter ships goods and sends commercial documents to buyer directly
Payment to exporter	after delivery of the goods, if importer satisfied with conditions of the delivery, and quantity and quality of the goods
Title/goods available to importer	on delivery
Bank involvement	• exporter may require normal working capital finance, particularly if the order is a large one • both importer and exporter may wish to take out a FX contract
Risk to importer	fraud or misunderstanding regarding goods
Risk to exporter	exporter loses all control over goods and depends on the buyer to make payment as per contract
Not advised if/when	importer and exporter are not well known to each other and don't have an established trading relationship

Activity bank

A Find 18 words from this unit in the wordsearch.
- Copy the words into your notebook.
- Check the definition of any words you can't remember.

```
L  L  E  G  I  S  L  A  T  I  O  N  F  B  P  F  R
M  J  T  T  G  O  V  E  R  S  E  A  S  J  M  L  Y
D  G  C  O  N  F  I  D  E  N  T  I  A  L  I  T  Y
K  E  K  X  T  J  T  M  N  M  A  S  S  E  T  S  D
S  G  C  J  M  Z  U  T  P  E  R  W  Z  R  K  K  J
Q  C  R  L  M  Z  N  R  C  R  X  C  S  Q  E  Z  K
P  B  R  Y  A  E  A  N  I  B  I  L  K  R  Y  V  L
P  O  L  E  D  R  E  U  K  S  O  V  U  W  W  D  W
P  L  F  I  E  C  A  E  T  R  D  S  A  Y  R  Q  X
Z  J  S  F  I  N  R  T  T  H  O  I  T  C  X  K  J
R  E  R  L  S  O  I  N  I  L  O  I  C  D  Y  Z  M
R  V  V  J  H  H  O  N  C  O  M  R  V  T  R  M  N
L  K  X  S  R  C  O  S  G  Y  N  D  I  K  I  J  T
R  K  N  X  Y  Y  I  R  N  W  T  H  G  T  R  O  V
P  O  Y  T  N  D  L  O  E  Z  L  M  R  V  I  V  N
L  C  G  B  R  X  N  I  D  E  N  T  I  T  Y  E  F
Y  R  T  L  Z  A  S  U  B  S  I  D  I  A  R  Y  S
```

B Rearrange the letters in the words below to form a correctly spelt word from this unit. The first letter of each word is underlined.

Jumbled word	Correct spelling
n_f_ciilaan	
nax_t_aito	
g_r_eatsoniul	
ordersup_c_e	
d_l_uanerngi	
tmves_i_nnet	
estump_i_	
antacrsnoi_t_	
littina_m_ulona	

Activity bank

A Solve the crossword.

Down

2 … is money earned.
4 An … is when one company buys or takes over another company.
6 Financial … is making laws or systems relating to money less strict.
7 … means government owned and operated; not controlled by private owners.
8 … is organizing a company in a new way to make it operate more efficiently.
9 The gross … product is the total value of goods and services produced by a country in a year.
10 A … is when two or more companies join together.
11 … is closing a company and selling its assets, often because it is unable to pay its debts.
12 … ownership means belonging to a company from another country.

Across

1 The per … income is the average amount of income for each individual person.
3 Economic … are various statistics (e.g., unemployment rate) which show short-term and long-term economic performance.
5 The … Bank is an international organization which was formed in 1945 to help economic development, especially of poorer countries.
13 … is the basic systems and services, such as transport and power supplies, that a country or organization uses in order to work effectively.
14 … is selling a nationalized industry to private owners.
15 The International … Fund is a part of the United Nations which encourages international trade and gives financial help to poor countries.

B Are the nouns in the box countable or uncountable? Use a dictionary to check.

acquisition   development   economy   income indicator
industry   infrastructure   merger   ownership   trade

Review reduce + recite + review	Notes record
Here you write only important words and questions; this column is completed after the lecture. Later this column becomes your study or revision notes. You can use it by covering the right hand column and using the cue words and questions here to remember the contents on the right.	This column contains your notes. You should underline headings and indent main ideas. After the lecture or reading you need to identify the key points and write them in the review column as questions or cue words.

Summary
reflect + recite + review
After the class you can use this space to summarize the main points of the notes on this page.

Table A (Student A)
Mergers and acquisitions (M & As) in commercial banking sectors 1995–2004

Type of M & A	1995–99			2000–4		
	Country	Number of M & As	Value (US $m)	Country	Number of M & As	Value (US $m)
M & As between domestic institutions	Colombia	6	20	Colombia	7	10
	Chile	2	480	Chile	2	530
	Mexico	6	64,600	Mexico	1	18,600
	Singapore	2	1,700	China	1	...
	Indonesia	1	...	Hong Kong	14	...
	Korea	10	13,500	Singapore	2	8,000
	Malaysia	2	20	Korea	5	23,480
	Philippines	2	6,900	Malaysia	15	40
	Thailand	1	47,700	Philippines	9	16,400
	Czech Rep.	4	...	Thailand	2	28,000
	Hungary	5	3,000	Czech Rep.	1	...
	Poland	9	...	Poland	11	...
	Russia	58	...	Russia	29	...
				Turkey	9	...
Total		108	137,920		99	95,060

Source: *National data (BIS questionnaire) www.bis.org*

Table B (Student B)
Mergers and acquisitions (M & As) in commercial banking sectors 1995–2004

Type of M & A	1995–99			2000–4		
	Country	Number of M & As	Value (US $m)	Country	Number of M & As	Value (US $m)
M&As between domestic institutions and foreign-owned institutions	Colombia	2	20	Colombia	1	10
	Chile	2	350	Chile	4	690
	Mexico	2	17,300	Mexico	4	152,000
	Korea	1	860	Korea	2	3,930
	Thailand	4	10,000	Philippines	3	300
	Czech Rep.	5	...	Czech Rep.	2	...
	Hungary	2	4,700	Hungary	2	12,200
	Poland	13	...	Poland	19	...
				Turkey	8	...
Total		31	33,260		45	169,130

Source: *National data (BIS questionnaire) www.bis.org*

Activity bank

A Complete the table.
- Identify the part of speech (n, v or both).
- Say whether nouns are countable (C), uncountable (U) or both.
- Say whether verbs are transitive (T), intransitive (I) or both.

Word	Part of speech	Noun – countable or uncountable?	Verb – transitive or intransitive?
account			
borrow			
client			
ethics			
lend			
monitor			
overheads			
project			
transparency			

B Think of a word or words that can go after each of the words or phrases below to make a phrase from banking . Explain the meaning.

Example: *bank = bank loan, bank account*

bank _____
business _____
capital _____
financial _____
investment _____
lending _____
operating _____
personal _____
transaction _____
working _____

Introduction		Examples of ideas
introduce the topic area give the outline of the essay		
Body	**Para 1:** situation: description and background	
	Para 2: problems (specific examples)	
	Para 3: solutions (benefits) and risks	
	Para 4: evaluations of solutions	
Conclusion		

Pair A Business representatives

> project:
>
> location:
>
> justification:
>
> benefits:
>
> risks:
>
> finance needs:
>
> conclusion:

To persuade the bank to invest in the project, Pair A will need to:

- identify a project with desirable social and environmental outcomes
- provide evidence of research that confirms the idea is sound
- prove their idea is sound and financially viable
- clearly identify the stages of the project
- explain what personnel is required and the cost
- detail other costs (set-up and operating)
- ensure that regulatory and legal aspects of the project are covered

Pair B Ethical bankers

> project:
>
> identifiable risks:
>
> identifiable benefits:
>
> SRI criteria:
>
> conclusion:

To identify all the risks, Pair B will have to assess:

- quality of proposal
- whether there are any possible adverse environmental and/or social consequences
- whether the project meets the SRI criteria set by the bank, as expected by their investors
- social (e.g., employment) and environmental benefits of the project
- amount of capital the shareholders will contribute
- quality and experience of the management team who will run the project
- whether all the statutory and regulatory requirements for the project to become operational can realistically be achieved
- whether the technology that is to be used by the project is proven and the most cost effective for the purpose

Sheleagh Heffernan, *Mod Banking* (2005) JW & Sons. Paperback

Shim, Jae K. and Costas, M. (2001) Encyclopedic dict internat fin & banking. (2001) Boca Raton: St. Lucie Press

R.C. Smith, & I.Walter, <u>*Global Banking*</u>. (2nd ed). New York: Oxford University Press (2003).

Sparkes, R. (2002) <u>*Socially Responsible Investment: A Global Revolution*</u> J.Wiley & Sons.

Vogel, D. (2006) The Market for Virtue: the Potential and Limits of Corporate Social Responsibility. Washigton: Brookings

A. Hardenbrook, "The Equator Principles: the private financial sector's attempt at environmental responsibility" in the Vanderbilt Journal of Transnational Law, 40(2007), 197-232.

Sheleagh Heffernan, *Mod Banking* (2005) JW & Sons. Paperback

Shim, Jae K. and Costas, M. (2001) Encyclopedic dict internat fin & banking. (2001) Boca Raton: St. Lucie Press

R.C. Smith, & I.Walter, <u>*Global Banking*</u>. (2nd ed). New York: Oxford University Press (2003).

Sparkes, R. (2002) <u>*Socially Responsible Investment: A Global Revolution*</u> J.Wiley & Sons.

Vogel, D. (2006) The Market for Virtue: the Potential and Limits of Corporate Social Responsibility. Washigton: Brookings

A. Hardenbrook, "The Equator Principles: the private financial sector's attempt at environmental responsibility" in the Vanderbilt Journal of Transnational Law, 40(2007), 197-232.

Activity bank

A Match a word in the first column with a word in the second column to make a two-word phrase. Make sure you know what they mean.

client	laundering
laser	security
log	horse
money	printer
online	server
proxy	numbers
serial	education
Trojan	management

B Find 20 words from this unit in the wordsearch.
- Copy the words into your notebook.
- Make two-word phrases.
- Check the definition of any words/phrases you can't remember.

```
D  L  W  F  R  Y  J  D  U  E  X  W  L  D  N  K  X
F  I  V  Y  M  V  R  O  M  B  U  D  S  M  A  N  Q
C  N  L  R  E  C  O  N  C  I  L  I  A  T  I  O  N
T  O  G  I  M  O  R  T  G  A  G  E  K  X  L  N  C
B  P  M  W  G  H  D  B  V  C  R  D  B  A  O  I  L
Z  O  Z  P  N  E  R  A  P  M  M  N  I  I  R  M  Z
B  R  U  W  U  H  N  Z  T  W  B  C  T  T  V  H  G
C  T  M  N  G  T  Z  C  P  A  N  P  E  V  Q  N  H
Z  A  V  T  C  L  E  D  E  A  Y  M  T  F  I  E  R
F  X  R  P  T  E  P  R  N  R  O  F  T  K  M  Q  L
K  T  M  D  M  D  D  I  C  I  E  N  C  I  T  E  B
X  J  Q  T  Z  P  F  N  B  H  U  A  R  K  U  N  W
S  M  A  R  T  X  E  J  T  O  H  P  W  Q  D  H  C
K  T  K  M  P  M  D  Y  C  W  -  W  E  D  F  B  T
D  L  R  Y  N  R  W  C  X  B  L  H  B  L  M  D  H
C  Y  Y  V  N  M  A  R  U  C  C  R  F  K  I  P  H
M  F  J  K  V  Y  J  S  O  F  T  W  A  R  E  D  F
```

Resource **11B**

A Match the phrase in column A with the correct definition in Column B.

Column A	Column B
computer hacking	1 sending an e-mail that falsely claims to be from a legitimate source, to obtain private information for use in identity theft
conflict of interest	2 infusing false information into a server so that users are directed to a fraudulent site
data compromise	3 software that gathers information (e.g., e-mail addresses, passwords, credit card numbers) by monitoring user activity on the Internet
fraudulent site	4 product unwittingly installed when the user installs something else
keylogger	5 surveillance software which records every keystroke to allow information to be transmitted to an unknown third party
pharming	6 web server that intercepts all requests to the real server
phishing	7 false location on the world wide web
proxy server	8 stealing information from a computer
scamming	9 when unauthorized user gains access to private information
	10 modifying a program, often in an unauthorized manner, by changing the code itself
spyware	11 presents which the recipient has not requested and may not be for legitimate business reasons
sub-prime mortgage	12 loan made to someone with poor credit record, which attracts very high interest rates
Trojan horse	13 a situation where an opportunity for private benefit clashes with a person's (or organization's) public responsibilities
unsolicited gifts	

English for Banking – Copyright © 2008 Garnet Publishing Ltd.

Activity bank

A Solve the crossword.

Down

2 openness (12)

3 more that half the total (8)

4 taking responsibility for one's actions (14)

5 the process of ensuring that a bank follows the rules established by regulatory bodies (10)

6 suggested but not communicated directly (8)

10 clear and well communicated (8)

11 set of agreed actions (10)

14 accepted standards or ways of behaving (5)

Across

1 honesty, moral principles (9)

7 less than half the total (8)

8 operating very badly (11)

9 relating to a big company or organization (9)

12 taking action without being asked (9)

13 sudden increase in numbers (13)

15 body that ensures that banks follow compliance procedures (9)

B Match the percentages with a suitable phrase to describe numbers of respondents.

95%	a significant majority
70%	a small proportion
53%	a tiny minority
50%	half
48%	just over half
10%	slightly less than half
2%	the great majority

Bank governance

Because banks have the potential, if badly run, to create severe economic dysfunction, they are subject to strict regulations. The Board of Directors and senior management of the bank must ensure transparency and accountability govern their actions. They also have a responsibility to maintain high fiduciary standards, and consequently must implement strong governance procedures. Furthermore, these procedures need to be reviewed regularly, as banking standards and norms continue to evolve.

A significant part of governance is compliance. The main compliance risks should be identified and addressed annually by senior management. The bank can do this, by means of a regular review of its corporate governance practices and procedures. As part of this review, managers should carry out an 'internal audit' in which they examine their compliance with their risk management programs. As a result of such reviews, they should be able to identify the opportunities and threats to the bank.

ABN AMRO bank voluntarily notified the US bank regulators, and De Nederlandesche Bank NV.

On top of the financial penalties, ABN AMRO was required to implement additional compliance measures.

ABN AMRO signed a 'written agreement' in July 2004 to improve its compliance procedures.

ABN AMRO's auditors found non-compliance in its Dubai branch.

ABN AMRO took action to improve controls based on the Basel principles.

In 2005, the US regulators issued a cease-and-desist order, plus monetary penalties of US$75 million.

Dubai branch employees modified payment instructions, allowing US dollar payments to be made to Iranians and Libyans.

US authorities identified non-compliance to some of their regulations by ABN AMRO bank.

ABN AMRO bank voluntarily notified the US bank regulators, and De Nederlandesche Bank NV.

On top of the financial penalties, ABN AMRO was required to implement additional compliance measures.

ABN AMRO signed a 'written agreement' in July 2004 to improve its compliance procedures.

ABN AMRO's auditors found non-compliance in its Dubai branch.

ABN AMRO took action to improve controls based on the Basel principles.

In 2005, the US regulators issued a cease-and-desist order, plus monetary penalties of US$75 million.

Dubai branch employees modified payment instructions, allowing US dollar payments to be made to Iranians and Libyans.

US authorities identified non-compliance to some of their regulations by ABN AMRO bank.

The People's Bank

Staff Survey

To all our staff:

A trained labour force is essential for a bank to thrive and compete, to be able to innovate and adapt to new technology, and for employment to expand over time.

Please help us to improve our services and our in-house operations by completing this questionnaire.

Please indicate your answer by circling your choice.

---

1 Have you received in-house training for your current position?

no   yes

If 'yes', how do you rate the training you have received?

A very good   B good   C satisfactory   D inadequate

---

2 What do you think of our job descriptions? Are they:

A accurate and complete   B adequate for the job   C unsatisfactory

---

3 What do you think of our staff training over the last five years? Has it:

A improved   B deteriorated   C remained the same

---

4 Do you think management are polite and helpful?

yes   no   don't know

---

5 Would you feel comfortable communicating concerns over inadequate management practices and procedures to management?

yes   no   don't know

---

6 Do you believe your performance reviews are properly linked to your duties?

yes   no   don't know

---

7 Has the bank's code of conduct been explained to you?

yes   no   don't know

---

8 Do you think that in performing your duties you are aware of the possible business risks?

yes   no   don't know

---

9 Any other comments?

Thank you for your help!

The People's Bank
Customer Survey

To all our customers:

Please help us to improve our services to you by completing this questionnaire.

Please indicate your answer by circling your choice.

---

1   Have you been advised on the returns and risks relating to your investments with us?

no   yes

If 'yes', how do you rate the advice you have received?

A very good   B good   C satisfactory   D unsatisfactory

---

2   What do you think of the quality of the assistance you have received from us? Is it:

A efficient and reliable   B adequate   C not reliable

---

3   What do you think of our customer service over the last five years? Has it:

A improved   B deteriorated   C stayed the same

---

4   Do you think our bank staff are polite and helpful?

yes   no   don't know

---

5   Would you feel comfortable communicating concerns over inadequate bank practices and procedures to bank management?

yes   no   don't know

---

6   Would you like the bank to provide more frequent information on its investment products?

yes   no   don't know

---

7   Are you familiar with the bank's procedures for customer complaints?

yes   no   don't know

If 'yes', do you think they are:

A very good   B good   C satisfactory   D unsatisfactory

---

8   Do you think that our website is informative?

yes   no   don't know

---

9   Do you have any suggestions for improvements in our customer services?

Thank you for your help!